윤희영의 News English

일러두기

1. 이 책에 수록된 원문 뉴스는 《ABC News》《AFP》《BBC News》《The Daily Mail》《Reuters》《The Guardian》 《The Observer》《The Mirror》《The Sun》 등 다양한 해외 언론사에 출처와 저작권이 있습니다.
2. 각 뉴스의 한글 번역은 저자에 의해 정리, 요약, 재구성되었으므로 해당 뉴스의 원문 문장과 완전히 일치하지는 않습니다.

월드 뉴스를 만나는 가장 쉽고 빠른 길!

윤희영 지음

샘터

Funny Funny World
웃음은 세계 공통어

12세 소년에게 붙잡힌 전과 50범 절도범 • **11**
A Burglar with Convictions Caught by a 12-year-old Boy

자신의 수배사진 불만 강도 용의자 • **21**
A Burglary Suspect Discontented with his Mugshot

생쥐의 엄청난 호화주택 • **29**
A Pretty Spendy House of a Mouse

육상 국가대표로 스카우트된 지각생 • **37**
A Tardy Student Headhunted as National Athlete

바람피우고 교차로에서 벌 받은 남편 • **45**
An Unfaithful Husband Standing at an Intersection

못난이 축구스타 웨인 루니와 살인 사건 • **53**
Football Star Wayne Rooney and a Murder Case

국회의원 얼굴 사진에 총 쏘기 • **61**
Shooting Lawmakers in the Face with Air Gun

구직자들의 색다른 전술 • **69**
Unconventional Tactics of Job Applicants

벼락치기 시험공부하는 야쿠자 똘마니들 • **79**
Yakuza Underlings Cramming for an Exam

Our Heart-warming World
언어는 달라도 마음은 하나

코 암(癌) 걸려 죽은 마약 탐지견 • **91**
A Drug Sniffer Dog Died of Nasal Cancer

눈먼 수캐 데리고 다니며 돌보는 암캐 • **99**
A Female Dog Taking Care of a Blind Male Dog

깨어진 사랑의 가슴 아픈 끝 • **107**
A Heartbreaking End of Shattered Love

10년 뒤에 배달된 연애편지 • **117**
A Love Letter Delivered 10 Years Later

생후 6주 아기의 기적적인 부활 • **125**
A Miracle Revival of a Six-week-old Baby

어느 어미새의 눈물겨운 모성 본능 • **135**
A Mother Bird's Maternal Instinct

어느 나치 돌격대원의 놀랍고 감동적인 보은 • **143**
A Nazi Stormtrooper's Amazing Requital of Kindness

가난한 아빠, 501억 원 로또 낭첨 • **153**
A Poor Father's $39 Million Jackpot

300전 4승 256패 은퇴하는 인간 샌드백 • **163**
A Retiring Human Punchbag

어느 알콜중독자의 비참한 죽음 • **173**
An Alcoholic's Miserable Death

마을 사람 모두에게 은혜 갚은 할머니 • **183**
An Old Woman's Way of Returning the Favor

아내를 대신한 그의 인생 전부 • **193**
His Whole Life Instead of his Wife

해고자를 위한 기도 • **201**
Prayer for Those Made Redundant

아들 따라 죽은 한 부부의 비극 • **209**
Tragedy of a Couple Following their Son to the Grave

Mysterious Science World
신비로운 과학의 세계

새신랑에게 알레르기 반응 보이는 새신부 • **221**
A Newlywed Bride Allergic to her Husband

내년 날씨 예보하는 물리학자 • **231**
A Physicist Predicting the Weather Next Year

도저히 막을 수 없는 페널티킥 비법 • **245**
A Secret Formula for Unstoppable Penalty

여성에게 인기 많은 남성들의 특징 • **253**
Features that Make a Man Appeal to a Woman

어머니에게 효도해야 하는 5가지 이유 • **281**
Five Scientific Reasons to Serve Parents with Devotion

남자가 감기에 걸리면? • **295**
'Man-flu'

잘못 알려진 의학상식 20가지 • **309**
Medical Common Sense Nobody Questions

27세부터 감소하는 사람의 정신 능력 • **327**
Mental Power Starting to Dwindle at 27

'투쟁'과 '도전'은 우리의 본능 • **335**
Our Instinctive 'Fight-or-flight Response'

천체물리학자가 발견한 최상의 비행기 탑승순서 • **349**
The Best Way to Load the Airplane

세계의 다양한 숙취(宿醉) 해소법 • **361**
Various Remedies for Hangover in the World

We are the Global Village
지구촌 이모저모 신기한 세상

85세 억만장자와 이혼한 24세 여성, 위자료 한 푼 못 받은 사연 • **373**
A Blonde in her 20s and her Octogenarian Husband

'맘마 미아' 노래 부르며 되살아난 소녀 • **389**
A Girl Resuscitated Singing 'Mamma Mia'

할머니 총명함에 붙잡힌 성폭행범 • **397**
A Rapist Arrested by an Elderly Woman of Sagacity

돌리 파튼 가슴보다 더 비싼 혓바닥 • **407**
A Tongue more Expensive than Parton's Breast

저주받은 아이들, 이른바 '독일놈의 자식들' • **417**
Accursed Children, So-called 'Boche Babies'

유럽에서 가장 돈 많은 여자와 한 남자 • **435**
Europe's Richest Woman and a Man

영국판 '미녀는 괴로워' • **445**
From an Ugly Duckling to a Beautiful Swan

자기 복제를 간절히 원했던 마이클 잭슨 • **453**
Michael Jackson, Desperate to Clone himself

미국과 중국의 닭발 전쟁 • **467**
War over Chicken Feet between U.S. and China

Epilog 독자가 영어로 꿈꿀 수 있는 날을 위해_윤희영 • **476**

A lie can travel half way around the world while the truth is putting on its shoes.

Charles H. Spurgeon

Funny Funny World

1st NEWS

웃음은 세계 공통어

News English

"A Burglar with Convictions Caught by a 12-year-old Boy"

As a fan of crime-solving TV series CSI, schoolboy Leon Yates knew exactly what to do when his neighbour was burgled. Although the terraced streets of his home town of Bolton are a long way from sun-drenched Florida, the 12-year-old proved he had been paying attention.

He had seen the suspect swigging lemonade before the break-in, and when he saw the entire can lying in the street outside he swept it into a plastic bag without touching it and handed it to police.

The budding detective's brainwave was rewarded after DNA tests unmasked the intruder as a serial burglar and he was sent to prison.

And Leon - who is in line for an award for his key role in solving the crime - has not surprisingly set his heart on a career in the police force.

"I watch CSI Miami and my sister Toni watches it on TV, and we knew what they do on it," he said yesterday. "I didn't want to get my fingerprints on the can or on it without touching it. Our neighbours would be quite impressed if they could keep a recording from the picture of it.

Leon was on his way to school last May when he spotted the man behaving suspiciously in the street.

The hooded pair let themselves into the unlocked home of his neighbour, Betty Hill, 59, and stole her handbag, which was in the back garden.

After alerting his neighbour Leon turned around with his mother to see if he could see the two men, but by then they had fled. But on returning to his home in Broughtnet, in Bolton, Greater Manchester, the schoolboy noticed an empty can of lemonade one had been swigging from.

With a technique that would have won the approval of the real-life experts from television's CSI, Leon found a plastic bag and swept it inside with a brush.

He then carefully bagging it up for evidence without touching it. The exhibit was handed over to police along with a detailed description of the offender - right down to his distinctive trainers, which are the same as Leon's own.

Yesterday a serial burglar was behind bars after DNA tests on the can confirmed that he had taken the handbag.

Daniel Jones, 26, pleaded guilty after his details matched forensic examination of the can, and he was jailed for two years and five months for last month's break-in. The hearing at Bolton Crown Court was told that Jones had been a drug abuser since the age of 14 and had already been convicted of 50 offences, most of them burglary.

After his taste of crime-busting Leon, who attends Thornleigh Salesian College, has not surprisingly decided on a career in the police when he's a little older.

"I want to catch a few more," he said.

head of Bolton CID, said: 'This was an absolutely superb bit of detective work from Leon, whose quick-thinking and brave efforts led directly to the arrest of a serial burglar.

television's CSI, Leon found a plastic bag and swept it inside with a brush.

He then carefully bagging it up for evidence without touching it. The exhibit was handed over to police along with a detailed description of the offender - right down to his distinctive trainers.

레온 예이츠와 연쇄 강도범 대니얼 존스

12세 소년에게 붙잡힌 전과 50범 절도범

과학수사드라마 CSI를 즐겨보던 12세 소년이 평소 TV에서 본 대로 기지를 발휘해(be equal to the occasion) 전과 50범인 연쇄 절도범을 잡는 데 결정적 역할을 해냈다(tip the balance).

영국 그레이터맨체스터 주(州) 볼턴에 사는 레온 예이츠라는 소년은 범죄수사 TV 시리즈 CSI의 골수팬(a diehard fan of crime-solving TV series CSI)이다. 그는 얼마 전 이웃집에 도둑이 드는(be burgled) 것을 보고 CSI의 한 장면을 떠올리며 어떤 행동을 취해야 할지 정확히 알 수(know exactly what to do) 있었다고 한다.

예이츠는 마침 용의자가 (이웃집에) 침입하기 직전 레모네이드를 들이키는 것을 목격했고(see the suspect swigging lemonade before the break-in), 용의자가 달아난 뒤 거리에 버려져 있던 빈 캔을 발견(see the empty can lying in the street outside)했다. 예이츠는 자신의 지문이 묻지 않도록(not to get his fingerprints on the can) 캔에 손을 대지 않은 채 비닐봉지에 쓸어담아(sweep it into a plastic bag without touching it) 경찰에 넘김으로써(hand it to police) 용의자 검거를 가능케 했다. DNA 테스트로 침입자가 연쇄 절도 범이라는 사실을 밝혀내게(unmask the intruder as a serial burglar) 한 것이다.

범죄 해결에 결정적 역할을 해 상을 받게 될(be in line for an award for his key role in solving the crime) 예이츠는 이미 이번 사건 이전부터 경찰 직업을 갖기로 마음을 정한(set his heart on a career in the police force) 것으로 알려졌다.

예이츠는 사건 당일 학교에서 집으로 돌아가다가(be on his way home from school) 집 밖 거리에서 한 남자가 수상하게 행동하고 있는 것을 보게(spot a man acting suspiciously in the street outside his home) 됐다. 두건을 둘러쓴 남자(the hooded man)는 예이츠의 이웃인 플로렌스 힐(59세) 씨가 뒤뜰에 있는(be in the back garden) 사이에 문이 잠기지 않은 집으로 들어가(let himself into the unlocked home) 그녀의 핸드백을 훔쳤다(steal her handbag).

예이츠는 우선 어머니에게 주의하도록 알린 뒤(after alerting his mother) 도둑을 찾아내기 위해(to spot the thief) 네 명의 손주를 둔 할머니인 힐 씨를 도와 함께 차로 돌아다녀봤으나(offer to drive around with the grandmother of four) 범인은 이미 도망간 뒤였다. 그러나 집으로 돌아오는 길에(on return to his home) 예이츠는 범인이 레모네이드를 들이켰던(take a swig of lemonade) 빈 캔에 주목해(notice the empty can), CSI에서 본 것처럼 비닐봉지를 구해 브러시로 조심스레 캔을 쓸어넣었다(carefully sweep it inside with a brush). 이 증거물(the exhibit)은 특이한 운동화(the distinctive sneakers) 등 범인에 대한 상세한 묘사와 함께 경찰에 넘겨졌다(be handed over to police along with a detailed description of the offender).

결국 빈 캔에 대한 DNA 테스트(DNA tests on the empty can) 결과로 경찰에 붙잡힌 연쇄 강도범 대니얼 존스(26세)는 자신의 세부사항들이 캔에 대한 법의학 검사와 일치하는(his details match forensic examination of the can) 것으로 드러나자 유죄를 인정(plead guilty), 투옥됐다(be put behind bars). 그에겐 2년 5개월의 징역형이 선고됐다(be sentenced to two years and five months in prison). 범인 존스는 14세 때부터 마약 중독자였으며(a drug addict since the age of 14), 주로 절도 또는 강도인 50건의 범죄 전과가 있는(be convicted of 50 offenses, most theft or burglary) 것으로 밝혀졌다.

CSI 매니아 12세 소년, 전과 50범 체포

Funny Funny World

CSI Bolton: Boy Detective Foils Serial Burglar after Collecting DNA Evidence from Drink Can

As a fan of crime-solving TV series CSI, schoolboy Leon Yates knew exactly what to do when his neighbour was burgled.

Although the terraced streets of his home town of Bolton are a long way from sun-drenched Florida, the 12-year-old proved he had been paying attention.

He had seen the suspect swigging lemonade before the break-in, and when he saw the empty can lying in the street outside he swept it into a plastic bag without touching it and handed it to police.

The budding detective's brainwave was rewarded after DNA tests unmasked the intruder as a serial burglar and he was sent to prison.

And Leon—who is in line for an award for his key role in solving the crime—has not surprisingly set his heart on a career in the police force.

'I watch CSI Miami because my sister Toni watches it on TV, and I have seen what they do on it,' he said yesterday. I didn't want to get my fingerprints on it so I picked it up without touching it. I think my mates will be quite impressed – I am quite proud of it.'

Leon was on his way home from school when he spotted two men acting suspiciously in the street outside his home.

The hooded pair let themselves into the unlocked home of his neighbour, Florence Hill, 59, and stole her handbag while she was in the back garden.

After alerting his mother, Leon offered to drive around with the grandmother-of-four to see if he could spot the thieves, but they had fled.

But on returning to his home in Breightmet, in Bolton, Greater Manchester, the schoolboy noticed an empty can of lemonade one had been swigging from.

With a technique that would have won the approval of the real-life experts from television's CSI, Leon found a plastic bag and swept it inside with a brush.

He then carefully bagging it up for evidence without touching it. The exhibit was handed over to police along with a detailed description of the offender – right down to his distinctive trainers, which are the same as Leon's own.

Yesterday a serial burglar was behind bars after DNA tests on the can confirmed that he had taken the handbag.

Daniel Jones, 26, pleaded guilty after his details matched forensic examination of the can, and he was jailed for two years and five months for last month's break-in. The hearing at Bolton Crown Court was told that Jones had been a drug addict since the age of 14 and had already been convicted of 50 offences, most theft or burglary.

After his taste of crime-busting, Leon, who attends Thornleigh Salesian College, has not surprisingly decided on a career in the police when he's a little older.

'I hope to catch a few more,' he said.

His mother Nikki, 36, who teaches beauty therapy, added: 'I am really proud of him. I would always look out for our neighbours and I would expect them to help me.

'A commendation from the police is something he can keep for life.'

Mrs Yates, whose 36-year-old husband Ian works at a hydraulics firm, has a 16-year-old son, Lewis, along with Leon and his 18-year-old sister.

Their neighbour has given Leon a box of chocolates for his quick-thinking.

'He's a very quiet unassuming lad who takes things in this stride and I am very grateful for what he did,' said Mrs Hill.

'I can't thank him enough.'

Leon now stands to receive an award from Greater Manchester Police.

Detective Chief Inspector Paul Hitchin, head of Bolton CID, said: 'This was an absolutely superb bit of detective work from Leon, whose quick-thinking and brave efforts led directly to the arrest of a serial burglar.

'I will be putting Leon forward for a commendation from the police.'

✅ 기억하면 좋을 구절!

be equal to the occasion 임기응변으로 잘 대처하다

➡ He *was* always *equal to the occasion*.
그는 늘 훌륭한 임기응변을 발휘했다.

be burgled 도둑 맞다 / 도둑이 들다

➡ We must have *been burgled* while we were asleep.
우리가 자고 있을 때 도둑이 든 게 분명하다.

sweep it into~ ~방향으로 쓸다 / 세거하다

➡ *Sweep* the dust out *into* the street!
먼지를 길가로 쓸어버려라.

be in line for 곧 ~하게 될 / ~을 얻을 공산이 있는

➡ If you keep it up, you may *be in line for* a promotion soon.
계속 그렇게 하면 곧 승진하게 될 겁니다.

hand over 건네주다 / 넘기다

➡ The man is *handing over* the book.
그 사람이 책을 건네주고 있다.

plead guilty 유죄를 시인하다 / 책임을 인정하다

➡ He *pleaded guilty* to the crime.
그는 범죄를 시인했다.

내 인생의 명언 — 믿음이 최선이다

▶ 진실이 신을 신고 있는 동안 거짓은 지구 반바퀴를 돌아다닌다.
찰스 스퍼전 (영국 침례교 설교자)

> A lie can travel half way around the world
> while the truth is putting on its shoes.
> Charles H. Spurgeon

▶ 아무도 믿어주지 않는 사람은 누구도
믿지 않는 부류의 사람인 경우가 많다.
해럴드 맥밀란 (영국 정치인)

> A man who trusts nobody is apt to be
> the kind of man nobody trusts.
> Harold Macmillan

▶ 신뢰하는 것을 배우는 것은 인생에서 가장 힘든 일 중 하나다.
이삭 와츠 (영국 시인 · 신학자)

> Learning to trust is one of life's most difficult tasks.
> Isaac Watts

▶ 순진한 사람의 신뢰는 거짓말쟁이의 가장 유용한 도구이다.
스티븐 킹 (미국 소설가)

> The trust of the innocent is the liar's most useful tool.
> Stephen Edwin King

▶ 믿음을 가진 한 사람은 단지 관심만 가진 99명의 사회적 세력과 맞먹는다.
피터 마샬 (영국 역사가)

> One person with a belief is a social power
> equal to ninety-nine who have only interests.
> Peter Marshall

News English

"A Burglary Suspect Discontented with hisMugshot"

As a wanted man, you might expect Matthew Maynard to be somewhat camera shy. But when his local paper published a mugshot of the 23-year-old in an attempt to track him down, he decided it didn't show his best side.

So he provided a replacement. And if that wasn't cheeky enough, he posed for the new photograph standing next to a police van.

Maynard is being hunted by police investigating a house burglary. Detectives sent the mugshot to local media in Swansea as part of a public appeal. When the picture appeared in the South Wales Evening Post, Maynard sent the paper a replacement photo of himself standing in front of a police van wearing luminous leggings and a policeman-like black jacket – which was then printed on the front page.

Yesterday officers at South Wales Police thanked him for helping. One said: 'He is a berk and he's not being clever by showing off like this. We'll have him in soon now.'

'Everyone in Swansea will know what he looks like now. When an officer from the South Wales Police issued his mugshot as part of a wanted appeal, which now 81 arrests in connection with robbery, in possession of drugs and in possession of drugs and fraud.

Spencer Feeney, editor of the South Wales Evening Post, said yesterday: 'We believed we were carrying out a public service by using his picture first time and even more so by using his new one on our front page.' As a wanted man, you might

Spencer Feeney, editor of the South Wales Evening Post, said yesterday: 'We believed we were carrying out a public service by using his picture first time and even more so by using his new one on our front page.'

'But if he has any sense at all then he should just give himself up to us.'

Spencer Feeney, editor of the South Wales Evening Post, said yesterday: 'We believed we were carrying out a public service by using his picture first time and even more so by using his new one on our front page.' As a wanted man, you might expect Matthew Maynard to be somewhat camera shy.

But when his local paper published a mugshot of the 23-year-old in an attempt to track him down, he decided it didn't show his best side.

So he provided a replacement. And if that wasn't cheeky enough, he posed for the new photograph standing next to a police van.

Maynard is being hunted by police investigating a house burglary. Detectives sent the mugshot to local media in Swansea as part of a public appeal. When the picture appeared in the South Wales Evening Post, Maynard sent the paper a replacement photo of himself

who led the operation, said: 'We hope that now many more people will know what he looks like and give us information which can lead to his arrest.'

'But if he has any sense at all then he should just give himself up to us.'

possession of drugs and fraud.

Four of the suspects were picked up within hours – but Maynard is one of four still on the run and is wanted for a house raid in Mount Pleasant, Swansea.

Acting Chief Inspector Nigel Whitehouse, who led the operation, said: 'We hope that now many more people will know what he looks like and give us information which can lead to his arrest.'

'But if he has any sense at all then he should just give himself up to us.'

Spencer Feeney, editor of the South Wales Evening Post, said yesterday: 'We believed we were carrying out a public service by using his picture first time and even more so by using his new one on our front page.' As a wanted man, you might expect Matthew Maynard to be somewhat camera shy.

But when his local paper published a mugshot of the 23-year-old in an attempt to track him down, he decided it didn't show his best side.

자신의 수배사진 불만 강도 용의자

　수배 중인 강도 용의자(a wanted burglary suspect)가 경찰이 신문에 공개한 자신의 사진이 마음에 들지 않는다며 새 사진을 보내오는 일이 영국에서 일어났다.
　한 가정집 강도 사건을 수사 중인 경찰의 추적을 받고 있던(be hunted by police investigating a house burglary) 용의자 매튜 메이너드는 경찰이 자신을 잡기 위해 한 신문에 게재한 자신의 얼굴 사진을 보게(see his mugshot appeared in a newspaper in attempt to track him down) 됐다.
　그런데 이게 마음에 들지 않았던 모양이다. 자신이 가장 잘 나온 모습을 보여주지 못하는(do not show his best side) 사진이라며 대신 쓸 사진을 신문사(사우스웨일스이브닝포스트)로 보내왔다(provide the newspaper with a replacement).
　그는 앞서 신문사에 전화를 걸어 신문에 실린 사진에 기분이 좋지 않다면서(saying he is not happy with the picture on the newspaper), 핸드폰을 이용해(use his mobile phone) 다른 사진을 보내주겠다(will send in another of his own)고 알려왔다고 한다.

수배자 신분인만큼(as a wanted man) 사진 찍히기를 좀 꺼려 할(be somewhat camera shy) 듯하지만 그는 전혀 달랐다. 새 사진을 보내오면서 경찰을 조롱하는 대범함까지 보였다. 보란 듯 경찰 밴 옆에 서서 포즈를 취한(pose for the new photo standing next to a police van) 모습이었다. 게다가 경찰관 같은 검은색 재킷과 야광 레깅스를 입어(wear a policeman-like black jacket and luminous leggings) 경찰 당국을 더욱 곤혹스럽게 만들었다. 이 사진은 신문 1면에 게재됐다(be printed on the front page).

이에 대해 경찰 관계자는 "그는 멍청이(a berk)다. 이렇게 과시함으로써 자신이 영리하다고(be clever by showing off like this) 생각하나 본데 곧 그를 잡게 될(will have him in soon) 것"이라며 불편한 심기를 드러냈다. "지역 주민들이 그가 어떻게 생겼는지 알게 됐으니(know what he looks like) 운신의 폭이 더 좁아질 것"이라면서 "그가 조금이라도 지각이 있다면(if he has any sense at all) 결국엔 자수할 수밖에 없게 될(should give himself up to us) 것"이라고 맞받아쳤다.

사우스웨일스 경찰은 대대적인 단속의 일환으로(as part of a major swoop) 범죄 용의자들의 얼굴 사진 원본을 공개(issue the original mugshots of criminal suspects)했으며, 그 결과 절도, 강도, 폭행, 마약 소지 및 사기 등 범죄와 관련해 48시간 만에 81명을 체포하는 성과를 올렸다(see 81 arrests in 48 hours for crimes including theft, burglary, assault, possession of drugs and fraud).

  그러나 메이너드는 아직도 잡히지 않은(be still on the run) 채 이 같은 경찰 농락 행각을 벌이고 있는 것이다. 이와 관련, 일부 주민들은 경찰이 신문의 독자편지 페이지도 확인해볼(check the newspaper's letters page) 필요가 있다며, "멍청한 메이너드가 한 줄 남기면서 자신의 주소도 써놓았을 수 있지 않느냐(may have dropped them a line with his address on it)"고 경찰을 비아냥대고 있다.

Unwanted: The Police Mugshot so Hated by Man on the Run that He Sent One He Liked Better

As a wanted man, you might expect Matthew Maynard to be somewhat camera shy.

But when his local paper published a mugshot of the 23-year-old in an attempt to track him down, he decided it didn't show his best side.

So he provided a replacement. And if that wasn't cheeky enough, he posed for the new photograph standing next to a police van.

Maynard is being hunted by police investigating a house burglary. Detectives sent the mugshot to local media in Swansea as part of a public appeal.

When the picture appeared in the South Wales Evening Post, Maynard sent the paper a replacement photo of himself standing in front of a police van wearing luminous leggings and a policeman-like black jacket – which was then printed on the front page.

Yesterday officers at South Wales Police thanked him for helping their campaign. One said: 'He is a berk. He thinks he is being clever by showing off like this – but we'll have him in soon now.

'Everyone in Swansea will know what he looks like now. What an idiot!'

South Wales Police issued the original mugshot as part of a major swoop which saw 81 arrests in 48 hours for crimes including robbery, burglary, assault, possession of drugs and fraud.

Four of the suspects were picked up within hours – but Maynard is one of four still on the run and is wanted for a house raid in Mount Pleasant, Swansea.

Acting Chief Inspector Nigel Whitehouse, who led the operation, said: 'We hope that now many more people will know what he looks like and give us information which can lead to his arrest.

'But if he has any sense at all then he should just give himself up to us.'

Spencer Feeney, editor of the South Wales Evening Post, said yesterday: 'We believed we were carrying out a public service by using his picture first time and even more so by using his new one on our front page.'

✅ 기억하면 좋을 구절!

mugshot [mʌgʃɑ:t] n. (경찰) 범인 얼굴 사진 / 상반신 사진

➥ Anyone who saw the *mugshots* of Ms Kim would be very depressed.
미스 김의 얼굴 사진을 보면 누구든 기분이 좋지 않을 것이다.

in attempt to ~ ~하려 시도하다 / ~하는 의도로

➥ I failed *in my attempt to* persuade him.
그를 설득하려다 실패했다.

camera-shy [kæmərə-ʃài] a. 사진 찍히기 싫어하는 / 사진을 피하는

➥ She is shy of camera.
(She is *camera-shy* / She is reluctant to be photographed.)
그녀는 사진 찍히는 것을 꺼려한다.

show off 자랑하다 / 뻐기다 / 내보이다

➥ He is always such a *show off*, I can't stand it.
그 사람은 늘 잘난 척해서 난 정말 못 참겠다.

swoop [swu:p] v. (위에서) 덮치다 / (경찰, 군인이) 급습(기습)하다

➥ The police made a *swoop* at my house.
경찰이 우리 집에 갑자기 들이닥쳤다.

내 인생의 명언 — 인간은 사회적 동물

▶ 쥐들의 경주(극심한 생존경쟁)에 있어 문제는
설혹 당신이 이긴다 해도 당신은 여전히 쥐라는 사실이다.
릴리 톰린 (미국 여배우 · 작가 · 프로듀서)

> The trouble with the rat race is that
> even if you win, you're still a rat.
> Lily Tomlin

▶ 사회는 사람을 조각상 따위로 만들어 사회가 갖고 있는
가장 편리한 자리에 배치하는, 하나의 방대한 음모다.
랜돌프 보른 (미국 작가)

> Society is one vast conspiracy for carving one
> into the kind of statue likes, and then placing it in
> the most convenient niche it has.
> Randolph Silliman Bourne

▶ 자유로운 사회의 제1원칙은 공개된 자리에서
속박받지 않는 말들의 흐름이다.
애들레이 스티븐슨 (미국 정치인)

> The first principle of a free society is
> an untrammeled flow of words in an open forum.
> Adlai Ewing Stevenson

▶ 어느 사회든 가장 위험한 창조물은 아무것도 잃을 것 없는 사람이다.
제임스 볼드윈 (미국 소설가)

> The most dangerous creation of any society is
> the man who has nothing to lose.
> James Arthur Baldwin

Funny Funny World

News English

"A Pretty Spendy House of a Mouse"

A mouse robbed the Gem Stop Chevron convenience store on Island Avenue Thursday.
A mouse with no larceny in its heart but a taste for $20 bills.
The tiny rodent squeezed into the automated teller machine inside the store and made a nest with $20 bills.
The ATM was operating well and nobody suspected anything. That is, until Millie Taylor, a Gem Stop employee, opened it around 9 a.m. Thursday and received the surprise of her life.
"I saw these beady eyes and a lot of chewed up $20 bills," she said.
She slammed the ATM's door shut and screamed. Then she composed herself.
"I stayed calm until the customers left." Taylor then carefully opened up the ATM machine and found a nest made from torn up $20 bills.
"It was a pretty spendy nest," Taylor said.
The mouse had completely torn up two $20 bills and damaged 14 others. Fortunately, a bank replaced the 14 bills that were not extensively damaged. But the two other $20 bills were a total loss.
No bills damaged by the mouse were dispensed to customers.
The mouse, unharmed, was taken outside and allowed to run away.
"There was not a trial or anything," Taylor said with a laugh.
Gem Stop employees are still mystified as to how the mouse got in the ATM machine.
The mystery will add to a story that may be retold in La Grande and on the Internet for years to come.

A mouse robbed the Gem Stop Chevron convenience store on Island Avenue Thursday.
A mouse with no larceny in its heart but a taste for $20 bills.
The tiny rodent squeezed into the

지폐를 벽지로 사용한 생쥐

생쥐의 엄청난 호화주택

'은수저를 입에 물고 태어나다(be born with a silver spoon in one's mouth)'라는 영어 표현이 있다. 부유한 집에서 태어났다는 뜻이다. 입에 은수저 없이 가난한 집에서 태어난(be born to poverty without a silver spoon in the mouth) 이들은 각고의 노력으로 자수성가하지(make one's fortune by one's own tireless effort) 않으면 돈 방석에 올라앉기 어렵다. 그런데 여기, 보잘것없는 출신임에도(being of humble birth) 집에 돈을 처바르고 살다가 졸지에 거리로 나앉은 안타까운(?) 사연이 있다.

힘닿는 대로(to the best of his ability) 지폐들을 긁어모았다(rake up bank notes). 그리고 집에다 차곡차곡 쌓아두기(pile up one by one) 시작했다.

미국 오리건 주(州) 라 그랜드의 한 편의점 현금자동인출기 속에서 쥐 한 마리가 발견됐다(be found inside an automatic teller machine at a convenience store). 20달러짜리 지폐들을 씹어 잘라 만든 둥우리와 함께(along with a nest built with chewed-up $20 bills)였다. 이 쥐는 지폐 두 장을 갈가리 찢어(thoroughly tear up two bills) 둥우리 바닥에 깔았다. 또 다른 열네 장은 둥우리 안 가장자리에 덧대느라 이리저리 훼손시킨(damage another 14 to line his nest) 상태였다.

이 장면을 발견한 편의점 직원 밀리 테일러는 평생 잊지 못할 놀라움을 겪었다(receive the surprise of her life). 현금지급기는 정상적으로 작동하고(be operating well) 있었다. 어느 누구도 무엇 하나 의심쩍게 여기지 않았다(do not suspect anything).

테일러는 이날 아침 9시쯤 현금지급기 문을 열었다가(open it around 9 a.m.) 말똥말똥 빛나는 두 개의 작은 눈과 잘게 씹어 찢어놓은 20달러싸리 지폐들을 보고 소스라치게 놀랐다(be frightened at a sight of two beady eyes and chewed-up $20 bills). 작은 쥐 한 마리(a tiny rodent)가 현금자동지급기 속으로 파고 들어가(squeeze into the automatic teller machine) 20달러짜리 지폐로 둥우리를 지어놓은 것이었다.

테일러는 놀란 나머지 소리를 지르며 현금지급기 문을 쾅 닫아버렸다(scream and slam the machine's door shut). 다행히 주변에 고객들은 없었다. 그녀는 한동안 마음을 진정시킨 뒤(after composing herself) 고객들이 다 나갈 때까지 평정을 유지하다가(stay calm until the customers leave) 다시 문을 열었다.

다행이라고 해야 하나, 그 쥐는 절도죄로 체포되지는(be arrested on charge of a larcenous act) 않았다. 재판이나 그 비슷한 것도 없었다(there was not a trial or anything). 말하자면(so to speak) '형 집행유예' 처분을

받고(just get 'a reprieve') 둥우리에서 퇴거 조치를 당하기는(be evicted from his nest) 했지만, 자유의 몸이 되어 바깥세상으로 돌아갔다(be set free outside). 은행 측에선 크게 훼손되지 않은(be not extensively damaged) 열네 장의 지폐는 모두 새 지폐로 바꿔줬다(replace all the 14 bills). 그러나 쥐가 잘게 찢어놓은 두 장은 완전 손실(a total loss)로 처리됐다.

그 쥐가 집에 처바른 돈은 총 320달러(약 39만 원)였다. 쥐에게는 엄청난 호화주택(a pretty spendy house)이었던 셈이다.

Mouse Strikes ATM

A mouse robbed the Gem Stop Chevron convenience store on Island Avenue Thursday.

A mouse with no larceny in its heart but a taste for $20 bills.

The tiny rodent squeezed into the automated teller machine inside the store and made a nest with $20 bills.

The ATM was operating well and nobody suspected anything. That is, until Millie Taylor, a Gem Stop employee, opened it around 9 a.m. Thursday and received the surprise of her life.

"I saw these beady eyes and a lot of chewed up $20 bills," Taylor said.

She slammed the ATM's door shut and screamed. Then she composed herself.

"I stayed calm until the customers left."

Taylor then carefully opened up the ATM machine and found a nest made from torn up $20 bills.

"It was a pretty spendy nest," Taylor said.

The mouse had completely torn up two $20 bills and damaged 14 others. Fortunately, a bank replaced the 14 bills that were not extensively damaged. But the two other $20 bills were a total loss.

No bills damaged by the mouse were dispensed to customers.

The mouse, unharmed, was taken outside and allowed to run away.

"There was not a trial or anything," Taylor said with a laugh.

Gem Stop employees are still mystified as to how the mouse got in the ATM machine.

The mystery will add to a story that may be retold in La Grande and on the Internet for years to come.

☑ 기억하면 좋을 구절!

make one's fortune 성공하다 / 재산을 모으다

All these people are *making fortunes* without contributing anything to society. It's a sort of criminal.
이들은 사회에 아무 기여도 없이 부를 축적하고 있다. 이는 일종의 범죄이다.

of humble birth 태생이 천하다 / 출신이 낮다

He is a man *of* very *humble birth*.
그는 비천한 집안 출신이다.

rake up 긁어모으다

Will you *rake up* the fallen leaves?
낙엽을 쓸어 모아 주시겠습니까?

be arrested on charge of ~의 혐의로 체포되다

He *was arrested on charges of* corruption and abuse of power.
그는 부패와 권력 남용 혐의로 체포되었다.

larcenous [láːrsənəs] a. 손버릇이 나쁜 / 절도의

She was arrested on a charge of *larcenous* act.
그 여자는 절도 혐의로 체포되었다.

내 인생의 명언 — 돈으로 살 수 없는 가치들

▶ 좋은 명성은 돈보다 더욱 값어치 있는 것이다.
퍼블릴리우스 사이러스 (시리아 출신 노예 작가)

> A good reputation is more valuable than money.
> Publilius Syrus

▶ 사람은 대개 자신의 원칙보다 자신의 돈에 더 주의를 기울인다.
올리버 홈즈 주니어 (미국 법학자)

> A man is usually more careful of
> his money than of his principles.
> Oliver Wendell Holmes, Jr.

▶ 돈을 가진 사람은 사명을 가진 사람의 적수가 되지 못한다.
도일 브런슨 (미국 직업도박사)

> A man with money is no match against a man on a mission.
> Doyle Brunson

▶ 돈이 행복을 가져올 것이라고 생각하는 사람은
아직 돈을 벌어보지 못한 사람이다.
데이비드 게펜 (미국 영화제작자·자선가)

> Anybody who thinks money
> will make you happy, hasn't got money.
> David Geffen

▶ 나는 돈이 아주 많은 가난한 사람으로 살고 싶다.
파블로 피카소 (스페인 입체파 화가)

> I'd like to live as a poor man with lots of money.
> Pablo Picasso

News English

"A Tardy Student Headhunted as National Athlete"

A novice runner is aiming for the Olympics - after he was spotted chasing a bus.

Jeffrey Lawal Balogun was just 19 when a scout from a top athletics club saw him racing after the No28.

Now, three years on, he is hoping to be part of Team GB for the 2012 London Games.

Jeffrey, currently ranked seventh in the UK at the 60m sprint, told yesterday how his lightning dash down the road in Bromley, Kent, changed his life. He said: "I always knew that I was fast, but I didn't really know how to get into running.

"Then one day I was on my way to college and had to run after the bus. I must have been quite fast because a girl came up to me afterwards and asked if I ran with a club."

It turned out the girl was from Kent Athletic Club and she introduced him to leading sprint coach Clarence Callender, who was immediately impressed. Jeffrey, now 23, of Mottingham, South London, is already carving out a name for himself - and encouraging children to take up athletics at an early age.

He said: "The ultimate goal has to be the Olympics. To win a medal would be the best feeling ever. I just wish I'd started earlier."

He added: "I never thought running after a bus would lead to all this. And the funny thing is, I missed it."

버스 뒤쫓다 육상선수 된 제프리 밸로건

육상 국가대표로 스카우트된 지각생

지각할 것 같았다. 그래서 이미 출발한 버스를 따라잡으려고 필사적으로 달려갔다. 그런데?

지각하지 않으려고 버스를 쫓아가다가 눈에 띄어(be spotted chasing a bus not to be late for school) 육상 국가대표 후보로 발탁된 선수가 있다.

영화 같은 이 이야기의 주인공은 영국 켄트 주(州)에 사는 제프리 밸로건(27세). 그는 현재 런던올림픽을 목표로(aim for the London Olympic Games) 훈련에 구슬땀을 흘리고(train with sweat running down in beads) 있다.

밸로건은 지난 2005년 어느 날 대학 강의를 들으러 가고(be on his way to college) 있었다. 하지만 정류장에 도착했을 때는 이미 버스가 출발한 뒤였다. 저만치 가고 있었다. 지각하지 않으려면 버스를 뒤쫓아가(run after the bus) 잡는 수밖에 없었다.

그때 그의 잽싼 달리기(his lightning dash down the road)가 삶을 뒤바

꿔(change his life)놓았다. 한 명문육상클럽 스카우트가 버스를 뒤쫓아가는 그의 모습을 목격(see him racing after the bus), 손꼽히는 단거리육상 코치인 클래런스 캘린더에게 소개했던 것.

밸로건은 "나도 내가 좀 빠르다는 것은 알고 있었지만 어떻게 달리기에 입문해야 할지 몰랐다(do not know how to get into running)"고 했다.

얼마 후 한 여성이 그에게 와서(come up to him afterwards) 클럽에서 뛰어보지 않겠느냐고 물었다(ask if he'd like to run with club).

그 여성이 켄트 주에서 가장 유명하다는 켄트 육상클럽의 스카우트였던 것이다. 이 스카우트로부터 밸로건을 소개받은 캘린더 코치는 깊은 인상을 받았고(be deeply impressed) 즉각 제자로 받아들이기로 했다.

현재 밸로건은 어린이들이 이른 나이에 육상을 시작하도록 용기를 북돋아 주는(encourage children to take up athletics at an early age) 등 이미 명성을 쌓아가고(carve out a name for himself) 있다.

밸로건이 런던올림픽 단거리 대표팀 선수로 선발되려면(to qualify for the national sprint team) 최소한 100미터를 10초 21 이내에 달려야 한다(must run the 100m in 10.21 seconds).

밸로건은 언론 인터뷰를 통해 "버스 뒤를 쫓아간 것(the running after a bus)이 이 모든 상황으로 이어질 줄(would lead to all these surroundings)은 꿈에도 몰랐다"며 "그런데 재미있는 것(the funny thing)은 내가 그때 그 버스를 놓쳤었다는 사실"이라고 털어놓았다.

Sprinter's Talent Spotted as He Ran for a Bus, Now He's Aiming for Olympics!

A novice runner is aiming for the Olympics—after he was spotted chasing a bus.

Jeffrey Lawal Balogun was just 19 when a scout from a top athletics club saw him racing after the No28.

Now, three years on, he is hoping to be part of Team GB for the 2012 London Games.

Jeffrey, currently ranked seventh in the UK at the 60m sprint, told yesterday how his lightning dash down the road in Bromley, Kent, changed his life. He said: "I always knew that I was fast, but I didn't really know how to get into running.

"Then one day I was on my way to college and had to run after the bus. I must have been quite fast because a girl came up to me afterwards and asked if I ran with a club."

It turned out the girl was from Kent Athletic Club and she introduced him to leading sprint coach Clarence Callender, who was immediately impressed. Jeffrey, now 23, of Mottingham, South London, is already carving out a name for himself – and encouraging children to take up athletics at an early age.

He said: "The ultimate goal has to be the Olympics. To win a medal would be the best feeling ever. I just wish I'd started earlier."

He added: "I never thought running after a bus would lead to all this. And the funny thing is, I missed it."

JEFFREY'S GOLD BID

To qualify for the 2012 sprint team Jeffrey must run the 100m inside 10.21secs. Team GB can enter three athletes if they finish inside this time.

✓ 기억하면 좋을 구절!

aim for ~을 목적으로 하다 / ~을 지향하다

Work hard if you *aim for* the sky.
큰 뜻을 품고 있다면 열심히 일하라.

dash down 급히 (달려) 내려가다 / 돌진하다

The horse *dashed down* the hill.
말 한 마리가 언덕을 달려 내려갔다.

take up ~을 하기 시작하다 / 차지하다

An old lady began to *take up* the tale in a loud voice.
한 노부인이 큰 소리로 이야기하기 시작했다.

qualify for ~의 자격을 얻다 / 출전권을 따내다

This training course will *qualify* you *for* a better job.
이 훈련 과정을 거치면 더 좋은 일자리를 구할 자격이 생긴다.

carve out 노력하여 얻다 / 자수성가하다

She *carved out* a niche market with a small capital.
그녀는 적은 자본으로 틈새 시장을 뚫었다.

내 인생의 명언 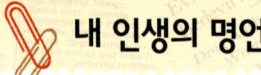 과거, 현재, 그리고 미래

▶ 나는 과거 속에서 사는 편이다.
그 이유는 생애 대부분이 거기 있기 때문이다.
허브 코헨 (퓰리처상 수상, 미국 칼럼니스트)

> I tend to live in the past because most of my life is there.
> Herb Cohen

▶ 미래는 어느 날 한꺼번에 들이닥친다.
에이브러햄 링컨 (미국 제16대 대통령)

> Future pays you a surprise visit one day at a time
> Abraham Lincoln

▶ 현재는 막 지나간 시점이다.
데이비드 러셀 (미국 시나리오작가 · 영화제작자)

> The present is a point just passed.
> David Russell

▶ 과거에 머물지 말고, 미래에 대해 몽상하지 말고,
현재 순간에 마음을 집중해라.
석가모니 (불교 창시자 · 인도의 성자)

> Do not dwell in the past, do not dream of the future,
> concentrate the mind on the present moment.
> Buddah

▶ 미래를 예측하는 가장 좋은 방법은 미래를 만들어나가는 것이다.
앨런 케이 (미국 컴퓨터과학자)

> The best way to predict the future is to invent it.
> Alan Kay

Favorite famous sayings!

▶ 언제나 기억하라. 미래는 어느 날 한꺼번에 온다.
  딘 애치슨 (미국 행정관료 국무장관)

> Always remember that the future comes one day at a time.
> Dean Acheson

▶ 현재란 과거의 생생한 총체이다.
  토마스 칼라일 (스코틀랜드 수필가 · 역사가 · 비평가)

> The present is the living sum-total of the whole past.
> Thomas Carlyle

▶ 과거의 위험은 사람이 노예가 되는 것이었는데,
  미래의 위험은 사람이 로봇이 될 수 있다는 것이다.
  에리히 프롬 (미국 정신분석학자)

> The danger of the past was that men became slaves.
> The danger of the future is that man may become robots.
> Erich Pinchas Fromm

▶ 사회의 적은 중산층이고, 인생의 적은 중년이다.
  조지 웰스 (미국 배우 · 영화감독)

> The enemy of society is middle class and the enemy of life is middle age.
> George Wells

News English

"An Unfaithful Husband Standing at an Intersection"

Jobless William Taylor was forced to wear the sign reading, "I cheated, this is my punishment" after his wife Karen found him texting "intimate pictures" to another woman.

He explained: "It kind of came out in an argument. I said, 'What do I have to do to show you I love you to death?'

"She said, 'How about you go and stand out on the street and tell everybody that you know what you are.'" "I thought she was kidding, but she was serious.

"I figured I got to do what I got to do to makes things right - so here I am."

William, of Washington DC, admitted he would have run naked through the US capital's shopping centre to win Karen over.

He admitted: "I would do anything to get her back. I made a huge mistake."

Meanwhile jilted Kim Eccott set fire to her boyfriend's designer suits as he turfed her out of his flat. The blaze caused $25,000 of damage to the two-bed apartment.

Eccott, 23, had become angry when club boss Mark Naylor, 47, ordered her to go, Ipswich crown court heard.

As he carried her cases out of the flat above his nightclub Jokers in Stowmarket, Suffolk, she set light to his clothes with a cigarette lighter.

Eccott of Stevenage, Herts, admitted arson and received a 52-week suspended jail sentence with two years' supervision.

Jobless William Taylor was forced to wear the sign reading, "I cheated, this is my punishment" after his wife Karen found him texting "intimate pictures" to another woman.

He explained: "It kind of came out in an argument. I said, 'What do I have to do to show you I love you to death?'

"She said, 'How about you go and stand out on the street and tell everybody that you know what you are.'" "I thought she was kidding, but she was serious.

"I figured I got to do what I got to do to makes things right - so here I am."

William, of Washington DC, admitted he would have run naked through the US capital's shopping centre to win Karen over.

He admitted: "I would do anything to get her back. I made a huge mistake."

Meanwhile jilted Kim Eccott set fire to her boyfriend's designer suits as he turfed her out of his flat. The blaze caused $25,000 of damage to the two-bed apartment.

Eccott, 23, had become angry when club boss Mark Naylor, 47, ordered her to go, Ipswich court heard.

"바람피워서 벌 받는 중이랍니다"

바람피우고 교차로에서 벌 받은 남편

남편이 바람을 피웠다. 애인에게 휴대폰 메시지를 보내다가 아내에게 딱 걸렸다. 용서를 빌었다. 어떻게 하면 변함없는 사랑을 증명해 보일 수 있겠느냐고 물었다. 아내가 말했다. "'나는 바람을 피웠다'는 간판을 목에 걸고 일주일 동안 시내 교차로에 서 있어요."

바람을 피웠던 한 미국인 남편(an unfaithful American husband)이 아내의 마음을 되찾기 위해(in a desperate bid to win back his wife) 2009년 8월 28일 워싱턴 시내의 한 붐비는 교차로에서 창피를 무릅썼다(humiliate himself at a busy intersection in Washington D.C.).

실업자 상태인 윌리엄 테일러(jobless William Taylor)는 최근 성관계를 묘사하는 문자를 다른 여성에게 보내다가(text intimate pictures to another woman) 아내 캐런에 의해 발각됐다.

이후 그는 참담한 역경(a wretched plight)을 당해야 했다. "나는 바람을 피웠다. 이것은 내가 받는 벌이다"라고 쓰인 간판을 목에 걸고 창피한 모습으로 길 가에 서 있어야 (have to stand looking suitably ashamed on the street corner with a sign draped around his neck, reading "I CHEATED. THIS IS MY PUNISHMENT")했다.

이런 진풍경은 "말다툼을 하다가 나온 것(come out in an argument)"이라고 했다. "당신을 죽도록 사랑한다는(love you to death) 걸 보여주려면 어떻게 해야 하겠느냐"고 했더니 "거리로 나가 서서(go and stand out on the street) 당신이 어떤 인간인지를 모든 사람들에게 얘기하라(tell everybody what you are)"고 했다는 것이다.

농담하는(be kidding) 줄 알았다」/ 했디. 하시만 아내는 진담(be serious)이었다. 테일러는 "아내를 되찾기 위해서라면 무슨 일이든 해야(do anything to get her back) 겠다"고 판단했다. "큰 실수를 한(make a huge mistake) 것은 사실이고, 불륜에 대한 속죄를 해야 한다고(must atone for his affair) 생각했기 때문"이라고 했다.

그는 "캐런을 설득하려면(to win Karen over) 워싱턴 시내 쇼핑센터에서 발가벗고 뛰어다니는(run naked through the US capital's shopping center) 짓이라도 했을 것"이라고 말한다. 아내와 화해하기를 간절히 원했다는(be desperate to make up with his wife) 것이다.

처음엔 간판을 걸고 일주일 동안 서 있으라고 요구했다(ask him to stand with it for a week). 하지만 두 시간 정도 지난 뒤(after a couple of hours) 그는 "당신의 벌은 이제 끝났다"는 아내의 전화를 받았다(receive a call to say "your punishment is over").

Unfaithful Husband Humiliated by Wife

Jobless William Taylor was forced to wear the sign reading, "I cheated, this is my punishment" after his wife Karen found him texting "intimate pictures" to another woman.

He explained: "It kind of came out in an argument. I said, 'What do I have to do to show you I love you to death?'

"She said, ' How about you go and stand out on the street and tell everybody that you know what you are.' "I thought she was kidding, but she was serious.

"I figured I got to do what I got to do to makes things right – so here I am."

William, of Washington DC, admitted he would have run naked through the US capital's shopping centre to win Karen over.

He admitted: "I would do anything to get her back. I made a huge mistake."

Meanwhile jilted Kim Eccott set fire to her boyfriend's designer suits as he turfed her out of his flat. The blaze caused $25,000 of damage to the two-bed apartment.

Eccott, 23, had become angry when club boss Mark Naylor, 47, ordered her to go, Ipswich crown court heard.

As he carried her cases out of the flat above his nightclub Jokers in Stowmarket, Suffolk, she set light to his clothes with a cigarette lighter.

Eccott, of Stevenage, Herts, admitted arson and received a 52-week suspended jail sentence with two years' supervision.

☑ 기억하면 좋을 구절!

in a bid to do ~을 목적으로 / ~하기 위하여

They take on a Korean pairing *in* their *bid to* reach the final tomorrow.
내일 결승전에 진출하기 위해 한국 선수 한 쌍과 경기한다.

humiliate oneself 면목을 잃다 / 창피를 당하다

I was *humiliated* because I couldn't answer a simple question.
간단한 질문에도 대답을 못해서 창피를 당했다.

atone [ətóun] v. 속죄하다

If we do wrong, we must *atone*.
우리는 잘못을 저지르면 속죄해야 한다.

be desperate to ~하기 위해 안간힘을 다하다 / 필사적으로 ~을 하다

I'm *desperate to* make a living.
먹고살 일이 막막하다.

make up with ~와 화해하다

Did you *make up with* your parents?
부모님과는 화해했니?

내 인생의 명언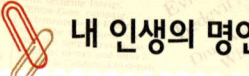

▶ 시각장애 아내와 청각장애 남편 부부는 늘 행복하다.
몽테뉴 (프랑스 사상가 · 수필가)

> A deaf husband and a blind wife are
> always a happy couple.
> Michel de Montaigne

▶ 성공적인 결혼은 늘 똑같은 사람과 몇번이고 다시
사랑에 빠지는 것을 필요로 한다.
미뇽 머클로플린 (미국 언론인 · 작가)

> A successful marriage requires falling in love many times,
> always with the same person.
> Mignon McLaughlin

▶ 모든 남자들이 실수를 한다. 그러나 결혼한 남자들은
더 빨리 실수에 대해 알아차리게 된다.
레드 스켈튼 (미국 코미디언)

> All men make mistakes, but married men
> find out about them sooner.
> Red Skelton

▶ 당신이 함께 살 수 있을 것 같다고 생각하는 사람과 결혼하지 마라.
없으면 못살 것 같다고 생각하는 사람과 결혼하라.
제임스 돕슨 (미국 작가 · 심리학자)

> Don't marry the person you think you can live with;
> marry only the individual you think
> you can't live without.
> James Dobson

Favorite famous sayings!

▶ 사랑과 결혼에 대해 읽고 싶으면 각각 다른 두 권의 책을 사야 한다.
앨런 킹 (미국 배우 · 코미디언)

> If you want to read about love and marriage,
> you've got to buy two separate books.
> Alan King

▶ 결혼이란 제1장은 시(詩)로 쓰여지고 나머지 장들은 산문(散文)으로 쓰여지는 책과 같다.
비벌리 니콜스 (영국 작가 · 언론인 · 작곡가)

> Marriage: a book of which the first chapter is
> written in poetry and the remaining chapters in prose.
> Beverly Nichols

▶ 내 충고는 결혼을 하라는 것이다. 좋은 아내를 만나면 행복할 것이요, 그렇지 못하면 철학자가 될 것이기 때문이다.
소크라테스 (그리스 철학자)

> My advice to you is to get married.
> If you find a good wife you'll be happy;
> if not you'll become a philosopher.
> Socrates

▶ 결혼을 잘 한 사람은 날개를 달고, 잘못한 사람은 족쇄를 차게 된다.
헨리 비처 (미국 성직자)

> Well married a person has wings,
> poorly married shackles.
> Henry Beecher

Funny Funny World | 51

News English

"Football Star Wayne Rooney and a Murder Case"

A MAN was killed by a drunken stranger after taunting him that he looked like Wayne Rooney, a court heard yesterday.

Reveller Anthony Corsi, 24, was at a taxi rank heading home when a group of men chanted "Rooney, Rooney".

He swung an uppercut at Christopher Jones, 21, who suffered bleeding to the brain. He died a short time later.

Rees, defender for Wales and Manchester United, has become a "figure" features.

He said of Corsi, that the stranger but was provoked.

"I don't want to say his looks have him and Corsi ask..."

The alleged attack October 21 last his way home after Christopher Aberg, was with Mr Jones attack and admitted Rooney' football-st Cardiff Crown Court as a joke because I th him and I could see h reaction on his face.

"He said, 'Do I look gi of the taxi as we were shouting, 'Rooney, Rooney'. The gentleman came towards Chris and hit him.

Corsi's gentleman has doesn't matter whether you think Corsi looks like Mr Rooney or not ? it was a drunken joke.

"Corsi should have gone home but was angry and annoyed and looking for trouble. It was wholly unnecessary."

Trainee accountant Mr Jones had been... Rooney". The gentleman came back, moved towards Chris and hit him.

Corsi admitted he "over-reacted" to the taunts and stopped the cab and got out to confront the men. He told police: "I was upset about what they called me, I was nervous, upset and drunk.

"It was the way he approached, I remember him coming towards me ...him, I suppose I felt threatened ...acted."

Roger Thomas told the jury: "It ...ter whether you think Corsi ...r Rooney or not ? it was a

I have gone home but was ...yed and looking for trouble. ...necessary."

...nt Mr Jones had been ...ke a full recovery from ...but collapsed and died a ...tal.

...th, Cardiff, denies ...rial continues

...by a drunken stranger ...that he looked like ...rt heard yesterday.

...rsi, 24, was at a taxi ...en a group of men

October 21 last year as Corsi was on his way home after a night out in Cardiff. Christopher Aberg, a British Gas adviser, was with Mr Jones at the time of the attack and admitted starting the "Rooney, Rooney" football-style chants. He told Cardiff Crown Court: "I called him Rooney as a joke because I thought he looked like him and I could see he was annoyed by the reaction on his face.

"He said, 'Do I look ginger?' I then got in the taxi as we were shouting, 'Rooney, Rooney'. The gentleman came back, moved towards Chris and hit him."

Corsi admitted he "over-reacted" to the taunts and stopped the cab and got out to confront the men. He told police: "I was upset about what they called me, I was angry, nervous, upset and drunk.

"Maybe it was the way he approached, I just remember him coming towards me and I hit him, I suppose I felt threatened and over-reacted."

Prosecutor Roger Thomas told the jury: "It doesn't matter whether you think Corsi looks like Mr Rooney or not ? it was a drunken joke.

"Corsi should have gone home but was angry, and annoyed and looking for trouble. It was wholly unnecessary."

Trainee Accountant Mr Jones had been ... make a full recovery from ... ...ury, but collapsed and died a ...hospital.

...Heath, Cardiff ...es The trial continues.

못생긴 축구스타 1위 웨인 루니와 우발 살인범 앤서니코시

못난이 축구스타 웨인 루니와 살인 사건

축구스타 웨인 루니를 닮았다는 놀림에 살인을 저지르는(commit murder) 사건이 영국에서 벌어졌다.

박지성과 한솥밥을 먹고 있는 잉글랜드 프로축구 프리미어리그 맨체스터 유나이티드의 루니는 영국 여성 스포츠팬들을 상대로 한 '가장 못생긴 축구선수' 설문조사에서 1위로 뽑혔다. 애니메이션 영화 주인공 슈렉을 닮았다고 해서 '슈렉'이라 불리기도 하는 루니는 '외계인' 별명을 가진 호나우지뉴(바르셀로나)를 제치고 최고의 '얼짱 축구스타'라는 불명예를 안았다.

사건은 2008년 10월 21일 새벽 5시 카디프의 한 택시정류장 근처에서 일어났다(take place near a taxi stand). 루니와 동갑내기인 앤서니 코시(24세)는 자신의 외모가 루니를 닮았다고 놀려대는(taunt him over his resemblance to Wayne Rooney) 또래의 남자를 때려 숨지게 했다(lash out and kill a man of his age).

사건 당시 주먹을 휘두른 코시와 그를 향해 "루니, 루니" 하고 외쳐대다(chant "Rooney, Rooney" at him) 사망한 크리스토퍼 존스와 일행 두 명은 모두 만취한 상태(be drunk like a fish)였다.

먼저 택시에 올라탔다가(hop in a taxi) 존스 일행의 '모욕'에 화가 난(get furious at the 'insult') 코시는 택시를 세우고 차에서 내려 존스에게 다가간 뒤(after moving towards Jones) 갑자기 주먹을 휘둘렀다(strike him with a clenched fist all of a sudden).

엉겁결에(in spite of himself) 주먹을 맞은 존스는 비틀거리다가 쓰러져(stagger away and collapse) 병원으로 옮겨졌으나 뇌출혈을 일으켜(suffer bleeding in the brain) 일주일 만에 숨지고 말았다.

맨 처음 코시를 향해 "루니 루니"라고 외쳤던 존스의 친구 크리스토퍼 애버그는 법정 증언을 통해 "루니를 많이 닮았길래 그냥 농담으로 그렇게 불렀던 것인데 그가 격분한(be goaded into fury) 것 같았다"고 말했다.

그는 "나와 존스 등 일행이 그날 밤 맥주, 물을 타지 않은 독주와 알코올 함유 음료(drink beer, shorts and alcopops) 등을 마셔 술에 취해 있었던 것은 사실"이라고 인정했다.

이에 대해 코시 변호인은 "루니를 모욕하는 것은 아니지만, 루니의 외모가 좀 재미있게 생긴 것은 사실이지 않느냐. 루니에 비교된 코시가 화를 낸(take offence) 것은 당연하다"며 재판부가 정상참작해줄(make allowances for the circumstances) 것을 호소했다.

앞서 코시는 경찰 진술에서 "술에 취한데다 신경이 예민해져 있어 존스가 나에게 다가오고 있는 모습을 보고 위협감을 느껴 과잉반응을 한(feel threatened and overreact) 것 같다"며 선처를 호소했다.

그러나 검찰 측은 "의도적 살인은 아니지만 불법적 폭력(unlawful violence)을 행사한 것은 분명하다"며 "문제를 일으켜 화를 자초(ask for trouble and bring misfortune on himself)한 코시에게 중형을 내려야 한다"고 주장하고 있다.

Killed for Rooney Jibe at Lookalike

A MAN was killed by a drunken stranger after taunting him that he looked like Wayne Rooney, a court heard yesterday.

Reveller Anthony Corsi, 24, was at a taxi rank heading home when a group of men chanted "Rooney, Rooney".

He swung an uppercut at Christopher Jones, 21, who suffered bleeding to the brain. He died a week later. John Charles Rees, defending, told the court that England and Manchester United star Rooney had become a "figure of fun" because of his features.

He said of Corsi: "This man was a total stranger but was goaded, wound up and provoked.

"I don't want to insult Wayne Rooney but his looks have become a bit of a figure of fun and Corsi took offence."

The alleged attack happened at 5 am on October 21 last year as Corsi was on his way home after a night out in Cardiff. Christopher Aberg, a British Gas adviser, was with Mr Jones at the time of the attack and admitted starting the "Rooney, Rooney" football-style chants. He told Cardiff Crown Court: "I called him Rooney as a joke because I thought he looked like him and I could see he was annoyed by the reaction on his face.

"He said, 'Do I look ginger?' – then got in the taxi as we were shouting, 'Rooney, Rooney'. The gentleman came back, moved towards Chris and hit him."

Corsi admitted he "over-reacted" to the taunts and stopped the cab and got out to confront the men. He told police: "I was upset about what they called me. I was angry, nervous, upset and drunk.

"Maybe it was the way he approached, I just remember him coming towards me and I hit him. I suppose I felt threatened and over-reacted."

Prosecutor Roger Thomas told the jury: "It doesn't matter whether you think Corsi looks like Mr Rooney or not – it was a drunken joke.

"Corsi should have gone home but was angry and annoyed and looking for trouble. It was wholly unnecessary."

Trainee accountant Mr Jones had been expected to make a full recovery from the head injury – but collapsed and died a week later in hospital.

Corsi, of Heath, Cardiff, denies manslaughter. The trial continues.

☑ 기억하면 좋을 구절!

commit murder 살인하다

> He was blinded by money and went as far as to *commit murder*.
> 그는 돈에 눈이 멀어 결국 살인까지 저질렀다.

take place 개최되다 / (계획된 일이) 일어나다

> The predicted earthquake may not *take place* at all.
> 예보된 지진이 전혀 일어나지 않을 수도 있다.

taunt [tɔ:nt] v. 놀리다 / 비웃다 / 조롱하다

> He became a *taunt* to his friends.
> 그는 친구들에게 놀림감이 되었다.

lash out 채찍질하다 / 강타하다 / 비난하다

> He *lashed out* angrily, hitting anyone within his reach.
> 그는 화를 내며 후려 갈겨 닥치는 대로 아무나 때려댔다.

stagger [stǽgə(r)] v. 비틀거리다 / 휘청대다

> I managed to stagger the last few steps.
> 나는 비틀대며 간신히 걸었다.

take offense 불쾌해하다 / 화내다

> Don't *take offense* at what I said.
> 내 말에 기분 상하지 마라.

내 인생의 명언   화는 마음의 독이다

▶ 당신이 화를 낼 때마다 당신은 자신의 몸에 독을 넣는 것이다.
알프레드 몬태퍼 (미국 작가)

> Every time you get angry, you poison your own system.
> Alfred Montapert

▶ 당신이 화가 나 있는 매 1분마다
당신은 마음의 평화를 60초씩 포기하고 있는 것이다.
랠프 에머슨 (미국의 사상가·시인)

> For every minute you remain angry,
> you give up sixty seconds of peace of mind.
> Ralph Waldo Emerson

▶ 화를 내라. 그러나 그것을 이겨내라.
콜린 파월 (미국의 전 국무장관)

> Get mad, then get over it.
> Colin Luther Powell

▶ 증오는 가슴의 문제이고, 경멸은 머리의 문제이다.
아서 쇼펜하워 (독일의 철학자)

> Hatred is an affair of the heart; contempt that of the head.
> Arthur Schopenhauer

▶ 화가 났을 때는 절대 아무것도 하지 마라.
모든 것을 그르칠 것이기 때문이다.
발타사르 그라시안 (스페인 예수회 신부·작가)

> Never do anything when you are in a temper,
> for you will do everything wrong.
> Baltasar Gracian

News English

"Shooting Lawmakers in the Face with Air Gun"

Two artists have offered Czechs angered by politics the chance to take revenge on their lawmakers by shooting them literally in the face, by turning their photos into air gun targets.

Tomas Cap and Michal Kraus have displayed the portraits of 200 lower-house deputies in plastic boxes on the wall of a Prague alternative gallery, in front of an air gun and a boxful of ammunition.

"We have seen lawmakers breach the promises they gave to voters so many times. The visitors of the gallery have a unique opportunity to show these politicians what they think," the artists said in a statement.

Two weeks after opening, the exhibition was a sad sight as most of the faces had been heavily damaged by air gun shots, some destroyed beyond recognition. Opposition chief Jiri Paroubek was the worst hit with most of his face missing in the picture, followed by the premier Bohuslav Sobotka and Interior Minister Ivan Langer.

Outgoing Prime Minister Mirek Topolanek, whose cabinet was toppled midway through the Czech European Union presidency last month, was also badly damaged, just like his primered, lawmaker Lucie Talmanova.

"It's mostly young that come but we just had teenagers in suits and pensioners, including an elderly woman on crutches who climbed to the 3rd floor just to take a shot," Milan Mikulastik, the curator of the display, told AFP.

He added the exhibition designed to "trigger a debate on the functioning of the political system" was a big success, but it had drawn angry reactions from some deputies.

He said he only hoped the crumbling photos would last till the end of the exhibition on Sunday as "the artists want to send them to the lawmakers afterwards."

Two artists have offered Czechs angered by politics the chance to take revenge on their lawmakers but it

국회위원 사진에 총 쏘는 행위예술(?)

Two artists have offered Czechs angered by politics the chance to take revenge on their lawmakers by shooting them literally in the face, by turning their photos into air gun targets.

Tomas Cap and Michal Kraus have displayed the portraits of 200 lower-house deputies in plastic boxes on the wall of a Prague alternative gallery, in front of an air gun and a boxful of ammunition.

"We have seen lawmakers breach the promises they gave to voters so many times. The visitors of the gallery have a unique opportunity to show these politicians what they think," the artists said in a statement.

Two weeks after opening, the exhibition as most of the faces had damaged by air gun shots, beyond recognition.

chief Jiri Paroubek was the with most of his face missing in followed by premier Bohuslav Sobotka Interior Minister Ivan Langer.

국회의원 얼굴 사진에 총 쏘기

동유럽 체코에 '통렬한 행위예술'(an incisive performance art) 작품이 등장해 큰 호응을 얻고 있다. 벽면에 국회의원들 사진을 한가득 붙여놓고 얼굴에 공기총을 쏘아대는(shoot the lawmakers in the face with an air gun) 것이 작품 내용이다.

토마스 캡과 미찰 크라우스라는 이름의 두 예술가는 수도 프라하의 한 갤러리에 이 작품을 전시, 정치에 화가 난 체코인들에게 국회의원 얼굴을 향해 총을 쏨으로써 '복수'할 기회를 제공하고(offer Czechs angered by politics the chance to take 'revenge' on their lawmakers by shooting them in the face) 있다.

두 예술가는 "유권자들에게 수많은 공약들을 해놓고 지키지 않는 국회의원들을 봐왔다(have seen lawmakers breach the promises they gave to voters so many times)"면서 "우리 갤러리 방문객들은 어떤 생각을 갖고 있는지 정치인들에게 보여줄 진기한 기회를 갖게 될 것(will have a unique opportunity to show the politicians what they think)"이라고 말했다.

개관 2주 만에(two weeks after opening) 전시회장은 난장판이 됐다. (국회의원들) 얼굴 대부분이 공기총 총알에 의해 심각하게 손상됐고(be heavily damaged by airgun slugs), 일부는 얼굴을 알아볼 수 없을 정도로 만신창이가 됐다(be destroyed beyond recognition).

그중에서도 야당 총재(the Opposition leader)인 지리 파로우벡은 사진에서 얼굴 대부분이 없어졌을 정도로 최악의 총알 세례를 받는 대상이 됐다(become the worst hit with most of his face missing in the picture).

그다음으로는 그와 동맹 관계인 정치인 데이비드 라스와 이반 랑거 내무장관 얼굴에 집중 공세가 가해졌다. 또 최근에 물러난 미렉 토폴라넥 전 총리와 그의 여자친구인 루시 탈마노바 의원의 얼굴이 심하게 훼손됐다.

이 행위예술 갤러리에는 주로 젊은이들이 많이 찾아왔으나 나이 든 방문객들도 적지 않았다. 꼭 총을 쏘고 싶은(want to take a shot) 의원들이 있다며 목발을 짚고 찾아온 나이 지긋한 여성(an elderly woman on crutches)도 있었다고 AFP통신은 전한다.

정계의 역할에 대한 논쟁을 유발하기 위해 기획된 이 전시회(this exhibition designed to trigger a debate on the functioning of the political system)는 대성공을 거뒀다. 물론 일부 의원들로부터 격한 반응을 불러일으키기도(draw angry reactions from some deputies) 했다. 이번 행위예술을 기획한 예술가들은 산산조각 난 사진들을 나중에 국회의원들에게 보내(send the crumbling photos to the lawmakers afterwards) 줄 계획이다.

Artists Offer Czechs Chance to Shoot Lawmakers in the Face

Two artists have offered Czechs angered by politics the chance to take revenge on their lawmakers by shooting them literally in the face, by turning their photos into air gun targets.

Tomas Cap and Michal Kraus have displayed the portraits of 200 lower-house deputies in plastic boxes on the wall of a Prague alternative gallery, in front of an air gun and a boxful of ammunition.

"We have seen lawmakers breach the promises they gave to voters so many times. The visitors of the gallery have a unique opportunity to show these politicians what they think," the artists said in a statement.

Two weeks after opening, the exhibition was a sad sight as most of the faces had been heavily damaged by airgun slugs, with some destroyed beyond recognition.

Opposition chief Jiri Paroubek was the worst hit with most of his face missing in the picture, followed by his ally David Rath and Interior Minister Ivan Langer.

Outgoing Prime Minister Mirek Topolanek, whose cabinet was toppled midway through the Czech European Union presidency last month, was also badly damaged, just like his girlfriend, lawmaker Lucie Talmanova.

"It's mostly youths that come, but we have also had managers in suits and pensioners," including an elderly woman on crutches who climbed to the first-floor room to take a shot, Milan Mikulastik, the curator of the display, told AFP.

He added the exhibition designed to "trigger a debate on the functioning of the political system" was a big success, but it had drawn angry reactions from some deputies.

He said he only hoped the crumbling photos would last till the end of the exhibition on Sunday as "the artists want to send them to the lawmakers afterwards."

✅ 기억하면 좋을 구절!

incisive [ɪnsáɪsɪv] a. 예리한 / 기민한 / 날카로운

➡ That is an example of *incisive* questioning.
그것은 예리한 질문의 표본이다.

breach [briːtʃ] n. 위반. v. 위반하다 / 파기하다

➡ Many countries are in *breach* of their obligations.
대다수 국가들이 의무를 어기고 있다.

beyond recognition 알아볼 수 없을 정도로, 원형을 찾아볼 수 없을 만큼

➡ It will be changed almost *beyond recognition*
거의 알아보기 힘들 정도로 달라질 것이다.

get(take) revenge on ~에게 복수하다 / 원한을 풀다

➡ I swear I'll get revenge on him.
맹세코 그에게 복수하고 말 것이다.

on crutches 목발을 하고(짚고)

➡ I walked *on crutches* for quite a while.
나는 한동안 목발을 짚고 다녔다.

Funny Funny World

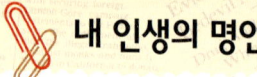
내 인생의 명언 — 인간은 정치적 동물이다

▶ 정치인이란 자신의 자리를 지키기 위해 뭐든지 하는 사람들이다. 심지어 애국자가 되는 것도 한다.
윌리엄 랜돌프 (미국 신문 경영인)

> A politician will do anything to keep his job
> — even become a patriot.
> William Randolph Hearst

▶ 민주주의란 서로 맞바꿔도 그만인 후보자들을 두고 아무런 이슈 없이 엄청난 비용을 들여 수많은 선거가 치러지는 장소다.
고어 바이덜 (미국 소설가·극작가)

> Apparently, a democracy is a place where
> numerous elections are held at great cost without
> issues and with interchangeable candidates.
> Gore Vidal

▶ 모든 정치인은 고아로 태어났어야 하고 미혼남으로 남았어야 한다.
레이디 버드 존슨 (린든 존슨 미국 36대 대통령의 부인)

> Every politician should have been born
> an orphan and remain a bachelor.
> Lady Bird Johnson

▶ 대통령보다 더 높은 한 자리가 있다. 나는 그것을 애국자라고 부른다.
게리 하트 (미국 정치인 변호사)

> I think there is one higher office than president
> and I would call that patriot.
> Gary Hart

Favorite famous sayings!

▶ 죄를 지어야 한다면 신에게 지어라. 관료주의에겐 짓지 마라.
 신은 용서할 것이다. 그러나 관료주의는 용서하지 않을 것이다.
 하이먼 리코버 (미국 해군제독)

> If you are going to sin, sin against God, not the bureaucracy.
> God will forgive you but the bureaucracy won't.
> Hyman Rickover

▶ 정치인들은 주인이 되기 위해 하인 시늉을 한다.
 드골 (프랑스의 군인 · 정치가)

> In order to become the master,
> the politician poses as the servant.
> Charles De Gaulle

▶ 정치인에게 나라의 열쇠를 주는 대신
 자물쇠를 바꿔버리는 것이 나을 것이다.
 더그 라슨 (미국 칼럼니스트)

> Instead of giving a politician the keys to the country,
> it might be better to change the locks.
> Doug Larson

▶ 사람들이 정치를 증오하는 이유 중 하나는
 진실이 정치인의 목표인 경우가 거의 없기 때문이다.
 그들의 목표는 오로지 당선과 권력뿐이다.
 칼 토마스 (미국 칼럼니스트)

> One of the reasons people hate politics is that
> truth is rarely a politician's objective. Election and power are.
> Karl Thomas

News English

"Unconventional Tactics of Job Applicants"

Facing the most difficult job market in decades, some job seekers have resorted to using unconventional methods to stand out from the crowd. According to a new survey from CareerBuilder, nearly one-in-five hiring managers (18 percent) reported that they are seeing more job seekers unusual tactics to cap 2009 compared to la 12 percent of hiring the same in 2008 as co years.

"The search for emp longer and is more co has been in past years," senior career adviser a

"To compensate, some turned to extreme men job search antics may attr of hiring managers, they ne with care and profession candidates are remembered reasons."

Some of the most memor identified by hiring managers i

• Candidate sent a shoe with "get my foot in the door."
• Candidate staged a sit-in in the lobby to get a meeting with a director.
• Candidate washed cars in the parking lot. Candidate sent a resume wrapped as present and said his skills were a "gift to the company.
• Candidate handed out resumes stoplights.
• Candidate sent a cake designed

Candidate told the receptionist he had an interview with the manager. When he met the manager, he confessed that he was driving by and decided to stop in on a chance.

identified by hiring managers include:
• Candidate sent a shoe with a resume to "get my foot in the door."
• te staged a sit-in in the lobby to ting with a director.
washed cars in the parking lot. sent a resume wrapped as a said his skills were a "gift to

e handed out resumes at

ent a cake designed as a with the candidate's picture: ent to the same barber as of the Board and had the his behalf. nded out personalized

dressed in a bunny suit r Exeter. receptionist he had the manager. When he confessed that he

survey from CareerBuilder, nearly one-in-five hiring managers (18 percent) reported that they are seeing more job seekers try unusual tactics to capture their attention in 2009 compared to last year. This is up from 12 percent of hiring managers who said the same in 2008 as compared to previous years.

"The search for employment is taking longer and is more competitive than it has been in past years," said Jason Ferrara, senior career adviser at CareerBuilder.

"To compensate, some candidates have turned to extreme tactics. While unusual job search antics may attract the attention of hiring managers, they need to be done with care and professionalism so that candidates are remembered for the right reasons."

Some of the most memorable tactics identified by hiring managers include:
• Candidate sent a shoe with a resume to "get my foot in the door."

이력서를 들고 거리에 선 구직자

68

구직자들의 색다른 전술

미국도 수십 년 만에 가장 어려운 취업 시장 위기에 직면한 가운데(facing the most difficult job market in decades), 일부 구직자들은 다른 다수의 구직자들로부터 돋보이기 위해 색다른 방법들을 쓰고(resort to using unconventional methods to stand out from the crowd) 있다.

고용주의 관심을 끌려고 진귀한 수법들을 사용하는(turn to unusual gimmicks to grab the attention of potential employers) 구직자 중엔 이력서와 함께 신발 한 짝을 보낸(send a shoe along with a resume) 경우도 있다. "귀사의 문에 내 발을 들일 수 있게(get my foot in the door of your company) 해달라"는 간곡한 표현이다.

미국의 온라인 구직·구인 사이트인 커리어빌더의 새 조사에 따르면(according to a new survey from CareerBuilder), 채용 담당자들 5명 중 1명(one-in-five hiring managers)은 올 들어 채용자의 관심을 끌기 위해 독특한 전술을 시도하는 구직자들을 더 많이 보게(see more job seekers try unusual tactics to capture hirers' attention) 됐다고 말한다.

일자리 찾기(the search for employment)는 과거 수년보다 경쟁이 더 심해졌고(be much more competitive than it has been in past years), 취업에 걸리는 기간도 훨씬 더 길어지고(be taking much longer) 있다.

25년 만에 가장 높은 실업에 직면해(be faced with the highest unemployment in 25 years) 있는 구직자들은 다음과 같은 다양한 수법들을 시도하고 (try a variety of tricks as follow) 있다.

- 구직자 사진이 들어간 명함 모양의 케이크를 보낸다(send a cake designed as a business card with the candidate's picture)
- 회사 앞 신호등에서 이력서를 배포한다(hand out resumes at stoplights in front of the company)
- 이력서를 선물처럼 포장해서 보내며(send a resume wrapped as a present) 자신의 능력과 경험이 회사에 선물이(a gift to the company) 될 것이라고 강조한다
- 회사 주차장에서 차들을 세차해준다(wash cars in a company parking lot)
- 회사 로비에서 간부와의 만남을 요청하며 앉아 있는다(stage a sit-in in a company lobby to demand a meeting with director)
- 자신의 이름 머리글자 등을 붙인 커피잔을 나눠준다(hand out personalized coffee cups)

- 회사 사장이 머리를 깎는 이발소에 가서 이발사에게 자신을 위해 유리한 말을 해줄 것을 부탁한다(go to the same barber as the company chairman to have the barber speak on his behalf)

이 밖에도 기발한 아이디어들이 많다. 하지만 채용 매니저들은 "독특한 구직 익살 행동들(unusual job search antics)이 채용 담당자들의 관심을 끌 수는(may attract the attention of hiring managers) 있지만, 올바른 동기로 기억되기 위해서는(to be remembered for the right reasons) 신중하고 전문성 있게 해야 한다고(need to be done with care and professionalism) 조언한다.

이번 조사는 미국 내 2543명의 풀타임 채용 담당자들과 인력관리 전문가들을 상대로 실시됐다. 전체 조사결과(the overall results)의 오차 범위는 플러스·마이너스 1.94%(have a margin of error of plus or minus 1.94 percentage points)다.

Employers Share the Most Unconventional Tactics Job Seekers Have Used to Get their Attention in New CareerBuilder Survey

Facing the most difficult job market in decades, some job seekers have resorted to using unconventional methods to stand out from the crowd. According to a new survey from CareerBuilder, nearly one-in-five hiring managers (18 percent) reported that they are seeing more job seekers try unusual tactics to capture their attention in 2009 compared to last year. This is up from 12 percent of hiring managers who said the same in 2008 as compared to previous years.

"The search for employment is taking longer and is more competitive than it has been in past years," said Jason Ferrara, senior career adviser at CareerBuilder. "To compensate, some candidates have turned to extreme tactics. While unusual job search antics may attract the attention of hiring managers, they need to be done with care and professionalism so that candidates are remembered for the right reasons."

Some of the most memorable tactics identified by hiring managers include:

- Candidate sent a shoe with a resume to "get my foot in the door."
- Candidate staged a sit-in in the lobby to get a meeting with a director.
- Candidate washed cars in the parking lot.
- Candidate sent a resume wrapped as a present and said his skills were a "gift to the company."
- Candidate handed out resumes at stoplights.
- Candidate sent a cake designed as a business card with the candidate's picture.
- Candidate went to the same barber as the Chairman of the Board and had the barber speak on his behalf.
- Candidate handed out personalized coffee cups.
- Candidate came dressed in a bunny suit because it was near Easter.
- Candidate told the receptionist he had an interview with the manager. When he met the manager, he confessed that he was driving by and decided to stop in on a chance.

Survey Methodology

This survey was conducted online within the U.S. by Harris Interactive on behalf of CareerBuilder.com among 2,543 hiring managers and human resource professionals (employed full-time; not self-employed; with at least significant involvement in hiring decisions; non government) ages 18 and over between February 20 and March 11, 2009. With a pure probability sample of 2,543, one could say with a 95 percent probability that the overall results have a sampling error of +/- 1.94 percentage points. Sampling error for data from sub-samples is higher and varies.

✓ 기억하면 좋을 구절!

along with ~와 함께 / ~와 마찬가지로

Dozens of militants were killed *along with* at least 13 policemen.
수십 여 명의 과격분자들이 사살됐으며, 경찰도 최소한 13명이 사망했다.

resort to ~에 의지하다

Do not ever *resort to* violent means.
어떤 경우라도 폭력적 수단에 의지해서는 안 된다.

gimmick [gímɪk] n. 술책 (관심 끌기 위한)

This is typical of the Government's *gimmicks*.
이는 전형적인 정부의 정치적 술책이다.

hand out ~을 나누어주다

Could you *hand* these books *out* please?
이 책들 좀 나눠주시겠어요?

the overall results 전체 결과

In many cases *the overall results* are published in their annual reports.
대개 전체 결과는 연간 보고서에 명시된다.

내 인생의 명언 — 일하는 자의 미덕

▶ 하루에 8시간 충실하게 일하면 마침내는 사장이 될 수 있고,
그러면 하루에 12시간 일할 수 있게 된다.
로버트 프로스트 (미국 시인)

> By working faithfully eight hours a day,
> you may eventually get to be a boss and
> work twelve hours a day.
> Robert Lee Frost

▶ 고된 일은 사람들의 성격을 드러내준다. 어떤 사람은 소매를 걷어올리고,
어떤 사람은 콧방귀를 뀌며, 어떤 사람은 아예 나타나지도 않는다.
샘 유잉 (미국 언론인 작가)

> Hard work spotlights the character of people:
> some turn up their sleeves, some turn up their noses,
> and some don't turn up at all.
> Sam Ewing

▶ 살기 위해, 다시 말해 돈을 위해 취직하는 사람은 노예가 되고 만다.
조셉 캠벨 (미국 신화학자)

> The person who takes a job in order to live—
> that is to say, for the money—turns himself into a slave.
> Joseph Campbell

▶ 일을 하기 전에 성공이 오는 유일한 곳은 사전 속에나 있다.
빈스 롬바르디 (미국 미식축구 감독)

> The dictionary is the only place that
> success comes before work.
> Vince Lombardi

Favorite famous sayings!

▶ 8시간 내내 먹을 수는 없다. 8시간 내내 술을 마시거나 사랑을
  나눌 수도 없다. 사람이 8시간 내내 할 수 있는 유일한 것은 일뿐이다.
  윌리엄 포크너 (미국 소설가)

> The only thing a man can do for eight hours a day
> is work. He can't eat for eight hours; he can't drink
> for eight hours; he can't make love for eight hours.
> William Falkner

▶ 일하는 즐거움을 찾아내는 것은 젊음의 원천을 발견하는 것이다.
  펄 벅 (미국 소설가)

> To find joy in work is to discover the fountain of youth.
> Pearl Buck

▶ 우리가 일하는 것은 무엇이 되기 위해서이지,
  무엇을 얻기 위해서가 아니다.
  앨버트 하버드 (미국 작가 · 예술가)

> We work to become, not to acquire.
> Albert Havard

▶ 두뇌는 놀라운 신체기관이다. 아침에 일어나는 순간 작동하기 시작해
  사무실에 들어갈 때까지 멈추지 않는다.
  로버트 프로스트 (미국 시인)

> The brain is a wonderful organ; it starts working
> the moment you get up in the morning
> and does not stop until you get into the office.
> Robert Lee Frost

Funny Funny World

News English

"Yakuza Underlings Cramming for an Exam"

They're members of the biggest, meanest organised crime group in Japan, but these tattooed gangsters are being sent back to school by their godfathers.

Under new laws, mob bosses can be sued for the misdeeds of their underlings. So the leaders of the feared Yamaguchi-gumi have begun testing their mobsters' knowledge of the laws.

They've drawn up a 12-page test paper which questions them on a range of banned activities, from bootlegging fuel to dumping industrial waste.

For decades, the Yakuza has been the violent underbelly of Japanese society. Tattooed toughs and punks with pinkies, celebrated and denigrated alike in movies, books and comics.

But these mobsters are feeling the pinch. For a start, the global economic downturn has been bad for business and now tough new anti-mob laws are also squeezing these enterprising gangsters.

"Yakuza dons can now be sued for crimes committed by their subordinates, meaning they can be cleaned out if their underlings mess up.

Masahiro Tamura is a former chief of the Fukuoka Prefectural Police, a veteran yakuza hunter who commanded a force of 12,000 officers.

"I think this is a good move because it puts the responsibility on the crime bosses to control their gangsters. It means innocent people are less likely to be caught up in activities are banned?" And the correct answer: Dumping industrial waste, phone fraud scams, bootlegging fuel and theft of construction equipment.

Former police chief Masahiro Tamura says the Yakuza are merely evolving to suit the new environment.

"I am not surprised at all that the Yakuza are studying the law. The last thing they want is to be fined large amounts dumping industrial waste.

For decades, the Yakuza has been the violent underbelly of Japanese society. Tattooed toughs and punks without pinkies, celebrated and denigrated alike in movies, books and comics.

But these mobsters are feeling the pinch. For a start, the global economic downturn

무시무시한 문신을 한 야쿠자들

And the godfathers of Japanese crime believe they've already found a few legal loopholes in the new laws.

This was one briefing note recently distributed to Yakuza members of one group:

"It is now illegal to give financial rewards or promote someone who was involved in a hit against a member of a rival gang. But it is not illegal to give them a salary through a front company and promote them within that organisation."

So there you have it: Some free legal advice from Japan's mafia bosses: Don't pay the hit man directly, instead give him a job in a front company and a salary.

So from busting heads on the street to cramming heads for exams, life has never been so cerebral for Japan's Yakuza hard men.

They're members of the biggest, meanest organised crime group in Japan, but these tattooed gangsters are being sent back to school by their godfathers.

Under new laws, mob bosses can be sued for the misdeeds of their underlings. So the leaders of the feared Yamaguchi-gumi have begun testing their mobsters' knowledge of the laws.

They've drawn up a 12-page test paper which questions them on a range of banned activities, from bootlegging fuel to dumping industrial waste.

For decades, the Yakuza has been the violent underbelly of Japanese society.

벼락치기 시험공부하는 야쿠자 똘마니들

일본의 폭력조직 조직원들(Japan's mobster underlings)이 마치 학교로 되돌아간(go back to school) 것처럼 '시험공부'를 하고 있어 화제다. 일본의 새 법률에 따르면(under new laws) 앞으로 일본의 폭력조직 두목들은 부하들의 범죄와 악행에 대해서도 제소를 당할 수(can be sued for the criminal acts and misdeeds of their underlings) 있게 된다.

상황이 이렇게 되자 폭력조직 두목들이 휘하 조직원들의 법률 지식을 테스트하기 시작한(begin testing their mobsters' knowledge of the laws) 것이다. 문신한 조직원들(the tattooed gangsters)이 자신들의 대부들에 의해 학교로 되돌려 보내지고(be sent back to school) 있는 셈이다. 부하들이 법을 잘 몰라서 위법행위를 할 경우 두목들이 배상 책임 등을 고스란히 뒤집어써야 하기 때문이다.

일본에서 가장 크고 가장 비열한 범죄조직인 야마구치구미(山口組·the

biggest and meanest organized crime group Yamaguchi-gumi)는 열두 쪽에 달하는 시험 문제지를 만들었다(draw up a 12-page test paper). 이 문제지는 가짜 연료 밀매부터 산업폐기물 폐기에 이르기까지 금지된 행위들에 대한 질문을 조직원들에게 묻고(question the mobsters on a range of banned activities, from bootlegging fuel to dumping industrial waste) 있다. 경찰이 최근 입수한 시험 문제지의 한 문제는 "어떤 행위들이 법으로 금지돼 있나(What kind of activities are banned?)"였다. 그리고 정답으로는 산업폐기물 폐기(dumping industrial waste), 전화 금융사기(phone fraud scams), 가짜 연료 밀매(bootlegging fuel), 건설장비 절도(theft of construction equipment) 등이 제시됐다.

문제지의 마지막 질문은 "꼭 지켜야 할 것은?"이었으며, 정답은 "무엇이든 위에 보고하고 상의할 것"이었다. 지난 수십 년 동안(for decades) 야쿠자는 일본 사회의 가장 취약한 지대였다(be the underbelly of Japanese society). 문신한 폭력배와 새끼손가락이 없는 똘마니들(tattooed toughs and punks without pinkies)이 활개 치고 다녔다(go around with a swagger).

하지만 최근 들어 야쿠자들도 곤경에 처하게(feel the pinch) 됐다. 우선(for a start) 세계경제 침체(the global economic recession)가 그들의 사업에도 악영향을 미쳤고(have a bad influence on their business), 이젠 엄격한 반(反)범죄조직 법까지 그들의 기업형태 조직을 옥죄고(be squeezing the enterprising gangsters) 있기 때문이다.

1만 2000여 명의 경찰을 지휘하며(command a force of 12,000 officers) 베테랑 야쿠자 사냥꾼으로 명성을 날렸던(be famous for a veteran Yakuza hunter) 다무라 마사히로 전 후쿠오카현 경찰청장은 새 법에 대해 "범죄조직 두목들에게 부하들을 관리할 책임을 지우는(put the responsibility on the crime bosses to control their gangsters) 것은 바람직한 조치(a desirable move)"라며 "무고한 사람들(innocent people)이 범죄대상이 되는 일이 적어지게(be less likely to be targeted) 될 것"이라고 말했다.

한편 범죄조직 두목들(the crime bosses)은 무사히 빠져나가기(save their own skins) 위해 새 법을 무력화시킬 수 있는 방도를 찾고 있으며(look for ways to beat the new laws) 이미 몇 가지 법적 허점들을 발견한(have already found a few loopholes in the new laws) 것으로 전해졌다.

한 예로 최근 한 조직의 야쿠자 조직원들에게 배포된 한 브리핑 자료(a briefing note recently distributed to Yakuza members of one group)에는 "라이벌 조직 조직원 습격에 연루된 자에게 금전적 보상을 해주거나 승진을 시켜주는 것은 불법(be illegal to give financial rewards or promote someone involved in a hit against a member of a rival gang)"이라고 적혀 있다.

이 자료는 이어 "하지만 위장회사를 통해 봉급을 주고 그 회사 내부적으로 승진을 시켜주는 것은 불법이 아니다(be not illegal to give them a salary through a front company and promote them within that organization)"라고 대안을 제시하고 있다. 공격 가담 조직원에게 직접 돈을 주지 말고(do not pay the hit man directly), 위장회사에 일자리를 주고 봉급을 주라는(give him a job in a front company and a salary) 얘기다.

미국 ABC방송 인터넷판은 "어쨌든 길거리에서 머리를 깨트리는 것부터 시험을 위해 머리에 쑤셔 넣는 것까지(from busting heads on the street to cramming heads for exams) 일본 야쿠자 조직원들의 인생이 그렇게 이지적이야 했던 적은 없었다(have never been so cerebral for Japan's Yakuza hard men)"고 전했다.

Japan's Mobster Underlings Go back to School

They're members of the biggest, meanest organised crime group in Japan, but these tattooed gangsters are being sent back to school by their godfathers.

Under new laws, mob bosses can be sued for the misdeeds of their underlings. So the leaders of the feared Yamaguchi-gumi have begun testing their mobsters' knowledge of the laws.

They've drawn up a 12-page test paper which questions them on a range of banned activities, from bootlegging fuel to dumping industrial waste.

For decades, the Yakuza has been the violent underbelly of Japanese society. Tattooed toughs and punks without pinkies, celebrated and denigrated alike in movies, books and comics.

But these mobsters are feeling the pinch. For a start, the global economic downturn been bad for business and now tough new anti-mob laws are also squeezing these enterprising gangsters.

For example, Yakuza dons can now be sued for crimes committed by their subordinates, meaning they can be cleaned out if their underlings mess up.

Masahiro Tamura is a former chief of the Fukuoka Prefectural Police, a veteran yakuza hunter who commanded a force of 12,000 officers.

"I think this is a good move, because it puts the responsibility on the crime bosses to control their gangsters. It means innocent people are less likely to be targeted," he said.

The crime bosses are looking for ways to beat the news laws so they can save their own skins. And to do that, they've sent their mobsters back to the classroom.

During a raid in central Japan this week, police found a 12-page test paper for yakuza members.

One question asks, "What kind of activities are banned?" And the correct answer: Dumping industrial waste, phone fraud scams, bootlegging fuel and theft of construction equipment.

Former police chief Masahiro Tamura says the Yakuza are merely evolving to suit the new environment.

"I am not surprised at all that the Yakuza are studying the law. The last thing they want is to be fined large amounts or have costs awarded against them in court," he said.

And the godfathers of Japanese crime believe they've already found a few legal loopholes in the new laws.

This was one briefing note recently distributed to Yakuza members of one group:

"It is now illegal to give financial rewards or promote someone who was involved in a hit against a member of a rival gang. But it is not illegal to give them a salary through a front company and promote them within that organisation."

So there you have it: Some free legal advice from Japan's mafia bosses: Don't pay the hit man directly, instead give him a job in a front company and a salary.

So from busting heads on the street to cramming heads for exams, life has never been so cerebral for Japan's Yakuza hard men.

✅ 기억하면 좋을 구절!

look for way to ~할 방법을 찾다

> We need to *look for ways to* reduce our carbon footprint.
> 온실 효과 유발 이산화탄소 배출량을 줄일 방법을 찾아야 한다.

be sued for ~로 소송을 당하다 / 피소되다

> I've *been sued for* sorts of crazy things.
> 황당한 일로 소송 당한 적이 있습니다.

be taken in by ~에 속아넘어가다

> She *was* completely *taken in by* his scam.
> 그녀는 그의 사기에 완전히 넘어갔다.

walk with a swagger 으스대며 걷다 / 뻐기며 걷다

> He *walked with* something of *a swagger*.
> 그는 으스대듯 걸었다.

feel the pinch 경제적으로 쪼들리다

> Lots of people who have lost their jobs are starting to *feel the pinch*.
> 실직한 많은 이들이 돈에 허덕이기 시작했다.

내 인생의 명언 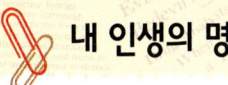 죽는 날까지 배워야 한다

▶ 교육은 더 높은 수준의 편견을 얻는 방법이다.
로렌스 피터 (미국 교육자)

> Education is a method whereby one acquires a higher grade of prejudices.
> Laurence J. Peter

▶ 진정으로 현명한 선생님은 당신에게 자신의 지식 안으로 들어오라고 하지 않고, 당신 안의 지성의 문턱에 이르도록 이끌어준다.
칼릴 지브란 (레바논계 미국 예술가 · 시인)

> The teacher who is indeed wise does not bid you to enter the house of his wisdom but rather leads you to the threshold of your mind.
> Khalil Gibran

▶ 교육은 한 세대가 다른 세대에게 건네주는 사회의 영혼이다.
길버트 체스터턴 (영국 작가 · 평론가)

> Education is simply the soul of a society as it passes from one generation to another.
> Gilbert Keith Chesterton

▶ 교육의 뿌리는 쓰다. 그러나 그 열매는 달다.
아리스토텔레스 (그리스 철학자)

> The roots of education are bitter, but the fruit is sweet.
> Aristoteles

▶ 교육의 목적은 거울을 창문으로 바꿔놓는 것이다.
시드니 해리스 (미국 언론인)

> The purpose of education is to turn mirrors into windows.
> Sydney Harris

> *To love is not to look at one another: it is to look, together, in the same direction.*
>
> Antoine de Saint-Exupery

2nd NEWS

Our Heart-warming World

언어는 달라도 마음은 하나

News English

"A Drug Sniffer Dog Died of Nasal Cancer"

He knew the perils of police work, but kept on sniffing until the end.

Max, a drug-detecting dog in England, has died of a rare form of nose cancer which likely developed during his years sniffing out cocaine in the line of duty, his owner said.

"It is ironic the wonderful organ that made him successful in his work has been his demise," owner Police Inspector Anne Higgins told the British newspaper the Telegraph.

He was a fighter until the end and always very dignified," she said.

The nine-year-old Springer spaniel was put down last week after an aggressive tumor developed in his nose.

Max had retired for work as a drug-sniffer last year after arthritis in his back legs limited his mobility. He was fitted with a wheeled contraption so he could continue to move on his own.

Max's veterinarian Kate Fairclaugh said death from nasal cancer is rare in dogs and that his police work likely contributed to the illness. "Sniffing drugs may well have been a factor. I certainly cannot rule it out," she said.

Higgins said it was difficult to let Max go, but she will focus on his legacy of good deeds.

"He has had a good life and a successful one as a police dog. Just think of all the drugs and people he managed to put away," she said.

평생 마약 탐지견으로 활약한 맥스

코 암(癌) 걸려 죽은 마약 탐지견

경찰 마약 탐지견(police drug sniffer dog)이 코 암(癌)에 걸려 죽었다(die of nasal cancer). 순직(a death on the job)이다. 마약류를 적발해내느라 숱한 냄새를 맡다가(sniff out hundreds of drugs) 코 암에 걸렸으니, 순직한(die at his post of duty) 셈이다.

영국 경찰청 소속 스프링어 스패니얼(Springer spaniel, 사냥감을 모는 스패니얼종의 사냥개)인 맥스(Max). 2009년 1월 9세로 생을 마감(end his life)했다. 개들 중에선 코카인으로 유발된 코 암의 첫 희생견(first casualty of cocaine-induced nasal cancer in canines)이 됐다.

수의사들은 공무집행 중 마약 냄새를 맡아온(sniff the drugs in the line of duty) 것이 맥스의 죽음에 원인을 제공했을(provide a cause to his death) 것이라고 말한다. "맥스는 끝까지 냄새 맡는 일을 계속했다(keep on sniffing until the end)"면서 "그를 업무에서 성공적으로 만들어줬던 코(the nose that made him successful in his work)가 아이러니컬하게도 그의 죽음을 불러왔다(bring about the demise)"고 애석해했다.

2006년 이후 맥스의 주치를 맡아온(Max's veterinarian since 2006) 수의사 케이트 페어클로우 박사는 "코 암은 개에게 전혀 흔한 것이 아니다(be not at all common)"면서 "개가 걸리는 모든 암의 단 1~2%(only about one or two percent of all cancers in dogs)만이 코에 나타난다"고 말한다.

모든 마약류를 냄새로 탐지해내는 훈련과 실전을 반복한 것이 그의 죽음을 불러온 병을 유발했다는(provoke the disease which led to him being put down) 얘기다.

맥스는 2008년 11월 엉덩이 쪽에 부상을 입은 뒤(after suffering a hip injury) 현역에서 은퇴했으나, 돌아다니는 데 도움을 주는 바퀴 장치를 달아(be outfitted with a wheeled contraption to help him get around) 활동에는 큰 지장을 받지 않았다.

영국 국민들은 맥스가 경찰 업무의 위험(perils of police work)을 무릅쓰고 일해준 덕분에 수많은 마약 밀매업자와 중독자들을 잡아낼(put away so many drug traffickers and narcotics) 수 있었다며 그의 죽음을 애도했다(express their regret over the death of Max).

Drug-detecting Police Dog Dies of Nose Cancer from Sniffing out Cocaine

He knew the perils of police work, but kept on sniffing until the end.

Max, a drug-detecting dog in England, has died of a rare form of nose cancer which likely developed during his years sniffing out cocaine in the line of duty, his owner said.

"It is ironic the wonderful organ that made him successful in his work has been his demise," owner Police Inspector Anne Higgins told the British newspaper the Telegraph.

He was a fighter until the end and always very dignified," she said.

The nine-year-old Springer spaniel was put down last week after an aggressive tumor developed in his nose, Higgins said.

Max had retired for work as a dug-sniffer last year after arthritis in his back legs limited his mobility. He was fitted with a wheeled contraption so he could continue to move on his own.

Max's veterinarian Kate Fairclaugh said death from nasal cancer is rare in dogs and that his police work likely contributed to the illness. "Sniffing drugs may well have been a factor. I certainly cannot rule it out," she said.

Higgins said it was difficult to let Max go, but she will focus on his legacy of good deeds.

"He has had a good life and a successful one as a police dog. Just think of all the bad people he managed to put away," she said.

✔️ 기억하면 좋을 구절!

end one's life 생을 마감하다

People have the right to *end one's life* in a peaceful and dignified manner.
사람은 평화롭고 존엄하게 죽을 권리가 있다.

bring about ~을 초래하다 / 유발하다

This event may *bring about* serious trouble.
이 사건이 심각한 문제를 야기할지도 모른다.

demise [dɪmáɪz] n. 종말 / 죽음, 사망

What was the cause of that *demise*?
그 죽음의 원인은 무엇이었을까?

put away (교도소, 정신병원 등에) ~를 집어넣다

They need to be punished and *put away* for life.
그들을 벌을 받아 평생 갇혀 있어야 한다.

express one's regret(sorrow) over ~에 애도의 뜻을 표하다

Koreans *expressed their regret over* the loss of life in Japan.
한국인들은 일본의 인명 손실에 대해 애도의 뜻을 표했다.

내 인생의 명언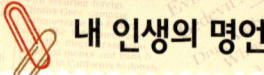

▶ 인생은 현명한 사람에게는 꿈이고, 어리석은 자에겐 게임이며,
부자에겐 코미디이고, 가난한 이에겐 비극이다.
숄름 알레이헴 (러시아 출신 미국 극작가 · 소설가)

> Life is a dream for the wise, a game for the fool,
> a comedy for the rich, a tragedy for the poor.
> Sholem-Aleichem

▶ 인생은 무엇인가 알기 전에 절반이 지나간다.
조지 허버트 (영국 시인 · 목사)

> Life is half spent before we know what it is.
> George Herbert

▶ 인생은 몽상하는 사람들에겐 결코 녹록하지 않다.
로버트 월러 (미국 작가)

> Life is never easy for those who dream.
> Robert James Waller

▶ 살아가는 기술은 춤이라기보다는 레슬링에 더 가깝다.
마르쿠스 아우렐리우스 (로마 황제 · 철학자)

> The art of living is more like wrestling than dancing.
> Marcus Aurelius

Favorite famous sayings!

▶ 어느 것의 가치라는 것은 당신이 그것과 바꾸는 인생의 양이다.
헨리 소로우 (미국 작가 · 사회평론가)

> The price of anything is the amount of
> life you exchange for it.
> Henry David Thoreau

▶ 인생은 지우개 없이 그림을 그리는 예술이다.
존 가드너 (미국 기업가 · 정치인)

> Life is the art of drawing without an eraser.
> John Gardner

▶ 인생이란 불충분한 전제로부터 충분한 결말을 이끌어내는 기술이다.
작자미상

> Life is the art of drawing sufficient conclusions
> from insufficient premises.
> anonymous

▶ 잘 보낸 하루가 행복한 잠을 가져오듯이,
보람있게 보낸 인생은 행복한 죽음을 가져다 준다.
레오나르도 다 빈치 (이탈리아 화가 · 건축가 · 조각가)

> As a well-spent day brings happy sleep,
> so life well used brings happy death.
> Leonardo da Vinci

Our Heart-warming World

News English

"A Female Dog Taking Care of a Blind Male Dog"

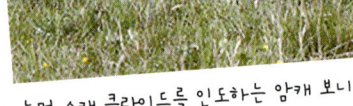

눈먼 수캐 클라이드를 인도하는 암캐 보니

눈먼 수캐 데리고 다니며 돌보는 암캐

'개 같은······' 어쩌고 하는 욕, 없어져야 한다. '개보다 못한 인간들 많다'는 말, 맞다.

여기 또 하나의 사례가 있다. 암수 한 쌍의 개가 폭풍우 몰아치던 어느 날 주인으로부터 버림받았다. 이들이 발견됐을 때 암컷은 수컷의 목줄을 물고 있었다. 눈이 멀어 앞이 안 보이는 수컷을 이끌고 살길을 찾아 헤매고 있었던 것이다.

시각장애를 가진 사람들이 맹도견(盲導犬)에 의지하는 경우는 드물지 않다(be not unusual for visually-impaired humans to rely on a guide dog). 하지만 눈이 먼 개를 같은 개가 앞장서서 인도해주는 경우는 알려진 적이 없다. 영국에서 일어난 일이다.

눈이 먼 수컷의 이름은 클라이드(5살), 클라이드를 줄곧 보살펴주고 있는 암컷은 보니(2살)라는 이름을 가졌다. 폭풍우 속에 길거리를 헤매다 발견돼(be found wandering the streets in a rain storm) 노포크 주(州)의 한 동물 보호소에 넘겨지면서(be brought to an animal shelter) 붙여진 이름. 1930년대 대공황 시절 악명을 떨쳤던 미국의 갱단 남녀 연인의 이름을 따서 지어졌다(be named after the American gangster lovers). 두 남녀의 스토리는 영화로도 만들어졌다.

보니와 클라이드는 양치기 개로 유명한(be famous as a sheepdog) 보더 콜리(Border collie) 종이다. 클라이드는 보니와 함께 있을 때는 멀쩡한 시력을 가진 개처럼 보인다(seem as capable as a fully sighted dog). 하지만 실제로는 퇴행성 질병으로 완전히 시력을 잃은(have lost his sight because of a degenerative disease) 상태다.

때문에 클라이드는 안내견 역할을 해주는 보니에게 전적으로 의존(rely entirely on Bonnie as his guide dog)하고 있다. 어디든 '그녀'만 따라다닌다(follow her everywhere). 어디인지 잘 모를(be unsure where he is) 때면 갑자기 보니 뒤를 찾아가(suddenly go behind Bonnie) 등에 얼굴을 갖다 댄다(put his face on the back of her). 보니에게 자신을 데리고 가달라는 의사표시다.

보니는 길을 가다가도 자주 걸음을 멈추고(walk and tend to stop) 뒤돌아본다. 클라이드가 곁에 있는지 확인해(to make sure he's there) 챙겨주고 돌봐주기(look out for him) 위해서다. 음식과 물이 있는 곳으로 가는 것도 이끌어준다(guide him on walks towards food and water). 클라이드가 방향감각을 잃어(become disoriented) 헤매고 있으면 그 곁으로 다가가 머리를 자신의 엉덩이에 기대고 쉬게(let him rest his head on her haunches)한다. 이렇다 보니 클라이드는 보니가 곁에 없으면(when she is not around) 꼼짝도 하려 하지 않는다(refuse to budge an inch).

현재 클라이드와 보니를 보호하고 있는 유기견보호소에선 이들을 위한 새 보금자리를 찾고 있다. 하지만 각각 다른 곳으로 입양 보낼 수 없는(there is no option of homing them separately) 상황이다. 어디로 가든 갈라놓을 수 없는 한 쌍으로 힘께 가야(have got to go as an inseparable pair) 한다.

영국 안내견협회(Guide Dogs for the Blind Association)의 빅기 벨 대변인은 "다른 개를 위해 자의적으로 안내견 역할을 하는 개에 대해선 들어본 적이 없다(have never heard of a dog voluntarily acting as a guide for another dog)"면서 "이들 두 마리 개의 사연은 대단히 희귀한 경우(be a very unusual case)로, 한 편의 러브 스토리를 보는 듯하다"고 말한다.

Blind Border Collie Gets His Own Guide Dog

Collies usually round up sheep not each other… but as the eyes of her blind canine companion, little Bonnie steers Clyde away from trouble.

The five-year-old long-haired border collie, who has lost his sight because of a degenerative disease, relies entirely on Bonnie as his guide dog. He follows her everywhere.

And like the American gangster lovers they have been named after, the friendly dogs are on the lookout for a safe, new hideaway.

They were recently dumped in the street during a storm and are currently being cared for at Meadow Green Dog Rescue Centre in Hales Green, near Loddon in Norfolk.

The centre's Cherie Cootes said: "If Clyde's unsure where he is, he will suddenly go behind Bonnie and put his face on the back of her so she can guide him. He totally relies on her.

"And when she walks she tends to stop and make sure he's there - she does look out for him. When she's about you wouldn't notice he is blind, but when she's not about he refuses to move. There's no option of homing them separately. They've got to go as a pair."

A driver found the dogs running through Blundeston, near Lowestoft, Suffolk, during a storm three weeks ago. Neither Clyde nor Bonnie—a short-haired border collie aged two or three—had identifying collars or chips.

Cherie, 40, added: "They've got very nice manners and they walk well on the lead.

"They really are a very sweet pair of dogs."

☑ 기억하면 좋을 구절!

be named after~ ~를 따 이름 붙여지다

> Wouldn't it be wonderful to have a comet *named after* him?
> 그의 이름을 딴 혜성이 있다니 대단하지 않나?

a degenerative disease 퇴행성 질환

> These include injuries and *degenerative disease*.
> 여기엔 부상과 퇴행성 질환이 포함됩니다.

look out for 보살피다 / 돌보다

> You should *look out for* yourself from now on.
> 지금부터는 당신 자신을 돌봐야 한다.

be disoriented 방향 감각을 잃다 / 혼란에 빠지다

> I'm so *disoriented*. Which way out should we take?
> 방향을 완전히 잃었습니다. 어디로 가야하는 거죠?

refuse to budge an inch 미동도 않다 / 꼼짝도 않다

> He *refused to budge an inch*.
> 그는 꼼짝도 하려 하지 않았다.

내 인생의 명언 — 신은 어디에 있는가

▶ 신은 죽었다면서 엘비스 프레슬리는 살아 있다고 하는
사회에 대해서 당신은 무슨 말을 할 수 있겠는가.
어브 컵시넷 (미국 언론인)

> What can you say about a society that says that
> God is dead and Elvis is alive?
> Irv Kupcinet

▶ 천국은 우리 머리 위뿐 아니라 우리 발밑에도 있다.
헨리 소로 (미국 사상가 · 문학가)

> Heaven is under our feet as well as over our heads.
> Henry David Thoreau

▶ 신이 없는 것처럼 인생을 살다가 죽어서 신이 있다는 것을
알게 되는 것보다 신이 있는 것처럼 인생을 살다가
죽어서 신이 없다는 것을 알게 되는 편이 나을 것 같다.
알베르 카뮈 (프랑스 소설가 · 극작가)

> I would rather live my life as if there is a God
> and die to find out there isn't, than live my life
> as if there isn't and die to find out there is.
> Albert Camus

▶ 당신 자신을 믿을 때까지 당신은 신을 믿을 수 없다.
스와미 비베카난다 (인도 종교 사회개혁 지도자)

> You cannot believe in God until you believe in yourself.
> Swami Vivekananda

News English

"A Heartbreaking End of Shattered Love"

SHE was the Miss Havisham of Sydney. Like the jilted bride-to-be in the Charles Dickens novel Great Expectations, Audrey Mountford was rejected by a man she was to marry.
To recover from the heartbreak and humiliation Ms Mountford, an artist, lived out her life until the age of 49 in a cave in remote bushland in the Blue Mountains.
Her remains were found on a banana lounge, and she was surrounded by household items including toothpaste, handbags, a knife and fork and a vinyl record of The Last Waltz, recorded in French.
Believing she might have gone overseas to recover from the shock, Ms Mountford's family had not contacted police to report her missing.
A NSW coroner yesterday ——— determine the cause of ——— death, although police ins——— foul play or suicide.
Instead, it is believed Ms ——— in April 1971 from expos——— out a simple existence ——— years in the cave.
Her remains, discovered ——— 14-year-old bushwalker ——— near jewellery, newspape——— tickets from April 1971 a——— passbook.
She still wore her trinket ——— and among her belongings ——— vellum weather-stained let——— attempted to transcribe.

of art and modelling, thus I packed my haversack and came bush," the letter reads.
"So far have had a lovely time except for ———

remains, but the case was reopened this year when the Missing Persons Unit conducted a review and was able to find family members.
Rather than providing comfort, news of ——— victim's remains had ———

was a half-written weather-stained letter that police attempted to transcribe.
"As work has been difficult to obtain since coming home in October 1968, I decided to revert to my old talent of art and modelling, thus I packed my ——— k and came bush," the letter ———

have had a lovely time except for ——— delayed by an undue ——— (possibly ——— ords in brackets added by police) ——— pped my strength.
——— me lovely ideas re oils and pastels ——— near future."

——— phew, John Mountford, now aged ——— members his aunt had converted ——— tholicism for a man she had met ——— ada and was about to marry." The ——— e did this for ended up leaving her ——— t think she ever recovered from ——— e told police.
"She was the type to think with her heart not her brain."
Mr Mountford said his aunt had loved the outdoors, had an adventurous personality and had travelled to New Zealand, Canada and Africa. She was "higher" and would "breeze in and out" of their lives, so her choice to move to the cave was not surprising.
"I know that being left by a man would have affected her very badly. She was a dreamer and a bit unrealistic, so for her to go and live in a cave is something I would believe suited her personality."

오드리 마운드포트와 블루마운틴 산

깨어진 사랑의 가슴 아픈 끝

한 남자를 사랑했다. 49세라는 적지 않은 나이에 찾아온 사랑이었다.

하지만 남자는 떠나갔고, 버림받은 그녀는 산속 깊은 동굴로 들어갔다. 거기서 그이를 원망하고, 하늘을 원망하며 안타까운 삶을 마감했다. 1971년이었다.

약 40년 전 머나먼 동굴 속에서 발견됐던(be found in a remote cave almost 40 years ago) 한 호주 여성 유해(the remains of an Australian woman)의 신원이 뒤늦게 밝혀졌다. 결혼을 원했던 남자로부터 버림받은 뒤(after being jilted by the man she wanted to marry) 산속으로 숨어버렸던(flee to the mountains) 오드리 마운드포트라는 여성의 유해로 확인(be identified as those of Audrey Mountford)됐다.

예술가였던 마운트포드는 지난 1969년, 캐나다인 연인으로부터 실연당한(be crossed in her love for her Canadian lover) 뒤 시드니의 집을 떠나 블루마운틴 신속 동굴로 들어갔다(move from her home in Sydney to a cave in the Blue Mountains). 그리고 12년 뒤, 그녀의 유골이 칫솔, 치약, 핸드백, 나이프와 포크 등 가재도구와 '마지막 월츠' 비닐 레코드 사이에 놓여 있는 것을 한 10대 등산가가 발견했다(be found among household items including toothbrush, toothpaste, handbags, a knife and fork and a vinyl record of The Last Waltz by a teenage mountaineer). 그녀의 손가락 뼈에는 어머니의 결혼반지(her mother's wedding ring)가 끼워져 있었다.

경찰은 동굴에서 발견된 신문, 기차표, 은행통장을 통해(from newspapers, train tickets and bankbooks found in the cave) 유해의 주인이 1971년 4월에 사망한 것으로 추정했다. 하지만 유해의 신원(the identity of the remains)은 검시 과정을 통해(through a coronial inquiry) 마운트포드의 것(belong to Ms Mountford)이라는 사실이 확인될 때까지 밝혀지지 않았다(be unknown).

마운트포드의 이야기는 오랫동안 알려지지 않았다(have gone untold for so long). 그녀가 충격에서 벗어나기 위해 외국으로 떠났다고 생각한(have gone overseas to recover from the shock) 가족들이 경찰에 실종 신고도 하지 않았기(do not contact police to report her missing) 때문이다.

검시관들은 그녀의 사망 원인이나 방식을 단정할 수 없다고(be not able to determine the cause or manner of her death) 밝혔으나, 경찰은 타살이나 자살에 의한 것은 아니라고(be not by foul play or suicide) 발표했다.

그녀의 조카 존 마운트포드는 "캐나다에서 만난 한 남자 때문에 가톨릭으로 개종했었다(convert to Catholicism for a man)"며 "결혼할 예정이었으나(be about to marry) 남자가 결국 그녀를 버리고 떠나버렸다(end up leaving her)"고 전한다.

조카에 따르면 마운트포드는 머리가 아니라 가슴으로 생각하는(think with her heart, not her brain) 타입이었다. 몽상가이며 약간은 비현실적이었던(be a dreamer and a bit unrealistic) 그녀가 남자에게 버림받은(being left by the man) 데 감당하기 어려운 상처를 입었던 것으로 추정된다.

1983년에 포기 처리됐던(be abandoned in 1983) 이 사건이 다시 다뤄지게 된 것은 한 실종자 단체(a missing person unit)가 재조사를 벌여(conduct a review) 그녀의 친척들을 찾아낸 덕에 가능했다.

그리고 친척들이 실종에 얽힌 깨어진 사랑 이야기를 공개하면서(reveal the story of shattered love behind her disappearance) 가슴 아픈 한 여인의 사연이 뒤늦게 세상에 알려지게 됐다.

The Jilted Bride who Retreated to a Cave in Heartbreak

SHE was the Miss Havisham of Sydney. Like the jilted bride-to-be in the Charles Dickens novel Great Expectations, Audrey Mountford was rejected by a man she was to marry.

To recover from the heartbreak and humiliation Ms Mountford, an artist, lived out her life until the age of 49 in a cave in remote bushland in the Blue Mountains.

Her remains were found on a banana lounge, and she was surrounded by household items including toothpaste, handbags, a knife and fork and a vinyl record of The Last Waltz, recorded in French.

Believing she might have gone overseas to recover from the shock, Ms Mountford's family had not contacted police to report her missing.

A NSW coroner yesterday could not determine the cause or manner of her death, although police insist it was not by foul play or suicide.

Instead, it is believed Ms Mountford died in April 1971 from exposure, having eked out a simple existence for up to two years in the cave.

Her remains, discovered in 1981 by a 14-year-old bushwalker, were found near jewellery, newspapers and train tickets from April 1971 as well as a bank passbook.

She still wore her mother's wedding ring, and among her belongings was a half-written weather-stained letter that police attempted to transcribe.

"As work has been difficult to obtain since coming home in October 1968, I decided to revert to my old talent of art and modelling, thus I packed my haversack and came bush," the letter reads.

"So far have had a lovely time except for … being delayed by an undue … (possibly wog) [words in brackets added by police] which sapped my strength.

Have some lovely ideas re oils and pastels for the near future."

Her nephew, John Mountford, now aged 65, remembers his aunt had converted to Catholicism for a man she had met in Canada and was about to marry. "The man she did this for ended up leaving her. I don't think she ever recovered from that," he told police.

"She was the type to think with her heart, not her brain."

Mr Mountford said his aunt had loved the outdoors, had an adventurous personality and had travelled to New Zealand, Canada and Africa. She was "flighty" and would "breeze in and out" of their lives, so her choice to move to the cave was not surprising.

"I know that being left by a man would have affected her very badly. She was a dreamer and a bit unrealistic, so for her to go and live in a cave is something I would believe suited her personality."

Ms Mountford's younger sister Nola Stewart, now 84, was the last family member to have seen her alive. Ms Mountford had left some clothes at her sister's home in Mortdale when she left in a taxi one day in 1969.

Mrs Stewart yesterday told the Herald it had been a shock when the family was told of her sister's fate, because they had searched for her for years. A 1983 coronial inquest had been unable to identify the remains, but the case was reopened this year when the Missing Persons Unit conducted a review and was able to find family members.

Rather than providing comfort, news of the discovery of her sister's remains had been difficult for Mrs Stewart.

"Actually it saddens me more to find out what happened to her because I thought that she was living somewhere and not bothering to get back in touch with me."

Mrs Stewart said she thought the Canadian man might have been a soldier her sister had met during World War II.

"I know that she did have an American lad [but] what one hurt her I don't know."

☑ 기억하면 좋을 구절!

be jilt by ~로부터 버림받다 / 차이다

She *was jilted by* her first lover.
그녀는 첫 번째 애인에게 차였다.

flee to ~로 달아나다 / 몰래 사라지다

He was caught trying to *flee to* the country.
그는 그 나라에서 달아나려다가 체포되었다.

be crossed in 사랑이 깨지다 / 실연당하다

I *was crossed in* my love.
나는 사랑에 실패했다. (실연당했다.)

household items 살림살이 / 생활용품

We have not stored *household items* at all.
우리는 살림살이가 거의 없다.

the identity of the remains 유해의 신원, 유골의 신분

DNA tests could be used to confirm *the identity of the remains*.
그 시체의 신원 파악에 DNA테스트가 사용될 수 있다.

내 인생의 명언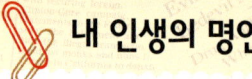

▶ 사랑함에 현명한 자는 최대한 사랑하고, 최소한 말한다.
알프레드 테니슨 (영국 계관시인)

> Who is wise in love, love most, say least.
> Alfred Tennyson

▶ 키스는 말이 더 이상 필요하지 않을 때 말하는 것을 막기 위해 자연에 의해 고안된 사랑스러운 술수이다.
잉그리드 버그먼 (스웨덴 출신 여배우)

> A kiss is a lovely trick designed by nature
> to stop speech when words become superfluous.
> Ingrid Bergman

▶ 사랑하는 마음은 모든 지식의 시작이다.
토마스 칼라일 (영국 평론가 · 사상가 · 역사가)

> A loving heart is the beginning of all knowledge.
> Thomas Carlyle

▶ 우정은 종종 사랑으로 끝난다.
그러나 사랑이 우정으로 끝나는 경우는 결코 없다.
찰슨 콜튼 (영국 성직자 · 작가)

> Friendship often ends in love but love in friendship, never.
> Charles Caleb Colton

▶ 미숙한 사랑은 "당신이 필요하기 때문에 당신을 사랑한다"고 말하고,
성숙한 사랑은 "당신을 사랑하기 때문에 당신이 필요하다"고 말한다.
에리히 프롬 (독일 태생 미국 정신분석학자)

> Immature love says: 'I love you because I need you.'
> Mature love says: 'I need you because I love you'
> Erich Pinchas Fromm

Favorite famous sayings!

▶ 사랑받지 못하는 것은 슬픈 일이다.
  사랑할 수 없는 것은 훨씬 더 슬픈 일이다.
  미겔 데 우나무노 (스페인 소설가 · 극작가 · 철학자)

> It is sad not to be loved but
> it is much sadder not to be able to love.
> Miguel de Unamuno

▶ 사랑은 두 사람이 해서 두 사람 모두 승리할 수 있는 게임이다.
  에바 가보 (헝가리 출신 여배우)

> Love is a game that two can play and both win.
> Eva Gabor

▶ 사랑은 두 몸에 사는 하나의 영혼으로 이뤄진다.
  아리스토텔레스 (그리스 철학자)

> Love is composed of a single soul
> inhabiting two bodies.
> Aristoteles

▶ 사랑은 전쟁과 같다. 시작하기는 쉽지만 끝내기는 대단히 힘들다.
  헨리 멘켄 (미국 언론인 · 문학평론가)

> Love is like war: easy to begin but very hard to stop.
> Henry menken

▶ 사랑한다는 것은 서로 마주보는 것이 아니라
  같은 방향을 바라보는 것이다.
  생텍쥐페리 (프랑스 작가 · 비행사)

> To love is not to look at one another:
> it is to look, together, in the same direction.
> Antoine de Saint-Exupery

News English

"A Love Letter Delivered 10 Years Later"

A couple have married after they were reunited when a long-lost love letter sent ten years ago was found unopened behind a fireplace.

Steve Smith and Carmen Ruiz-Perez, both 42, walked down the aisle on Friday following a separation of a decade. The pair fell in love in their 20s after Carmen arrived in the UK as a foreign student.

But after a year-long relationship the couple drifted apart when Carmen had to move back to France.

A few years later, Steve wrote to Carmen in a bid to rekindle their relationship, but Carmen's mother hid the letter in the mantelpiece and it slipped down the back of the fireplace.

It remained there for more than a decade until the family decided to plan for renovations. Carmen, who had remained single and never forgot Steve, was given the letter by her mother. Steve had written 'I hope you are well. I was just writing to ask if you ever got married and if you ever still thought of me.'

fell in love. Steve, of Paignton, Devon, said: 'When we met again it was like a film. We ran across the airport into each other's arms.'

'We met up and fell in love all over again. Within 30 seconds of setting eyes on each other we were kissing.'

'Now we're married, I'm just glad the letter did eventually end up where it was supposed to be.'

Carmen, who is now living with Steve in Paignton, said the wedding was the pinnacle of an 'amazing' love story.

She added: 'I never got married and now I'm marrying the man I have always loved.'

A couple have married after they were reunited when a long-lost love letter sent ten years ago was found unopened behind a fireplace.

great to hear from you, please great in touch if you can. Steve XXX'.

Factory supervisor Steve said: 'I didn't write much because I assumed she would be remarried. I never thought it would take ten years to hear back.'

Carmen said she was initially too nervous to call as so much time had passed but plucked up the courage and the pair arranged to meet.

They met up in Paris a few days later and have now wed. 17 years after they first fell in love. Steve, of Paignton, Devon, said: 'When we met again it was like a film. We ran across the airport into each other's arms.'

'We met up and fell in love all over again. Within 30 seconds of setting eyes on each other we were kissing.'

'Now we're married, I'm just glad the letter did eventually end up where it was supposed to be.'

Carmen, who is now living with Steve in Paignton, said the wedding was the pinnacle of an 'amazing' love story.

the letter in which Steve had written: 'I hope you are well. I was just writing to ask if you ever got married and if you ever still thought of me.'

'It would be great to hear from you, please great in touch if you can. Steve XXX'.

Factory supervisor Steve said: 'I didn't write much because I assumed she would be remarried. I never thought it would take ten years to hear back.'

Carmen said she was initially too nervous to call as so much time had passed but plucked up the courage and the pair arranged to meet.

They met up in Paris a few days later and have now wed. 17 years after they first fell in love. Steve, of Paignton, Devon, said: 'When we met again it was like a film. We ran across the airport into each other's arms.'

'We met up and fell in love all over again. Within 30 seconds of setting eyes on each other we were kissing.'

'Now we're married, I'm just glad the letter did eventually end up where it was supposed to be.'

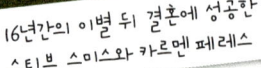

16년간의 이별 뒤 결혼에 성공한 스티브 스미스와 카르멘 페레스

10년 뒤에 배달된 연애편지

뜻하지 않게 헤어졌다가 10년 전 연애편지가 다시 인연이 돼 결혼한 남녀의 사랑 이야기가 화제다.

42세 동갑내기인 영국인 남성 스티브 스미스와 스페인 여성 카르멘 페레스는 16년간의 이별 끝에(following a separation of 16 years) 2009년 7월 17일 꿈에 그리던 결혼식을 올렸다(walk down the aisle).

두 사람은 페레스가 외국인 학생 신분으로 영국에 오면서(move to England as a foreign student) 만나 사랑에 빠졌다(fall in love with each other). 하지만 1년가량 교제 후(after a year-long relationship) 페레스가 갑자기 프랑스로 떠나면서 헤어지게(drift apart) 됐다. 페레스는 프랑스에 있는 집안의 가게 운영 때문에 급히 영국을 떠나면서 연락처도 제대로 남기지 못했다.

몇 년 뒤 스미스는 사랑의 불꽃을 되살리기 위해 그녀에게 편지를 썼다(write to Perez in a bid to rekindle their romance). 스페인 집주소를 우여곡절 끝에 알아냈다.

하지만 페레스의 어머니가 그 편지를 벽난로 장식장 위에 올려둔(put it on the mantelpiece) 것이 두 사람의 재회를 10년이나 늦추고 말았다. 편지가 벽난로 뒤로 떨어지면서(slip down the back of the fireplace) 페레스에게 전달되지 못했던 것이다.

편지는 이후 10년 동안 개봉되지 않은 채 그 자리에 그대로 떨어져 있다가(remain there unopened for the next decade) 시설 보수를 위해 벽난로가 치워지면서(be removed for renovations) 발견됐다.

편지는 그때까지 미혼으로 있으면서 평생의 사랑을 잊지 못하고 있닌(remain single and never forget the love of her life) 페레스에게 10년 만에 전달됐다. 편지에는 "잘 지내고 있기를 바라(I hope you are well). 네가 결혼했는지, 그리고 아직 나를 생각하고 있는지 물어보려고 편지 보내는 거야(write to ask if you are married and if you still think of me). 답장이 온다면 정말 좋을 텐데……(would be great to hear from you). 가능하다면 연락해줘(get in touch with me if possible)"라고 쓰여 있었다.

페레스는 너무 많은 시간이 흘러(since so much time has passed) 긴장돼서 전화도 하지 못하다가 용기를 내서(pluck up the courage) 편지에 적힌 전화번호로 연락을 해봤다. 스미스는 "그 편지를 보내고 답장을 받는 데 10년이 걸릴(take ten years to hear back) 것이라고는 생각도 하지 못했다"고 했다.

그리고 두 사람은 며칠 뒤 파리에서 재회했고(meet up in Paris a few

days later), 마침내 처음 사랑에 빠진 후 17년 만에(17 years after they first fell in love) 결혼식을 올리게 됐다.

스미스는 영국 언론과의 인터뷰를 통해 "우리가 다시 만났을 때 그것은 한 편의 영화 같았다(be like a film)"며 "공항을 가로질러 달려가 서로 껴안았고(run across the airport into each other's arms) 눈을 마주친 지 30초도 안 돼(within 30 seconds of setting eyes on each other) 키스를 했다"고 말했다.

영국 데본 주(州) 페이턴에 신혼살림을 차린 페레스는 "우리의 결혼은 놀라운 러브 스토리의 절정(be the pinnacle of an amazing love story)"이라면서 "결혼을 한 번도 하지 않았던(have never got married) 내가 마침내 늘 사랑해오던 남자와 결혼하게(marry the man I have always loved) 됐다"며 행복해했다.

How Long-lost Love Letter Led to Couple Marrying after 16 Years Apart

A couple have married after they were reunited when a long-lost love letter sent ten years ago was found unopened behind a fireplace.

Steve Smith and Carmen Ruiz-Perez, both 42, walked down the aisle on Friday following a separation of 16 years.

The pair fell in love and got engaged in their 20s after Carmen moved to England as a foreign student.

But after a year-long relationship the couple drifted apart when she had to move back to France.

A few years later Steve wrote to her in a bid to rekindle their romance —but Carmen's mother put it on the mantlepiece and it slipped down the back of the fireplace.

It remained there unopened for the next decade until the fireplace was removed for renovations. Carmen – who had remained single and never forgot the love of her life – was given the letter in which Steve had written: 'I hope you are well. I was just writing to ask if you ever married and if you ever still thought of me?

'It would be great to hear from you, please great in touch if you can. Steve XXX.'

Factory supervisor Steve said: 'I didn't write much because I assumed she would be remarried. I never thought it would take ten years to hear back.'

Carmen said she was initially too nervous to call as so much time had passed but plucked up the courage and the pair arranged to meet.

They met up in Paris a few days later and have now wed – 17 years after they first fell in love. Steve, of Paignton, Devon, said: 'When we met again it was like a film. We ran across the airport into each other's arms.

'We met up and fell in love all over again. Within 30 seconds of setting eyes on each other we were kissing.

'Now we're married, I'm just glad the letter did eventually end up where it was supposed to be.'

Carmen, who is now living with Steve in Paignton, said the wedding was the pinnacle of an 'amazing' love story.

She added: 'I never got married and now I'm marrying the man I have always loved.'

✅ 기억하면 좋을 구절!

fall in love with 사랑에 빠지다

> She was a beautiful girl that Charles immediately *fell in love with*.
> 그녀는 무척 아름다운 소녀였기에 찰스는 순식간에 사랑에 빠졌다.

drift apart 헤어지다 / 사이가 멀어지다

> As children we were very close, but as we grew up we just *drifted apart*
> 어릴 적에는 매우 친했지만 우리는 자라면서 멀어져갔다.

get in touch with ~와 연락하다 / 접촉하다

> *Get in touch with* me as soon as you arrive
> 도착하자마자 나한테 연락해줘.

pluck up the courage 용기를 내다

> I finally *plucked up the courage* to ask her for a date
> 나는 마침내 용기를 내 그녀에게 데이트를 신청했다.

be the pinnacle of 정점이 되다 / 중심이 되다 /

> *The pinnacle of* the mountain can't be seen here at all.
> 그 산봉우리는 여기서는 전혀 보이지 않는다

내 인생의 명언 — 가정은 최고의 별장이다

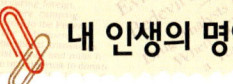

▶ 가정에서 행복하지 않으면 다른 어디에서도 행복할 수 없다.
앤지 하먼 (미국 여배우 · 모델)

> If you're not happy at home, you're not happy anywhere else.
> Angie Harmon

▶ 가정은 우리가 가장 많이 사랑하고 가장 많이 투덜대는 곳이다.
빌리 선데이 (미국 복음전도가)

> Home is the place we love best and grumble the most.
> Billy Sunday

▶ 가정은 하루아침에 이뤄지지 않는다.
제인 에이스 (미국 라디오쇼 진행자)

> Home wasn't built in a day.
> Jane Ace

▶ 집안일은 여자가 하지 않으면 아무도 알아채지 못하는 일이다.
에반 에사르 (미국 유머작가)

> Housework is something that nobody notices
> unless women haven't done it.
> Evan Esar

▶ 인간은 자기 새끼들로 하여금 집에 돌아오게 하는
지구상 유일한 동물이다.
빌 코스비 (미국 코미디언 · 배우 · 작가)

> Human beings are the only creatures on earth
> that allow their children to come back home.
> Bill Cosby

News English

"A Miracle Revival of a Six-week-old Baby"

They are holding her as tightly as they can because they know it will be for the very last time.

After deciding to turn their six-week-old daughter's life-support system off, Pete Vincent and Emily Ashurst cradled her in their arms and waited for her to slip quietly away.

But Grace had other ideas. The baby, given only a 1 per cent chance of life after contracting meningitis, suddenly started to breathe on her own.

To her parents' amazement, not only has she surely and steadily continued her extraordinary recovery, yesterday she was well enough to leave hospital and go home.

Grace's father, a 26-year-old soldier and member of 45 Commando who returned from Afghanistan in April, said it's all about fighting spirit. 'And it seems my daughter does too.

'It was all doom and gloom and we thought Grace had a chance,' he said. 'They just didn't want to get our hopes up but we are overjoyed with what has happened.

'The fact she's recovered is incredible — she's obviously a real fighter. She has defied all the odds and proved everyone wrong.'

Grace was taken to Newcastle General Hospital on May 16 after her parents noticed she was listless and struggling to breathe.

Tests showed she had late onset group B streptococcus meningitis, a condition which affects one in 1,000 babies and is contracted through the mother during childbirth. After four days in intensive care, doctors told her devastated parents there was virtually no hope for Grace.

'The decision to turn off her life support machine was based on what the doctors were telling us,' Mr Vincent said.

'The scan results were very bad so we thought it would be best for her.

but also hoping things will improve.'

Late onset meningitis, known as GBS, is present in a quarter of women of childbearing age and is passed on to one in every 1,000 babies during labour.

It is first... support machine was based on what the doctors were telling us,' Mr Vincent said.

'The scan results were very bad so we thought it would be best for her.

'We were told she would take a few last breaths. But she kept stopping breathing and starting again for the next six hours. Six months in Afghanistan was easy compared to that.'

Soon it was apparent that Grace had absolutely no intention of giving up. In the weeks since that rollercoaster day on May 20, her heart rate, temperature and blood pressure have all returned to normal.

She has however, lost her sight although doctors are not yet sure whether this is permanent.

Grace's mother Emily, 26, works as a ward clerk at the hospital but now has a very clear patient's perspective as well.

She said the family, including Grace's big sister Megan, six, are 'looking forward to the future'. 'We are over the moon,' she said at the family home in Holystone, Newcastle.

'We were told Grace had catastrophic brain damage and had no chance of living. But she managed it and we are really happy and looking forward to enjoying her future as a family. Every day she is making slow progress. She cried on Tuesday for the first time in four weeks and for me that was the nicest sound in the world — it was amazing to hear her do that.'

기적적으로 살아난 아기 그레이스와 부모

생후 6주 아기의 기적적인 부활

엄마와 아빠가 생후 6주 된 딸을 마지막으로 안아 들었다(cradle their six-week-old daughter for the last time). 생명유지장치를 떼어낸 뒤(after life support is lifted)였다. 의사들은 마지막 인사를 나누라고 했다.

그 순간 엄마 품에 안겨 있던 딸이 기적적으로 되살아났다(come back to life). 2009년 5월 20일 영국 뉴캐슬에서 일어난 일이다. 그들은 있는 힘을 다해 딸을 껴안았다(hold their daughter as tightly as they can). 정말 마지막이 될 것(will be for the very last time)이라 생각했다.

딸의 생명유지장치를 끄기로 결정한 후(after deciding to turn their daughter's life-support system off), 아빠 피트 빈센트(26세)와 엄마 에밀리 아셔스트(26세)는 딸을 팔에 안아 들고 딸이 조용히 떠나가는 것만을 기다리고(wait for her to slip quietly away) 있었다.

그런데 딸 그레이스의 생각은 달랐던(have other ideas) 모양이다. 뇌막염에 감염돼 생존 가능성이 1%밖에 안 된다던 그 어린 소녀(the little girl given only a 1% chance of survival after contracting meningitis)가 갑자기 자력으로 숨을 쉬기 시작한(start to breathe on her own) 것이다.

부모가 놀라움과 기쁨에 겨워 어쩔 줄 모르도록(to her parents' amazement and delight) 어린 딸은 그 역경을 이겨내며 확실하고 꾸준하게 놀라운 회복을 계속해(surely and steadily continue her extraordinary recovery against all odds)나갔다. 그리고 마침내 며칠 만에 병원에서 퇴원해 집으로 돌아갈 만큼 건강 상태가 좋아졌다(get well enough to leave hospital and go home).

그레이스의 아빠 빈센트는 같은 해 4월 아프가니스탄에서 돌아오(return from Afghanistan) 영국 해병대원이다. 투지에 관한 한 모든 것을 아는(know all about fighting spirit) 아빠처럼, 딸 그레이스도 그랬던 모양이다.

빈센트는 "모든 것이 정말 절망적이었다(be all doom and gloom)"고 말한다. 의사들을 비롯해 어느 누구도 그레이스가 회생할 수 있을 것으로(be restored to life again) 생각하지 못했다. 그런데 그 어린 그레이스가 숱한 어려움을 이겨내고 모두가 잘못 생각했음을 보여준(defy all the odds and prove everybody wrong) 것이다.

앞서 그레이스는 뉴캐슬종합병원 응급실로 옮겨졌다. 생기가 없고 가까스로 호흡을 이어가는(be listless and struggle to breathe) 것을 부모가 발견하고 앰뷸런스를 불렀다.

그레이스는 후발성 B형 연쇄상구균 뇌막염에 걸린(have late onset group B streptococcus meningitis) 것으로 밝혀졌다. 신생아 1000명 중 1명이 걸리는 병(a condition which affects one in 1000 newborn babies)으로, 출산 때 엄마로부터 감염됐다는(be contracted from the mother during childbirth) 진단을 받았다.

나흘간의 집중 치료 끝에(after four days in intensive care) 의사들은 그레이스 부모에게 "사실상 희망이 없다"(there is virtually no hope for Grace)고 통보했다. 아빠 빈센트는 "생명유지장치를 떼기로 한 결정(the decision to turn off her life support machine)은 의사들의 말에 따른 것"이라며 "스캔 결과가 너무 나빠, 그렇게 하는 것이 그레이스를 위해서도 최선이 될(would be best for Grace) 것으로 생각했다"고 한다.

아빠 빈센트에게는 딸이 죽어가는 모습을 지켜보는 것이 너무 큰 고통이었다. 의사들은 "그레이스가 마지막 몇 차례 숨을 쉬게(take a few last breaths) 될 것이며, 여섯 시간 동안 호흡을 그쳤다가 다시 숨 쉬는(keep stopping breathing and starting again for the next six hours) 과정을 거칠 것"이라고 했다. 그에 비하면 아빠가 아프가니스탄에서 보낸 6개월은 아무 것도 아니었다(six months in Afghanistan was easy compared to that).

롤러코스터와 같았던 그날 이후 수 주 동안(in the weeks since that rollercoaster day) 그레이스의 심박수, 체온, 혈압은 모두 정상으로 돌아왔다(her heart rate, temperature and blood pressure have all returned to normal).

하지만 그레이스는 시력을 잃고 말았다(lose her sight). 의사들은 시력 상실이 평생 갈 것인지에 대해 아직 확실히 알 수 없다(be not yet sure whether this is permanent)고 말한다.

그레이스의 엄마 에밀리는 병원 병동 직원으로 일하고(work as a ward clerk at the hospital) 있다. 어린 딸의 불행을 겪은 에밀리는 이제 환자의 관점도 아주 명확하게 이해할(have a very clear patient's perspective as well) 수 있게 됐다고 말한다.

에밀리는 "그레이스가 4주 만에 처음 울음소리를 냈다(cry for the first time in four weeks)"며 "세상에서 가장 아름다운 소리(the most beautiful sound in the world)였다"고 감격해했다.

그레이스의 언니인 메건(6세)을 포함한 모든 가족(the whole family including Grace's big sister Megan, six)은 너무나 행복해(be over the moon)하고 있다. 앞으로 그레이스에게 어떤 일이 일어날지는 어느 의사도 단언하지 못한다(none of the doctors cannot assure what the future will hold for Grace). 부모는 여전히 걱정을 떨치지 못한 채(be still worried for her), 다만 더 나아질 것(things will improve)이라는 희망을 붙들고 있을 뿐이다.

Amazing Grace: Parents Cradle Baby for Last Time after Life support is Switched Off······ But Then She Came Back to Life

They are holding her as tightly as they can because they know it will be for the very last time.

After deciding to turn their six-week-old daughter's life-support system off, Pete Vincent and Emily Ashurst cradled her in their arms and waited for her to slip quietly away.

But Grace had other ideas. The little girl given only a 1% chance of survival after contracting meningitis suddenly started to breathe on her own.

To her parents' amazement and delight, she has surely and steadily continued her extraordinary recovery. Yesterday, she was well enough to leave hospital and go home.

Grace's father, a 26-year-old Royal Marine and member of 45

Commando who returned from Afghanistan in April, knows all about fighting spirit. And it seems his daughter does too.

'It was all doom and gloom and no one thought Grace had a chance,' he said.

'They just didn't want to get our hopes up but we are overjoyed with what happened.

'The fact she's recovered is incredible – she's obviously a real fighter. She's defied all the odds and proved everybody wrong.'

Grace was taken to Newcastle General Hospital on May 16 after her parents noticed she was listless and struggling to breathe.

Tests showed she had late onset group B streptococcus meningitis, a condition which affects one in 1,000 babies and is contracted from the mother during childbirth.

After four days in intensive care, doctors told her devastated parents there was virtually no hope for Grace.

'The decision to turn off her life support machine was based on what the doctors were telling us,' Mr Vincent said.

'The scan results were very bad so we thought it would be best for her.

'We were told she would take a few last breaths. 'But she kept stopping breathing and starting again for the next six hours. Six months in Afghanistan was easy compared to that.'

Soon it was apparent that Grace had absolutely no intention of giving up. In the weeks since that rollercoaster day on May 20, her heart rate, temperature and blood pressure have all returned to normal.

She has however, lost her sight although doctors are not yet sure whether this is permanent.

Grace's mother Emily, 26, works as a ward clerk at the hospital but now has a very clear patient's perspective as well.

She said the family, including Grace's big sister Megan, six, are 'looking forward to the future'. 'We are over the moon,' she said at the family home in Holystone, Newcastle.

'We were told Grace had catastrophic brain damage and had no chance of living.

'But she managed it and we are really happy and looking forward to enjoying our future as a family. Every day she is making slow progress. She cried on Thursday for the first time in four weeks and to me that was the nicest sound in the world—it was amazing to hear her do that.

'None of the doctors know what the future will hold for Grace and we are still worried for her, but also hoping things will improve.'

Late onset meningitis, known as GBS, is present in a quarter of women of childbearing age and is passed on to one in every 1,000 babies during labour.

It is fatal for one in eight of those affected.

☑ 기억하면 좋을 구절!

slip away　사라지다 / 없어지다 / 죽다

> She knew that time was *slipping away*.
> 그녀는 시간이 간다는 사실을 알았다.

against all odds　모든 역경에도 불구하고 / 숱한 방해물을 넘어서

> *Against all odds*, he won gold in the Games.
> 온갖 역경을 넘어, 그는 대회에서 금메달을 땄다.

be all doom and gloom　보는 것이 절망적이고 우울한

> But this speech was far from *being all doom and gloom*.
> 그러나 그 연설은 절망과 우울과는 거리가 먼 것이었다.

be over the moon　무척 황홀한 / 매우 행복한 / 행복에 겨운

> I felt I *was over the moon*.
> 나는 너무 행복했다.

be contracted　감염되다

> I was bitten by a mosquito and I *was contracted* Japanese encephalitis.
> 모기에 물려 일본 뇌염에 걸렸다.

내 인생의 명언

▶ 인류는 불평하고 싶은 필요성을 충족하기 위해 언어를 발명했다.
릴리 톰린 (미국 여배우 · 작가 · 프로듀서)

> Man invented language to satisfy his need to complain.
> Lily Tomlin

▶ 화가 났을 때는 말하기 전에 10까지 세라.
대단히 화가 많이 났을 때는 100까지 세라.
토머스 제퍼슨 (미국 3대 대통령)

> When angry, count ten before you speak;
> if very angry, a hundred.
> Thomas Jefferson

▶ 적은 말에 많은 뜻을 담아 간단히 하라.
작자미상

> Comprehend much matter of thought in few words.
> anonymous

▶ 사람들은 눈보다 귀를 덜 믿는다.
헤로도투스 (그리스 역사가)

> Men trust their ears less than their eyes.
> Herodotos

News English

"A Mother Bird's Maternal Instinct"

These amazing photographs show the moment a mother bird saved her chicks from being washed away by using her own body as a dam.

The mistle thrush had unwittingly built her nest on top of a downpipe, blocking the water's passage and causing it to flood.

Desperate to protect her young, the clever bird puffed herself up to twice her normal size and sat in the pipe to stop the tide of rain water flooding the nest.

Amateur wildlife photographer Mr Bright, who captured the amazing scene in Fareham, Hampshire, said he had never seen a bird do this before.

"The nest was tucked away out of the weather in the shade of a bush but was so close to the downpipe it would be flooded when it rained; he said.

"It was only a matter of seconds before the pipe flooded, and water cascaded over the sides."

Mr Bright said he was astonished by the bird's ingenuity.

He said: "She had to come up with a solution so she puffed herself up until she was twice the size of her mate and used her body as a cork to stop the water – it was absolutely amazing.

"She was very dedicated, sitting there even when the rain was hammering down.

"Then every half an hour she would get off and come back."

Her mate was left to feed their young and the mother herself, Mr Bright noticed. RSPB expert Hester Phillips said the society had heard of birds nesting in sites as bizarre as the top of traffic lights but she had never seen one in a situation like this.

But she added: "Birds can be amazingly hardy creatures, their endurance is incredible – especially when protecting their young.

"Mistle thrushes prefer natural nesting like tall trees or shrubs. If they can't find this natural habitat, they'll look for something that closely resembles it, and this small flooded spot appears to do the job.

"It's a precarious beginning in life but the chicks were perfectly healthy and the parents successfully."

"These photographs show the moment a mother bird saved her chicks from being washed away by using her own body as a dam."

자기 몸을 부풀려 홈통의 넘치는 물을 막고 있는 어미새의 모습

어느 어미새의 눈물겨운 모성 본능

　지붕 홈통 위에 지어놓은 둥지가 휩쓸릴(be washed away) 위기에 처하자, 자신의 몸으로 홈통에 댐을 만들어 넘치는 물로부터 새끼들을 구한(use her own body as a dam to save her chicks from overflowing rain leader) 어미새 사진이 공개돼 감동을 자아내고 있다.

　이 놀라운 사진들(these amazing photographs)은 영국의 아마추어 야생 사진작가 데니스 브라이트 씨가 햄프셔 주(州) 페어햄의 한 주택에서 촬영한(capture the scene at a house in Fareham, Hampshire) 것으로, 어미새(a mother bird)가 몸으로 댐을 만들어 새끼들을 보호하는(protect the chicks by using herself as a dam) 사이 아빠 새는 새끼들에게 먹이를 먹이는 장면이 포착됐다.

　개똥지빠귀 종류인 이 부모 새들은 우연히 홈통 위에 둥지를 지었다(unwittingly build a nest on top of a downspout). 빗물이 흘러내리는 길목을 막아 홈통 물이 넘쳐흐를(block the rainwater's passage and cause the gutter to flood) 수밖에 없는 위치였다.

　새끼들을 보호하기 위해 절박해진(be desperate to protect her young) 어미새는 자신의 몸을 평상시 크기의 두 배 가까이 부풀렸고(puff herself up to twice her normal size), 둥지가 빗물에 잠기는 것을 막기 위해(to stop the tide of rain water swamping the nest) 홈통 안을 가로막고 앉았다(sit in the drainpipe).

　둥지는 악천후를 피할 수 있게 지붕 그늘 아래 한적한 곳에 지어졌지만(be tucked away from the weather in the shade of the roof) 수직 홈통에 너무 가까워(be so close to the downpipe) 비가 많이 오면 빗물에 잠길 수밖에 없었다.

　홈통이 넘치는 것은 시간 문제(be only a matter of time before the pipe flooded)였다. 그 순간 사진을 찍던 브라이트 씨는 어미새의 독창력에 놀라지(be astonished by the mother bird's ingenuity) 않을 수 없었다.

　브라이트 씨는 "해결 방안을 내놓아야(have to come up with a solution) 했는데, 자기 짝 크기의 두 배가 될 때까지 몸을 부풀리더니(puff herself up to be twice the size of her mate) 그 몸을 코르크 마개처럼 해서 빗물을 막더라(use her body as a cork to stop the rainwater)"며 감탄해 마지 않았다.

　어미 새는 비가 억수처럼 퍼붓는(be hammering down)데도 그 자리에 앉아 있는 대단히 헌신적인(be very dedicated, sitting there) 모습을 보였다. 그사이 아빠 새는 새끼들에게 먹이를 먹이고(feed their young) 있었다. 어미 새는 30분마다 한 번씩 밖으로 나가(get out every half an hour) 몸을 말리고 다시 돌아오곤(dry herself off and come back) 했다.

영국 왕립조류보호학회의 헤스터 필립스 박사는 "신호등 꼭대기처럼 이상한 장소에 둥지를 트는 새들의 이야기는 들어봤지만(hear of birds nesting in sites as bizarre as the top of traffic lights) 이런 상황은 본 적이 없다(have never seen one in a situation like this)"면서 "새는 놀라울 정도로 강건한 생물(an amazingly hardy creature)이다. 특히 새끼를 보호할 때(especially when protecting their young)의 인내력은 믿기지 않을 정도"라고 말한다.

개똥지빠귀는 높은 나무나 관목 위와 같은 곳에 자연적인 둥지 틀기를 선호하지만(prefer natural nesting like tall trees or shrubs) 그런 자연 서식지를 찾지 못할(can't find such a natural habitat) 경우엔 비슷한 곳을 구하는(look for somewhere similar) 것으로 알려져 있다.

둥지 안에 있던 네 마리의 새끼들(the four chicks in the nest)은 위태로웠던 삶의 시작에도 불구하고(despite their precarious beginning in life) 모두 성공적으로 둥지를 떠났다고 사진작가 브라이트 씨는 전했다.

Bird Bath··· Mother Thrush Uses herself as Dam to Protect Nest from Overflowing Drainpipe

These amazing photographs show the moment a mother bird saved her chicks from being washed away by using her own body as a dam.

The mistle thrush had unwittingly built her nest on top of a downpipe, blocking the water's passage and causing the gutter to flood.

Desperate to protect her young, the clever bird puffed herself up to twice her normal size and sat in the drainpipe to stop the tide of rain water swamping the nest.

Amateur wildlife photographer Dennis Bright, who captured the scene at a house in Fareham, Hampshire, said he had never seen a bird do this before.

'The nest was tucked away from the weather in the shade of the roof but it was so close to the downpipe the gutter flooded when it rained,' he said.

'It was only a matter of seconds before the pipe flooded, and water cascaded over the sides.'

Mr Bright said he was astonished by the bird's ingenuity.

He said: 'She had to come up with a solution so she puffed herself up until she was twice the size of her mate and used her body as a cork to stop the water - it was absolutely amazing.

'She was very dedicated, sitting there even when the rain was hammering down.

'Then every half an hour she would get out, dry herself off and come back.'

Her mate was left to feed their young and the mother herself, Mr Bright noticed. RSPB expert Hester Phillips said the society had heard of birds nesting in sites as bizarre as the top of traffic lights but she had never seen one in a situation like this.

But she added: 'Birds can be amazingly hardy creatures, their endurance is incredible – especially when protecting their young.

'Mistle thrushes prefer natural nesting like tall trees or shrubs. If they can't find this natural habitat, they'll look for something which closely resembles it, and this small, secluded spot appears to do the job.'

Despite their precarious beginning in life the four chicks were perfectly healthy and all flew the nest successfully.

✓ 기억하면 좋을 구절!

be only a matter(question) of time 단지 시간문제다

➥ So far as I know it's only a matter of time.
내가 아는 바로는 그건 시간문제예요.

unwittingly [ʌnˈwɪtɪŋli] ad. 부지불식간에, 자기도 모르게

➥ It was clear that, wittingly or *unwittingly*, he had offended her.
일부러 그랬든 아니든 간에, 그가 그녀를 불쾌하게 만든 것은 사실이다.

come up with ~을 제시하다 / 생산하다

➥ She had to *come up with* a new idea for sales rise.
그녀는 매출 증가를 위해 새 아이디어를 제시해야 했다.

be tucked away 한적한 곳에 위치하다 / 눈에 안 띄는 곳에 두다

➥ The village *is tucked away* in a quiet valley.
그 마을은 조용한 계곡 안에 있다.

hammer down 전속력을 내다 / 강하게 내려치다

➥ Rain was *hammering down* onto the roof.
비가 지붕 위로 쏟아지고 있었다.

내 인생의 명언 자연은 아름다워라

▶ 봄이란 설사 눈녹은 진창물에 발이 빠졌다 하더라도
휘파람을 불고 싶은 때이다.
더그 라슨 (미국 칼럼니스트)

> Spring is when you feel like whistling
> even with a shoe full of slush.
> Doug Larson

▶ 가을은 모든 잎이 꽃이 되는 제2의 봄이다.
알베르 카뮈 (프랑스 소설가 · 극작가)

> Autumn is a second spring where every leaf is a flower.
> Albert Camus

▶ 모든 꽃은 자연 속에 피어나는 영혼이다.
제라르 드 네르발 (프랑스 시인 · 소설가)

> Every flower is a soul blossoming in nature.
> Gerard de Nerval

▶ 나는 신을 믿는다. 다만 '자연'이라고 쓸 뿐.
프랭크 라이트 (미국 건축가)

> I believe in God, only I spell it Nature.
> Frank Lloyd Wright

▶ 자연은 언제나 영혼의 색을 입는다.
랠프 에머슨 (미국 사상가 · 시인)

> Nature always wears the colors of the spirit.
> Ralph Waldo Emerson

News English

"A Nazi Stormtrooper's Amazing Requital of Kindness"

He was a soldier in one of the most fanatical divisions in Hitler's war machine. As a member of the SS, Heinrich Steinmeyer expected little mercy as he surrendered to British troops towards the end of the Second World War. But instead, he says he was treated with humanity by both the troops who captured him and the guards at the Scottish prison camp where he was kept until the end of the war.

Sixty-five years later, Mr Steinmeyer has pledged to leave his home and life-savings of $430,000 to elderly residents in the village of Comrie, Perthshire, as a gesture of gratitude.

Mr Steinmeyer was held at Cultybraggan camp near Comrie, which was built to house ardent Nazis.

He was [...] in Norm[...] been sav[...] He says [...] treated h[...] remain in[...] the war.

Now 84 a[...] Bremen, M[...] "I always w[...] they showe[...] I have to g[...] they have it [...]

"Cultybragg[...] compared to [...] prisoners wo[...] my heart and [...] fighting till the[...] "They were so[...]

not just the enemy, but a Nazi.' Such friendliness was a surprise, but it is in the British nature. It was so much better than being told to lie in a filthy foxhole - and to die there.'

When Mr Steinmeyer dies, his a[...] be scattered at Cultybraggan [...] estate passed to a trust he has s[...] help the elderly in the area.

After the war he decided t[...] Comrie after learning that his ho[...] had become a part of Poland[...] stunned by the kindness of vill[...] though he made no secret of [...] past.

They even sent parcels to his [...] Germany after learning [...]

Bulge in 1944 and later the Red Army, it withdrew to Austria and the 10,000 survivors surrendered in May 1945.

Mr Steinmeyer, as an SS soldier, was expected to die defending the Fuhrer, but [...] fight for a bridge in

lie in a filthy foxhole - and to die there. When Mr Steinmeyer dies, his ashes will be scattered at Cultybraggan and his estate passed to a trust he has set up to help the elderly in the area.

After the war he decided to stay in [...]earning that his home [...] a part of Poland. He [...] kindness of villagers, [...] made no secret of his [...]

[...]arcels to his mother in [...]rning she had fallen ill [...] of Comrie, who knew [...]yer by his nickname [...] are delighted by his gift. [...]ck to the village - which [...]on of around 1,800 [...] become 'Uncle Heini' [...] to whom he sends gifts

[...]raggan - which once held Hitler's [...] Rudolf Hess - became notorious [...]he inmates hanged one of their [...] 1944 after accusing him of leading [...]e plot.

[...]meyer joined the Nazis in 1941 [...]e of 17, and joined the Hitler [...] 12th Panzer Division - which [...] linked to war crimes, notably [...]v of 140 Canadian prisoners

[...]uited from the ranks of the [...]and, with 20,000 men, first [...] June 1944 in the Normandy [...]ontested with only 12,500 [...]wing the Americans in the [...]otten in 1944 Stichstein the [...] Wehrmacht to Russia this [...] wiped outsurrender in May

히틀러를 둘러싼 나치 대원들과 젊은 시절의 스타인마이어

142

어느 나치 돌격대원의 놀랍고 감동적인 보은

'원수'나 다름없던 자신을 가족처럼 대해준 사람들의 은혜에 그 '원수'가 65년 만에 전 재산을 털어 보답했다.

84세인 독일인 하인리히 스타인마이어는 제2차 세계대전 당시 히틀러의 '전쟁 기계'에서 가장 광적이었던 사단들 중 하나에 속한 나치 돌격대원(a Nazi stormtrooper in one of the most fanatical divisions in Hitler's 'war machine')이었다.

그는 2차 대전 말기(towards the end of World War Two)인 1944년 노르망디의 진흙투성이 참호에 숨어 있다가 며칠째 이어진 영국 공군의 집요한 폭격을 당한 뒤(after being relentlessly bombarded for days in his muddy Normandy foxhole by the Royal Air Force) 영국군에 투항했다(surrender to British troops).

어떤 자비도 기대하지 않았다(expect little mercy). 하지만 그를 포로로 잡은 영국군, 전쟁이 끝날 때까지(until the end of the war) 머물렀던 포로수용소 경비원들(the troops who captured him and the guards at the prison camp)은 그를 인간적으로 대해(treat him with humanity)줬다.

65년이 지난 지금(now 65 years on) 그 독일군은 그곳에서 받았던 대우에 대한 감사의 표시로(as a gesture of gratitude for his treatment there) 퍼스 주(州)의 작은 마을 콤리의 노인 주민들에게(to the elderly residents in the tiny village of Comrie, Perthshire) 40만 파운드(약 7억 6000만 원)의 전 재산을 증여키로(bequeath his all equivalent to 400000 pounds) 했다. 자신의 집과 3만 파운드(약 5600만 원)의 노후대비저축금을 모두 내놓기로(leave his home and life savings of 30,000 pounds) 한 것이다.

스타인마이어는 소속 부대가 노르망디 상륙작전 기간 연합군에 의해 궤멸된(be decimated by the allies during the D-day landings) 후 열성 나치들을 수용하기 위해 특별히 지어진(built specially to house ardent Nazis) 컬티브래건 포로수용소로 보내졌다.

증오스러운 적군으로 대우할 것으로 예상했지만(expect to be treated as a hated enemy) 경비원이나 마을 주민들은 따뜻하게 그를 보듬어주었다. 그 은혜에 감복한 그는 전쟁이 끝난 후에도 7년간 그곳에 머물기로 결정했다(decide to remain there for seven years after the war).

그는 자신의 고향이 폴란드의 일부가 된(become a part of Poland) 것을 알고 난 뒤 콤리 마을에 남아 농장 노동자로 일했다(stay in Comrie and work as a farmhand). 그는 나치 전력을 숨기지 않았음에도 불구하고(despite making no secret of his Nazi past) 마을 주민들이 보여준 친절

함에 너무나 놀랐다(be stunned at the kindness of local residents)고 한다.

한번은 마을에서 하일랜드게임(스코틀랜드 전통 스포츠축제)이 열려 어렴풋이나마 엿보려고 언덕에 올라가 서 있었다(stand on a hill to catch a glimpse). 그랬더니 한 여성이 다가와(come up to him) 들어가서 볼 수 있는 티켓(a ticket to go in and watch)뿐만 아니라 10실링짜리 지폐까지 용돈으로(not only that, but a ten shilling note as well to spend) 손에 쥐여주는 것이 아닌가.

또 주민들은 스타인마이어의 어머니가 병에 걸렸다는(fall ill) 소식에 독일에 있는 그의 어머니에게 소포들을 보내주기도(send parcels to his mother in Germany) 했다. 스타인마이어는 "사람이 그렇게 좋을 수 있다는(could be so nice) 사실에 너무나 놀랐다(be utterly astonished)"고 한다.

그는 "포로수용소 주변 전체(the whole place around the prison camp)가 너무나 아름다웠다"며 "내가 왜 이 피비린내 나는 전쟁에서 싸우고 있나(fight the bloody war) 하는 생각에 마음이 아팠다(go to my heart)"고 회고했다.

현재 독일 브레멘에 살고 있는 스타인마이어는 "나는 그들이 나에게 보여준 관대함에 보답하기를(repay the generosity they showed me) 늘 바라왔다"며 "그들은 내가 그들에게 주어야 할 모든 것을 받을 자격이 있다(deserve everything I have to give them). 다른 어느 누구보다 그들이 갖는 것이 훨씬 낫다(be far better they have it than anyone else)"고 말했다.

스타인마이어가 사망하면 그의 유골은 컬티브래건 포로수용소 자리에 뿌려질(his ashes will be scattered at Cultybraggan Prisoner of War camp)

예정이다. 그의 재산은 지역 노인들을 돕기 위해 그가 설립한(set up to help the elderly in the area) 특별신탁기금에 넘어가게(be passed to a special trust) 된다.

'하인즈'라는 별명으로 스타인마이어를 기억하고(remember him by his nickname 'Heinz') 있는 콤리 마을의 노인 주민들(elderly residents of Comrie)은 마을에 대한 그의 놀라운 보은에 기쁨을 감추지 못하고(do not conceal their delight about his amazing requital of kindness to the village) 있다.

SS Soldier Leaves Life Savings to British Village Where He was Kept Prisoner

He was a soldier in one of the most fanatical divisions in Hitler's war machine.

As a member of the SS, Heinrich Steinmeyer expected little mercy as he surrendered to British troops towards the end of the Second World War.

But instead, he says he was treated with humanity by both the troops who captured him and the guards at the Scottish prison camp where he was kept until the end of the war.

Sixty-five years later, Mr Steinmeyer has pledged to leave his home and life savings of $430,000 to elderly residents in the village of Comrie, Perthshire, as a gesture of gratitude.

Mr Steinmeyer was held at Cultybraggan camp near Comrie which was built to house ardent Nazis.

He was taken there after being captured in Normandy. His SS Panzer division had been savaged by the Allies.

He says both the guards and villagers treated him so well that he decided to remain in Scotland for seven years after the war.

Now 84 and living in Delmenhorst, near Bremen, Mr Steinmeyer said:

'I always wanted to repay the generosity they showed me. They deserve everything I have to give them. And it is far better they have it than anyone else.

'Cultybraggan was a holiday camp compared to the fighting. The whole place was so beautiful. It went straight to my heart, and I thought "why have I been fighting this bloody war?".

'They were tough, but always fair. I didn't expect to find this attitude – I was not just the enemy, but a Nazi.

'Such friendliness was a surprise, but it is in the British nature. It was so much better than being told to lie in a filthy foxhole – and to die there.'

When Mr Steinmeyer dies, his ashes will be scattered at Cultybraggan and his estate passed to a trust he has set up to help the elderly in the area.

After the war he decided to stay in Comrie after learning that his home town had become a part of Poland. He was stunned by the kindness of villagers, even though he made no secret of his Nazi past.

They even sent parcels to his mother in Germany after learning she had fallen ill. Elderly residents of Comrie, who knew Mr Steinber-meyer by his nickname 'Heinz' say they are delighted by his gift.

He has been back to the village – which has a population of around 1,800 – regularly, and has become 'uncle Heinz' to five families, to whom he sends gifts every year.

Cultybraggan – which once held Hitler's deputy Rudolf Hess – became notorious after the inmates hanged one of their numin 1944 after accusing him of leaking an escape plot.

Mr Steinmeyer joined the Nazis in 1941 at the age of 17, and joined the Hitler Youth SS 12th Panzer Division – which has been linked to war crimes, notably the execution of 140 Canadian prisoners in 1944.

It was recruited from the ranks of the Hitler Youth and, with 20,000 men, first saw action in June 1944 in the Normandy campaign. It emerged with only 12,500 men. After fighting the Americans in the Battle of the Bulge in 1944 and later the Red Army, it withdrew to Austria and the 10,000 survivors surrendered in May 1945.

Mr Steinmeyer, as an SS soldier, was expected to die defending the Fuhrer, but was captured in the fight for a bridge in Caen.

☑ 기억하면 좋을 구절!

a token of gratitude 감사의 표시로 / 고마움의 징표로

→ Please accept this small gift as *a token of our gratitude*.
이 작은 선물을 저희의 감사 표시로 받아주세요.

bequeath [bɪkwíːð] v. (유산 등을) 물려주다 / 유산으로 남기다

→ He *bequeathed* his entire estate to his daughter.
그는 전 재산을 딸에게 남겼다.

be stunned at 깜짝 놀라다

→ He *was stunned at* being informed of his wife's pregnancy.
아내의 임신 소식에 그는 소스라치게 놀랐다.

catch a glimpse 힐끗 보다 / 일견하다

→ He *caught a glimpse of* her in the crowd.
그는 군중 속에서 그녀를 스쳐 보았다.

be scattered at ~에 뿌려지다 / 흩어지다 / 드문드문하다

→ In accordance with his wishes,
his ashes *were scattered at* sea.
그의 바람에 따라, 재는 바다에 뿌려졌다.

go to one's heart 마음에 찔리다

→ Things he did yesterday was *going to his heart*.
어제 저질렀던 일들이 그는 마음에 찔렸다.

내 인생의 명언 — 용서는 최고의 복수이다

▶ 언제나 적들을 용서하라. 그처럼 적들을 몹시 약오르게 하는 것이 없다.
오스카 와일드 (영국 극작가 · 소설가)

> Always forgive your enemies –
> nothing annoys them so much.
> Oscar Wilde

▶ 용서는 네 스스로에게 주는 선물이다.
수잔 소머스 (미국 배우 · 가수 · 작가)

> Forgiveness is a gift you give yourself.
> Suzanne Somers

▶ 용서는 용감한 자의 미덕이다.
인디라 간디 (인도 여성정치인 네루의 딸)

> Forgiveness is a virtue of the brave.
> Indira Gandhi

▶ 용서는 사랑의 최종 형태이다.
라인홀트 니부어 (미국 문명비평가 · 신학자)

> Forgiveness is the final form of love.
> Reinhold Niebuhr

▶ 용서처럼 완전한 복수는 없다.
조쉬 빌링스 (미국 유머작가)

> There is no revenge so complete as forgiveness.
> Josh Billings

Our Heart-warming World

News English

"A Poor Father's $39 Million Jackpot"

복권 당첨의 순간들

가난한 아빠, 501억 원 로또 당첨

가족 부양을 위해 아침부터 밤 늦게까지 세 개의 직업을 갖고 일해 온(work three jobs to support his family) 가난한 아빠가 3900만 달러(약 501억원)짜리 로또에 당첨(win a $39 million jackpot)됐다. 이 로또 티켓은 한인 동포가 운영하는 마켓에서 판매된 것으로 확인됐다.

미국 캘리포니아 주(州) 산타크루즈에 사는 클라이드 퍼슬리(51세) 씨는 2009년 6월 23일 캘리포니아 슈퍼로또 플러스 당첨 티켓을 제시(turn in his winning ticket), 3900만 달러 로또 당첨 사실을 공식 확인받았다.

네 살 난 딸을 둔 기혼남(a married man with a 4-year-old daughter)인 퍼슬리씨는 가족의 생계를 위해(to bring home the bacon) 산타크루즈 뉴트리셔널이라는 식품업체의 사탕 제조기 노동자와 파트타임 리무진 운전기사로 일하면서(operate candy-making machines for Santa Cruz Nutritionals and work part time as a limousine driver), 남는 시간엔 식당 일을 거들어 돈

을 벌어왔다(pick up extra hours at a restaurant). 지난 6년간(for the past 6 years) 일주일에 60시간 이상씩 일을 했다(work more than 60 hours a week).

그는 당첨 로또 티켓을 한 한인이 운영하는 산타크루즈의 한 마켓에서 구입했으며(buy his winning ticket at Santa Cruz market run by a Korean), 지난 수년간 일주일에 두 차례씩 로또를 해온(have played the lottery twice a week for several years) 것으로 전해졌다.

그는 "나는 늘 가게 안으로 걸어 들어가(walk into the store) 내가 당첨됐다는 사실을 알게(find out that I win) 되는 상상을 하곤 했다"면서 "그런데 그것이 현실이 됐다(come true)"며 기뻐했다.

버슬리 씨는 가게에 로노 티켓을 사러 갔다가(go into the market to buy lotto tickets) 한인 가게주인(the Korean store owner)인 최봉국 씨가 "지난번 우리 가게에서 팔린 티켓이 당첨됐으니 당신 것도 확인해보라"는 말을 들었다.

그는 근무 중이던 아내 폴린의 직장으로 찾아가(go to visit his wife, Pauline, at work) 주차장에서 번호를 확인(check the numbers in the parking lot)해봤다. 그런데 여섯 개 번호가 모두 맞는(all six numbers match) 것 아닌가.

그 순간 그는 "담담하면서 그냥 행복했다(feel calm and just so happy)"고 말한다. 아내에게 당첨 사실을 알려주자 아내는 기쁜 나머지(in the excess of her joy) 소리를 지르며 위아래로 팔짝팔짝 뛰기 시작(start screaming and jumping up and down)했다. 이번 슈퍼로또 1등 당첨 확률은 4100만분의 1이었다.

퍼슬리 씨는 당첨금으로 "함께 고생해온 아내에게 우선 하와이 여행부터 시켜주고(take his wife on a trip to Hawaii) 싶다"고 했다. "딸 대학진학 대비 펀드 가입, 어머니와 의붓아버지 부양도 최우선 순위에 올려놓았다(my priorities include a college fund for my daughter and the support for my mother and my father-in-law)"고 말했다.

이후 다른 계획들은 재무설계사를 고용해(hire a financial adviser) 상의하면서 "절대 낭비하지 않도록 하겠다(be definitely not going to waste it)"고 다짐했다.

퍼슬리씨는 산타크루즈 토박이(be a Santa Cruzan through and through)다. 산타크루즈에서 태어나 1977년 산타크루즈고교를 졸업(graduate from Santa Cruz High School in 1977)했다.

당첨 티켓을 판매한 가게 주인인 한인 최봉국 씨도 1등 당첨금의 0.5%에 해당하는 19만 5000달러(약 2억 5000만 원)를 받았다. 최씨는 지역언론과의 인터뷰에서 "상금은 주택 융자금 상환과 두 아들 대학 등록금에 보태겠다"고 밝혔다.

Calif. Man with 3 Jobs Wins $39M Lottery Jackpot

For 20 years, Clyde Persley of Santa Cruz worked more than 60 hours a week making candy, driving limousines and waiting by the phone to pick up extra hours at a restaurant. He bought lottery tickets and hoped for his big break.

And he got it.

Persley, 49, turned in his winning SuperLotto Plus ticket to the California Lottery office Tuesday night, said California Lottery spokeswoman Cathy Doyle Johnston, and will receive a check for about $16 million in four to six weeks.

"I'm so happy for my family," said Persley, who is married with a 4-year-old daughter. "We gotta' get the money first, but we are definitely not going to waste it."

Persley's big plans? To sit on it.

"The next step is to get financial advisers," he said Wednesday outside his apartment building off Soquel Drive near Dominican Hospital. "But I have to take my wife to Hawaii. She really wants that."

Persley is a Santa Cruzan through and through. He was born in Santa Cruz and he graduated from Santa Cruz High School in 1977.

Twice a week, Persley would stop in at the Santa Cruz Market, the store that will get $140,000 for selling the winning ticket, to play the lottery.

"I always imagined I would walk into the store and find out that I won," he said.

And that's what happened Monday.

When he went into the market to buy lotto tickets, Bankook Choi, the store owner, told him the store had won and to check his tickets. Persley went to visit his wife, Pauline, at work and checked the numbers in the parking lot. All six numbers matched.

"I felt calm, and just so happy," he said. "I told my wife and she started screaming and jumping up and down."

Persley has been working three jobs for the past six years to support his family. He worked part time as a limousine driver and on-call at El Palomar restaurant, but he worked full time for Santa Cruz Nutritionals, formerly Harmony Foods, operating candy-making machines.

Although he no longer has to work, Persley finds it hard to think about leaving his job.

"I really appreciate my life with Harmony Foods," he said of his 26-year stint there. "I can't say enough how much my work has meant to me."

While there are no plans for penthouses or private jets just yet, Persley does see relaxation and family time in his future.

"People think we are going to jump up and start spending all our money," he said. "But that's just not the way this works."

His priorities include a college fund for his daughter, support for his mother and his father-in-law and traveling.

"I want to live a quiet life without stress," Persley said. "There is not much more you could ask for."

☑ 기억하면 좋을 구절!

turn in 제출하다 / 반납하다

 I *turned in* books to the library.
도서관에 책을 반납했다.

find out 발견하다 / 생각해내다 / 답을 얻다

 I can't wait to *find out*.
빨리 답을 알고 싶다.

bring home the bacon 생활비를 벌다

 Both of us *bring home the bacon*.
우리는 맞벌이 부부입니다.

in the excess of one's joy 기쁜 나머지

 She ended up crying *in the excess of her joy*.
그녀는 기쁜 나머지 그만 울고 말았다.

check the answer to a test 시험 답안을 맞춰보다

I was afraid of *checking my answers to the test*.
나는 시험 답안을 맞춰보는 것이 두려웠다.

내 인생의 명언 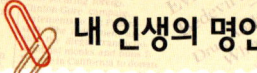 돈은 잘못이 없다

▶ 부의 창출이 잘못된 것이 아니다. 돈 그 자체를 위한 사랑이 잘못된 것이다.
마거릿 대처 (영국 최초 여총리)

> It is not the creation of wealth that is wrong,
> but the love of money for its own sake.
> Margaret Hilda Thatcher

▶ 돈 없이도 행복할 수 있다고 사람들이 생각하게 만드는 것은
정신적 우월의식의 일종이다.
알베르 카뮈 (프랑스 소설가·극작가)

> It's a kind of spiritual snobbery that makes
> people think they can be happy without money.
> Albert Camus

▶ 당신을 부자로 만드는 것은 봉급이 아니라 씀씀이 버릇이다.
찰스 제프 (벨로루시 출신 미국 체스챔피언)

> It's not your salary that makes you rich,
> it's your spending habits.
> Charles Jeff

▶ 많은 사람들은 돈이 거의 바닥날 지경에 이를 때까지
돈에 대해 주의하지 않는다. 시간에 대해서도 똑같이 한다.
요한 괴테 (독일 시인·극작가·정치가·과학자)

> Many people take no care of their money
> till they come nearly to the end of it,
> and others do just the same with their time.
> Johann Wolfgang von Goethe

Favorite famous sayings!

▶ 돈은 도구일 뿐이다. 돈이 당신을 원하는 곳 어디든
데려다주기는 해도 그 운전자로 만들어주지는 않는다.
아인 랜드 (러시아 출신 미국 소설가)

> Money is only a tool. It will take you wherever
> you wish, but it will not replace you as the driver.
> Ayn Rand

▶ 돈은 쫓아가기엔 진저리나지만, 만나기에는 매력적이다.
헨리 제임스 (미국 출신 영국 작가)

> Money's a horrid thing to follow,
> but a charming thing to meet.
> Henry James

▶ 돈이 모든 악의 근원이라고 생각한다면
모든 돈의 근원은 무엇인지 생각해보았는가.
아인 랜드 (러시아 출신 미국 소설가)

> So you think that money is the root of all evil.
> Have you ever asked what is the root of all money?
> Ayn Rand

▶ 돈을 가진 사람이 있고, 부자인 사람이 있다.
코코 샤넬 (프랑스 디자이너)

> There are people who have money and
> people who are rich.
> Coco Chanel

"A Retiring Human Punchbag"

'인간 샌드백' 피터 버클리의 미소

300전 4승 256패 은퇴하는 인간 샌드백

영국의 프로복서 피터 버클리(39세). 슈퍼페더급(super-featherweight)인 그는 최근 5년간 단 한 번도 이겨보지 못했다.

88차례 연속 경기 결과(a sequence encompassing 88 straight fights)는 0승 88패. 버밍햄에서 벌어진 프로통산 300번째 경기(the 300th bout of a professional career)에서도 졌다. 통산 전적 300전 4승 256패.

용기 있는 패자를 성원해주는(root for the plucky underdog) 것이 영국 스포츠문화라고는 하지만, 버클리의 기록은 앞으로도 좀처럼 깨지기 어려울(take some beating) 것으로 보인다.

버클리는 떠오르는 신예들의 스파링파트너로 겨우 생계를 이어(manage to earn a living as a sparring partner for rising stars)왔다. 마흔두 명의 세계, 유럽, 영국, 영연방 챔피언들이 타이틀을 차지하는 과정에서 버클리를 이기고(have defeated Buckley on the way to taking titles) 올라갔다.

그 버클리가 오랫동안 '인간 샌드백' 노릇을 해온 끝에(after years of being the equivalent of a 'human punchbag') 은퇴하기로(hang up his gloves) 결심했다고 발표했다. "더 이상 경기를 하고 싶지 않다(do not want to fight on)"고 선언하면서.

256패를 기록하는 동안 버클리가 얻어맞은 펀치는 이루 헤아릴 수 없을(be innumerable) 정도다. 그렇다면 영국 프로복싱협회는 왜 그의 프로복서 자격을 취소시키지(revoke his license) 않았을까.

버클리는 그 동안 복싱협회의 메디컬 테스트를 매번 통과(repeatedly pass the medical test)했고, 협회로선 테스트에서 아무 문제가 발견되지 않는 그가 커리어를 이어나가는 것을 막을 권한이 없었다(be powerless to prevent him from continuing his career). 그런 상황에서 협회가 경기를 하지 못하도록 금지하려(try to ban him from fighting on in those circumstances) 했다면 자유거래 제한에 관한 법적 대응에 직면(face a legal action for restraint of trade)했을 것이다.

버클리가 언제나 뛰어난 상대들의 먹잇감으로 여겨졌던(be always regarded as fodder for talented opponents) 것만은 아니다. 1990년대 초엔 다른 선수들이 기피할 정도로 뛰어난 기량을 발휘(show his distinguished ability)했었다.

하지만 버클리는 챔피언벨트를 노리는(have an eye on the champion belt) 전도유망한 선수의 경기 상대로 더 많은 돈을 벌 수 있다는(make more money as an opponent for an up-and-coming boxer) 것을 알게 됐다. 버클리는 거의 이기지는 못했지만, 엄청나게 두들겨 맞지도 않았다(rarely get badly beaten up either).

시간이 지나면서(with the passing of time) 버클리는 경기 시작 공이 울리기 수 시간 전 제의받는 스파링게임에도 응하는 선수로 알려졌다(be known to agree to a contest just hours before the opening bell). 그는 "벽돌공에게 전화를 걸어 담을 쌓아달라고 요청(phone up a bricklayer and ask him to build a wall)하면 벽돌공이 준비하는 데 3주일을 달라고 하지 않는 것(do not ask for three weeks to prepare)과 마찬가지"라고 말한다.

은퇴 후에도 복싱과 관련된 생활을 하고 싶다(would like to stay involved in boxing)는 버클리는 "나는 어릴 때(when I was a youngster) 경찰과 문제를 일으키는(be in trouble with the police) 등 굉장히 거친 아이(a really wild kid)였다"면서 "복싱은 내게 인생의 초점을 갖게 해준(give me a focus in life) 친구였다"고 은퇴 소회를 밝혔다.

Final Bell Tolls for Serial British Boxing Loser

In a country where rooting for the plucky underdog is as much a part of the sporting culture as Wembley Stadium, the Lord's Test and strawberries and cream at Wimbledon, the record of British boxer Peter Buckley takes some beating.

Or perhaps that should be losing.

This Friday, Buckley steps into the ring in Birmingham, central England, for the 300th bout of a professional career which has witnessed 256 defeats.

Buckley, who hasn't won for five years, a sequence encompassing 88 straight fights, has managed to earn a living as an opponent for rising stars.

In all, 42 future world, European, British and Commonwealth champions, have defeated Buckley on the way to taking titles.

But after years of being the equivalent of a 'human punchbag' the 39-year-old Englishman has, not unreasonably, decided to hang up his gloves.

"I've had my eye on the 300 mark for a while, and it's a little milestone I want to achieve, but I don't want to fight on," Buckley told The Times newspaper here Wednesday.

"People keep saying to me that I'll get a call in a few weeks' time offering me a fight and I'll say yes, but I mean it when I say this is it."

Given his record, it is tempting to ask why the British Boxing Board of Control (BBBC), the governing body for the professional sport in the UK, has not revoked his licence.

After all, were he to be seriously injured his whole career would provide those who want boxing banned, such as the British Medical Association, with easy publicity for their cause.

However, given that Buckley has repeatedly passed BBBC medical tests, the Board has been powerless to prevent him continuing his career.

Had they tried to ban him in those circumstances they might well have faced legal action for restraint of trade.

Buckley was not always regarded as fodder for talented opponents. In the early 1990s the super-featherweight won the English Midlands area title.

However, he then found he could make more money as an opponent for those on their way to greater things. Buckley rarely won, but he rarely got badly beaten up either. But with the passing of time and the slowing of his reflexes, he has become easier to hit.

Unlike those tilting at world championships, who go into training camps for weeks or even months, Buckley has been known to agree to a contest just hours before the opening bell.

"I'm always in the gym, so if I get a call a couple of hours before a fight, I usually say yes," he said. "If you phone up a bricklayer and ask him to build you a wall, he doesn't ask for three weeks to prepare."

And whatever else Buckley, who would like to stay involved in boxing in some other capacity, wants, it's certainly not pity.

"Boxing has been good to me over the years. When I was a youngster I was in trouble with the police, a really wild kid. But the sport has given me a focus in life."

✓ 기억하면 좋을 구절!

root for ~을 성원하다 / 응원하다

Which team do you *root(cheer) for*?
어느 팀을 응원하세요?

the plucky underdog 용감한 약자

I am *the plucky underdog* who did not win.
나는 이긴 적은 없지만 용감한 약자이다.

earn one's living at ~로 생계를 꾸리다 / 생활비를 벌다

He *earns his living at* the pen.
그는 글을 써서 생계를 꾸려나간다.

hang up one's gloves 권투계에서 은퇴하다

Mayweather suggested he would now *hang up his gloves*.
메이웨더는 이제 권투계에서 은퇴할 것임을 시사했다.

have an eye on ~을 노리다

He *had an eye on* her property.
그는 그녀의 재산을 노렸다.

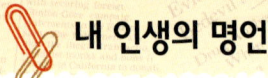

내 인생의 명언 — 노력하는 자에게 불가능은 없다

▶ 사람들을 뛰어남의 정점으로 평가해서는 안 된다.
처음 출발했던 지점부터 그가 지나온 거리로 평가해야 한다.
헨리 비처 (미국 성직자)

> We should not judge people by their peak of excellence;
> but by the distance they have traveled from
> the point where they started.
> Henry Beecher

▶ 목표에 다다를 수 없는 것이 분명해보이면
목표를 조정할 것이 아니라 행동 걸음걸이를 조정해라.
공자 (중국 유교의 시조)

> When it is obvious that the goals cannot be reached,
> don't adjust the goals, adjust the action steps.
> Confucius

▶ 총총걸음으로 돌아다니는 개가 뼈다귀를 찾는다.
골다 메이어 (이스라엘 여성정치인)

> The dog that trots about finds a bone.
> Golda Meir

▶ 한계에 달했더라도 거기에 매듭을 묶고 매달려라.
프랭클린 루즈벨트 (미국 32대 대통령)

> When you come to the end of your rope,
> tie a knot and hang on.
> Franklin Roosevelt

Favorite famous sayings!

▶ 매일매일을 당신이 거둔 수확으로 심판하지 말고,
당신이 심은 씨앗으로 심판하라.
로버트 스티븐슨 (스코틀랜드 소설가 · 시인)

> Don't judge each day by the harvest you reap but by the seeds that you plant.
> Robert Stephenson

▶ 불가능한 것은 없다. '불가능하다'는 단어 자체가
"나는 할 수 있다"라고 말하지 않는가.
오드리 헵번 (미국 여배우)

> Nothing is impossible, the word itself says 'I'm possible'.
> Audrey Hepburn

▶ 행운의 여신은 대담한 사람을 사랑한다.
마로 베르질리우스 (로마 시인)

> The goddess of fortune favors the bold.
> Vergilius

▶ 가장 하기 힘든 일은 아무 일도 하지 않는 것이다.
유대인 격언

> The hardest work is to go idle.
> Jewish proverb

News English

"An Alcoholic's Miserable Death"

A young alcoholic denied a liver transplant because he was too ill to prove he could stay sober outside hospital had begged his mother to help him live.

Gary Reinbach, 22, was terrified and pleaded with his mother to do something hours before his death. His last words to her were: 'Please help me Mum, I don't want to die.'

Mr Reinbach, of , died of cirrhosis that a man of his age   him a 'new life

his life.
National guideli
for a donor org
must prove he h
stop drinking by
six months'.
This is to ma
more cases like
the football leg
drink after recei
subsequently die
Gary's mother Mad
told how she beg
give him the vital t
before he died.
'Gary had done ev
convince doctors h
had even begged the
him a second chance

But by then, I think
going on he put on a
I could tell no one w
and it would all be O

including giving up smoking and staying in bed to try to show he would stay off alcohol.

'All he wanted to do was prove that he was serious, and that he wouldn't drink again. But he never had the chance to prove himself properly be

clinicians have some discretion to override the rules but this rarely happens. His mother said: 'He was in a wheelchair for the past two months - he couldn't eat, he couldn't talk. How could he have discharged himself to sh

the day before he died. 'Gary had done everything he could to convince doctors he deserved one. He had even begged them straight out to give him a second chance to live,' she told the Mirror
en. I think he knew he wasn't
  put on any transplant list. All
  to him what that I loved him
d all be OK.'
w her son had co-operated
  demand from the doctors
ving up smoking and staying
y to show he would stay off

ed so was prove that
  ous, and that he wouldn't
  ut he never had the chance
  self properly because he
  to be sent home. Miss

against the doctors, but
  he couldn't have the
  he wanted so much
  uthorities to change the
  Wouldn't want anyone
  watch their child die the

o lived in Dagenham,
  king at the age of 13
  akup of his parents
ol at 16, he got a job

영국에서는 6개월간 금주한 사람만 간 이식 수술을 허가한다

어느 알콜중독자의 비참한 죽음

영국에서 한 청년이 숨졌다. 간 이식수술을 받아야 했다. 하지만, 병원 측에서 시술을 거부했다. 장기간 폭음으로 간경변에 걸린 청년이 다시는 술을 마시지 않을 것임을 입증하지 못했다는 이유였다. 음주가 아닌 다른 원인으로 간 이식이 필요한 환자들도 줄을 잇고 있어서 알콜중독자에게는 이식해 줄 간이 없다는 것이었다.

22세인 알콜중독자 게리 라인배치(an alcoholic aged 22 Gary Reinbach)가 간 이식을 거부당한 뒤 사망(die after being refused liver transplant)했다. 병원 밖에 나가 술을 마시지 않고 견딜 수 있다는(can stay sober outside hospital) 사실을 증명하지 못했기 때문이다.

영국의학협회(BMA) 지침에 따르면(according to the guidelines of BMA), 잠재적 장기이식 대상자(a potential recipient)는 6개월 동안 금주를 해서(by remaining abstinent for six months) 술을 끊을 결심을 증명해보여야 장기를

기증받을 자격이 주어진다(be qualified for a donor organ). "기증되는 장기들이 귀한 만큼 마땅한 결과가 나올 곳에 사용되어야 한다"는 취지다.

이 같은 BMA의 지침은 조지 베스트와 같은 경우가 더 이상 없도록 하기 위해서다(to make sure there are no more cases like that of George Best). 조지 베스트는 영국의 전설적인 축구선수(the British football legend)로, 기증 장기 이식을 받고 나서도 계속 술을 마셔(continue to drink after receiving a donor liver) 끝내 사망하고 말았다.

결국 게리는 장기이식 요청이 거부됐고, 의사들이 그의 나이 또래에서 본 것 중 최악이었다는 간경변에 목숨을 내주고(succumb to the worst case of cirrhosis doctors have seen in a man of his age) 말았다. 어머니 매들린 핸쇼(44세)로서는 가슴이 찢어지는 노릇이었다. 그녀는 아들을 잃고 몇 시간 후(just hours after losing her son) 관련 규정을 맹렬히 비난하고(furiously criticize the related rules) 나섰다.

"아이가 지난 두 달 동안 휠체어 신세를 지며(be in a wheelchair for the past two months) 아무 말도 하지 못할 정도로 아팠는데 어떻게 술을 마시지 않겠다는 것을 보여주는 의무를 다할 수(discharge himself to show that he could stay off the drink) 있었겠느냐"는 것이다. 그녀는 "스스로 자신을 계속 망가뜨리는 사람에게도 장기이식을 해줘야 한다는(should give a transplant to someone who keeps damaging him or herself) 얘기는 아니다"라면서 "하지만 게리와 같은 사람들에게 있어서는(just for people like Gary) 해당 규정들이 정말 부당하다(be really unfair)"고 주장했다. "한 번 실수를 했는데 두 번째 기회조차 아예 가질 수 없다(make a mistake and never get a second chance)는 것은 너무 가혹하다"고 하소연했다.

22세 젊은 나이에 세상을 떠난 게리는 부모의 불화와 이별 이후(following the break-up of his parents' relationship)인 13세 때부터 술을 마시기 시작했다(begin drinking at the age of 13). 16세 때 학교를 자퇴한 후에는(after leaving school at 16) 창문설비 견습공으로 취직했지만(get a job as a trainee window fitter), 그나마 그것도 술 때문에 몇 주 가지 못했다(last only a few weeks because of his alcohol problem).

게리는 병원에 입원하기 전(before being admitted to hospital)까지 매일 보드카 큰 병 한 병씩을 마시곤(consume a large bottle of vodka a day) 했다. 건강이 악화되면서(as his health deteriorates) AA에 가입도 했지만(sign up for AA= Alcoholics Anonymous=알콜 중독에서 벗어나고자 하는 사람들의 친목 모임), 결국 병원에 입원할 수밖에 없었다(cannot help being admitted to hospital). 게리는 의사들로부터 폭음에 따른 질병(a condition brought on by heavy drinking)인 말기 간경변 진단을 받았다(be diagnosed with terminal liver cirrhosis). 수많은 최신 요법들을 받아보았지만(receive a variety of the most advanced therapies), 마지막 희망(his last hope)은 그에게 생존 가능성 75%를 안겨줄(give him a 75% chance of survival) 장기이식 밖에 없었다.

하지만 앞서 언급된 것처럼 영국의학협회의 지침은 알콜중독 간질환 환자들(alcoholic liver patients)은 병원 밖 환경에서 6개월 동안 금주해야 간 이식을 허용한다는 규정을 엄격히 적용했고, 게리 역시 예외가 되지 못한 채 병상에서 그대로 죽어가야 했다.

"Please Help me Mum, I don't Want to Die": Last Words of Alcoholic, 22, who Died after being Refused Liver Transplant

A young alcoholic denied a liver transplant because he was too ill to prove he could stay sober outside hospital had begged his mother to help him live.

Gary Reinbach, 22, was terrified and pleaded with his mother to do something hours before his death. His last words to her were: 'Please help me Mum, I don't want to die.'

Mr Reinbach had the worst case of cirrhosis that doctors had ever seen in a man of his age but they refused to give him a new liver which could have saved his life.

National guidelines dictate that to qualify for a donor organ, a potential recipient must prove he has the determination to stop drinking by remaining abstinent for six months.

This is to make sure there are no more cases like that of George Best – the football legend who continued to drink after receiving a donor liver and subsequently died.

Gary's mother Madeline Hanshaw, 44, told how he begged medical staff to give him the vital transplant just the day before he died.

'Gary had done everything he could to convince doctors he deserved one. He had even begged them straight out to give him a second chance to live,' she told the Mirror.

'But by then, I think he knew he wasn't going to be put on any transplant list. All I could say to him what that I loved him and it would all be OK.'

She told how her son had co-operated with every demand from the doctors including giving up smoking and staying in bed to try to show he would stay off alcohol.

'All he wanted to do was prove that he was serious, and that he wouldn't drink again. But he never had the chance to prove himself properly because he was too fragile to be sent home, Miss Hanshaw said.

'He couldn't go against the doctors, but because of that he couldn't have the second chance he wanted so much.'

She urged the authorities to change the rules, insisting: 'I wouldn't want anyone else to have to watch their child die the way Gary died.'

Mr Reinbach, who lived in Dagenham, Essex, began drinking at the age of 13 following the break-up of his parents' relationship.

After leaving school at 16, he got a job as a trainee window fitter which lasted only a few weeks because of his alcohol problem.

Before being admitted to hospital, he was consuming a large bottle of vodka a day.

As his health deteriorated he signed up for Alcoholics Anonymous but was admitted to hospital two months ago. Doctors at London's University College Hospital diagnosed advanced liver cirrhosis – a condition brought on by heavy drinking.

He received a variety of the most advanced therapies but his last hope was a transplant that would have given him a 75% chance of survival.

However, guidelines state alcoholic liver patients must abstain for six months outside a hospital environment.

Patients' clinicians have some discretion to override the rules but this rarely happens.

His mother said: 'He was in a wheelchair for the past two months - he couldn't eat, he couldn't talk. How could he have discharged himself to show that he could stay off the drink?

'These rules are really unfair. I'm not saying you should give a transplant to someone who is in and out of hospital all the time and keeps damaging themselves, but just for people like Gary, who made a mistake and never got a second chance.'

Sarah Matthews, spokesman for the British Liver Trust, said that the criteria for liver transplants are strict.

It was a 'difficult situation', she added, but 'with alcohol still being sold at pocket money prices, coupled with the UK's "any time anywhere any place" mentality, it is not surprising that young people are drinking to excess'.

☑ 기억하면 좋을 구절!

stay sober 취하지 않은 채로 있다

I promised her that I'd *stay sober* tonight.
오늘밤에는 취하지 않겠다고 그녀와 약속했다.

be qualified for 조건(자격)을 갖추다

I don't feel *qualified for* comment.
저는 평할 자격이 없는 듯합니다.

succumb to ~에 굴복하다 / 무릎 꿇다

Don't *succumb* to the temptation to have just one cigarette.
담배 한 개비의 유혹에 넘어가지 마세요.

remain abstinent 금욕하다 / 금주하다

Priests are required by the Catholic church to remain abstinent.
가톨릭 교회는 사제들에게 금욕을 요구한다.

be admitted to hospital 병원에 수용되다

She *was admitted to hospital* again in September last year.
그녀는 작년 9월 다시 병원에 수용되었다.

내 인생의 명언 — 참는 자에게 복이 있나니

▶ 모든 일이 그렇다. 쉽기 전에는 어렵다.
토마스 풀러 (영국 성직자·역사가)

> All things are difficult before they are easy.
> Thomas Fuller

▶ 달팽이는 인내로 방주에 닿았다.
찰스 스퍼전 (영국 침례교 설교자)

> By perseverance the snail reached the ark.
> Charles H. Spurgeon

▶ 자연의 속도를 받아들여라. 자연의 비밀은 인내다.
랠프 에머슨 (미국 평론가·시인·철학자)

> Adopt the pace of nature, her secret is patience.
> Ralph Waldo Emerson

▶ 인내는 현명함의 동반자다.
아우구스티누스 (로마 철학자 사상가)

> Patience is the companion of wisdom.
> Aurelius Augustinus

▶ 인내는 장거리 경주가 아니다.
하나 뒤에 또 하나 잇닿은 수많은 단거리 경주들이다.
월터 엘리엇 (영국 정치인)

> Perseverance is not a long race;
> it is many short races one after another.
> Walter Elliot

News English

"An Old Woman's Way of Returning the Favor"

When Margaret Allan and her husband retired to the tiny village of Solva, their golden years were enriched by the welcome they received.

Now, from beyond the grave, Mrs Allan has returned the favour.

Before she died at the age of 90 last year, she wrote a will that benefits every single resident – including gifts to more than 100 of her fellow villagers.

Mrs Allan's £400,000 will provides £40,000 to be shared among a small group of her close friends and carers.

In all, she left around £150,000 to the village. That includes £60,000 to provide gifts in the region of £500 to around 120 residents over 60 who have lived in the seaside Pembrokeshire village for 20 years or more.

In addition, Mrs Allan left:
- £16,000 to local animal charities
- £10,000 to the village ...
- £10,000 to local churches
- £5,000 to the village foot...
- £5,000 to the local surg... facilities.

She also bequeathed ... Solva Luncheon Club ... drinks at Christmas, an... Pembrokeshire Conserv...

Her only living relative... grandson in Norway rec...

Yesterday Solva reside... to the generosity of the ... remarkable life pictu...

in 1990, had no children. While they were still living in London they took regular holidays in the seaside village in West Wales as a break from the foreign travel that was an essential part of Mr Allan's job with the Foreign O...

... ions for her ... rose bushes ... s were ... er husband ... Solva, their ... d by the ... Mrs Allan ...

learned to parachute and was about to be dropped behind German lines in Norway when the war ended.

'She was a member of Mensa and a very ... It was typical ... er will ...

... that year ... ry single ... re than ... being ... ovides ... small ... yers. ... around £150,000 to the ... seaside ...

London they took regular holidays in the seaside village in West Wales as a break from the foreign travel that was an essential part of Mr Allan's job with the Foreign Office.

When they moved there permanently 30 years ago, locals welcomed them with open arms and the Allans were soon busily involved in village life. After Mr Allan died the community rallied around his widow, and when her own health started to fail she was determined to make sure she repaid the kindness.

Her companion in those final years – a cat called Brutus – was also not forgotten in her six-page will, which says: 'To any person whom the executors agree to taking care of my cat, to avoid it being put down or going into a cattery – the sum of $3,000.

That job has been taken on by neighbour Dave Phillips, a 56-year-old retired BT engineer, who said: 'Margaret was a remarkable woman who was friends with ... body in the village.

... and her husband built a home here ... he retired and they quickly became ... of the community.

... y were regulars at the local Ship Inn ... she always entertained there on her ...

... war housebound for a while before ... e died but she would still be interested ... the affairs of the village and the people ...

... 53-year-old will added: 'As they had ... o children they regarded the village as ... eir kin.' ...

마을 사람 모두에게 유산을 남긴 마가렛 앨런과 그녀가 살았던 솔바 마을

마을 사람 모두에게 은혜 갚은 할머니

지난 2008년 90세로 생을 마친 영국의 한 할머니가 살아생전 환대해준 데 대한 고마움의 표시로, 동네 사람 모두에게 일일이 유산을 남긴 것으로 밝혀져 잔잔한 감동을 주고 있다. 영국 웨일즈의 펨브로크셔 해변가 솔바라는 마을에서 노년을 보낸 마가렛 앨런은 자신의 유언장을 통해 마을주민들에게 40만 파운드(약 8억 원)를 남겨 주민들의 친절에 보답(repay villagers' kindness by leaving them £400,000 in her will)했다.

앨런은 30년 전 외교부에서 은퇴한 뒤(after leaving the Foreign Ministry) 남편 해리와 함께 솔바로 이사했다(move to Solva 30 years ago with husband Harry). 그런데 그 직후인 1990년 남편이 세상을 떠났다. 낯선 타지에 홀로 남게 된 것이다. 자식도 없었다. 마을 주민들은 남편을 잃은 그녀가 삶을 되찾을 수 있도록 도왔고(help the widow rebuild her life), 말년까지 돌봐줬다(care for her until her final years).

앨런과 죽은 남편은 은퇴하기 이전부터 해안가의 솔바 마을에서 휴가를 보내곤(be used to holiday in the waterfront village) 했다. 그랬다가 일단 이사를 오고 난 뒤에는 곧바로 마을 생활에 몰입해(throw themselves into village life) 빠르게 그 일부가 되어(quickly become part of the community) 갔다.

남편이 죽었을 때 그녀가 이겨낼 수 있도록 해준 이들도 그러면서 사귄 친구들이었다. 앨런은 40만 파운드 유산 중 1만 파운드(약 2000만 원)가량을 이들 절친했던 친구와 돌봐준 사람들 10여 명에게 남겼다(leave up to £10000 to more than a dozen of her close friends and carers). 그녀는 20년 이상 마을에 살아온(have lived in the village for more than 20 years) 60세 이상의 주민 모두에게(to everyone over the age of 60) 별도의 유산을 남겼다. 이에 따라 120여 명(around 120 people)이 각각 약 500파운드(약 100만 원)씩을 받게 됐다.

그녀는 말년의 동반자였던 황갈색 수코양이 브루터스를 챙기는(take care of her companion in her final years, her ginger tom, Brutus) 것도 잊지 않았다. 유언장에 "내 고양이가 죽임을 당하거나 고양이 사육장으로 가지 않도록(to avoid it being put down or going into a cattery) 돌봐주겠다는 사람에게는 3000파운드(약 600만 원)를 주도록 한다"는 구절을 남겼다.

고양이 브루터스를 맡아 기르기로 한 이웃주민 데이브 필립(56세) 씨는 "앨런은 마을의 모든 이들과 친구였던(be friends with everybody in the village) 훌륭한 여인(a remarkable woman)이었다"며 "자식이 없어서인지 마을 주민들을 자신의 가족처럼 생각했다(regard the villagers as her family)"고 전했다.

그녀의 인생 마지막 몇 년을 돌봐줬던(look after her in the last few years of her life) 사람들에게는 2만 5000파운드(약 5000만 원)의 유산을 나눠 갖도록 했다(have £25000 to be shared between them). 또 마을 기념관에 1만 파운드, 동네 교회에 1만 파운드, 그리고 크리스마스 행사 경비로 5000파운드를 남겼다.

그런가 하면 마을 축구클럽에 5000파운드, 환자시설 개선을 위해 마을 외과병원에(to the village surgery to improve patient facilities) 5000파운드, 자신의 고양이 브루터스에게 남긴 돈 외에 마을 개·고양이 자선재단에 1만 5000파운드, 오소리 그룹에 1000파운드를 기탁했다.

앨런이 유산을 남긴 살아 있는 유일한 친척(her only living relative)은 단 1명이었다. 지금은 노르웨이에 살고 있는 배다른 자매의 손자(her paternal half-sister's grandson)에게 1만 파운드를 전해달라고 유언장에 적었다.

그리고 앨런은 유언장에 자신의 유골을 17년 전 남편이 그랬던 것처럼 자신의 집 정원 장미덤불에 뿌려달라는(scatter her ashes in the rose bushes at the garden of her home) 마지막 당부를 남겼다.

Wealthy Widow Repays Villagers' Kindness by Leaving them £400,000 in her Will

When Margaret Allan and her husband retired to the tiny village of Solva, their golden years were enriched by the welcome they received.

Now, from beyond the grave, Mrs Allan has returned the favour.

Before she died at the age of 90 last year, she wrote a will that benefits every single resident – including gifts to more than 100 of her fellow villagers.

Mrs Allan's £400,000 will provides £40,000 to be shared among a small group of her close friends and carers.

In all, she left around £150,000 to the village. That includes £60,000 to provide gifts in the region of £500 to around 120 residents over 60 who have lived in the seaside Pembrokeshire village for 20 years or more.

In addition, Mrs Allan left:

- £16,000 to local animal charities
- £10,000 to the village memorial hall
- £10,000 to local churches
- £5,000 to the village football club
- £5,000 to the local surgery to improve facilities.

She also bequeathed £5,000 to the Solva Luncheon Club to be spent on drinks at Christmas, and £2,000 to the Pembrokeshire Conservative Association.

Her only living relative, her halfsister's grandson in Norway, receives £10,000.

Yesterday Solva residents paid tribute to the generosity of Mrs Allan, whose remarkable life included being trained as a secret agent to be dropped behind German lines during the Second World War.

She and her husband Harry, who died in 1990, had no children.

While they were still living in London they took regular holidays in the seaside village in West Wales as a break from the foreign travel that was an essential part of Mr Allan's job with the Foreign Office.

When they moved there permanently 30 years ago, locals welcomed them with open arms and the Allans were soon busily involved in village life. After Mr Allan died the community rallied around his widow, and when her own health started to fail she was determined to make sure she repaid the kindness.

Her companion in those final years – a cat called Brutus – was also not forgotten in her six-page will, which says: 'To any person whom the executors agree to taking care of my cat, to avoid it being put down or going into a cattery – the sum of £3,000.'

That job has been taken on by neighbour Dave Phillips, a 56-yearold retired BT engineer, who said: 'Margaret was a remarkable woman who was friends with everybody in the village.

'She and her husband built a house here when he retired and they quickly became part of the community.

'They were regulars at the local Ship Inn and she always entertained there on her birthdays.

'She was housebound for a while before she died but she was still so interested in the affairs of the village and the people here.'

His 53-year-old wife added: 'As they had no children they regarded the village as their family.'

Mrs Allan's close friend Susan King, 71, said: 'Margaret was an amazing woman. She had learned to parachute and was about to be dropped behind German lines in Norway when the war ended.

'She was a member of Mensa and a very kind and intelligent woman. It was typical of her to think of others in her will.'

Mrs Allan also left instructions for her ashes to be scattered under rose bushes in her garden, as her husband's were.

☑ 기억하면 좋을 구절!

return somebody's favor ~의 은혜에 보답하다

I want to *return your favor* somehow.
선생님의 은혜에 어떻게든 보답하고 싶습니다.

throw oneself into 몸을 던지다 / (사업, 일)에 투신하다

My dad's been *throwing himself into* his company since 2000.
아버지는 2000년부터 회사에 전념하고 있다.

a paternal half-brother 배다른 형제 / 이복형제

My paternal half-brother and I have the same father but different mothers.
이복동생과 나는 아버지는 같으나 어머니가 다르다.

look after 돌보다 / 건사하다

I can *look after* myself.
내 한몸은 돌볼 수 있다.

the only living relative 살아 있는 유일한 친척

The inheritance fell to *his only living relative*.
유산은 그의 살아 있는 유일한 친척에게 상속됐다.

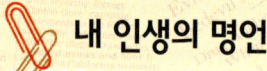

내 인생의 명언 — 내 슬픔을 등에 지고 가는 사람

▶ 우정은 돈과 같아서 만드는 것보다 지키는 것이 더 어렵다.
새뮤얼 버틀러 (영국 소설가 · 시인)

> Friendship is like money, easier made than kept.
> Samuel Butler

▶ 모든 사람에게 친구인 사람은 누구에게도 친구가 아니다.
아리스토텔레스 (그리스 철학자)

> A friend to all is a friend to none.
> Aristoteles

▶ 단 한 송이의 장미가 내 정원이 될 수 있듯이
한 명의 친구가 내 세계가 될 수 있다.
리오 버스킬리아 (미국 작가 · 교수)

> A single rose can be my garden…… a single friend, my world.
> Leo Buscaglia

▶ 진실되지 않고 사악한 친구는 야수(野獸)보다 더 두려워해야 한다.
야수는 몸에 상처를 남기지만 사악한 친구는 정신에 상처를 입힌다.
석가모니 (불교 창시자 · 인도의 성자)

> An insincere and evil friend is more to be feared than
> a wild beast; a wildbeast may wound your body,
> but an evil friend will wound your mind.
> Buddah

▶ 우정과 돈은 물과 기름 같다.
마리오 푸조 (미국 소설가 · 작가)

> Friendship and money: oil and water.
> Mario Puzo

Favorite famous sayings!

▶ 우정은 두 몸에 사는 하나의 영혼이다.
아리스토텔레스 (그리스 철학자)

> Friendship is a single soul dwelling in two bodies.
> Aristoteles

▶ 나는 내가 변할 때 변하는 친구, 내가 끄덕일 때
끄덕이는 친구는 필요하지 않다. 그건 내 그림자가 훨씬 더 잘한다.
플루타르크 (그리스 철학자)

> I don't need a friend who changes when I change
> and who nods when I nod;
> my shadow does that much better.
> Plutarchos

▶ 친구는 당신을 속속이 알지만 그래도 당신을 좋아해주는 사람이다.
앨버트 하버드 (미국 작가 · 예술가 · 철학자)

> Your friend is the man who knows all about you,
> and still likes you.
> Albert Havard

▶ 진짜 친구는 앞에서 찌른다.
오스카 와일드 (영국 극작가 · 소설가)

> True friends stab you in the front.
> Oscar Wilde

"His Whole Life Instead of his Wife"

마이클 다이어 씨를 지켜낸 개 미키와 보즈 (왼쪽부터)

아내를 대신한 그의 인생 전부

아내가 암으로 죽은 뒤 아내의 빈자리에서 길러온 개 두 마리가 죽어가던 남편의 목숨을 구했다.

66세인 영국인 마이클 다이어는 데번 주(州) 피시콤 코브라는 한 관광 명소에서(at a beauty spot) 미키(3살)와 보즈(5살)를 운동시키다가(as he exercise Mickey, three and Boz, five) 약 10미터 높이의 비탈에서 떨어졌다(fall down a 10m slope). 그는 떨어지면서 팔꿈치가 골절되고 목이 부러져(fracture an elbow and break his neck in the fall) 섭씨 7도의 쌀쌀한 기온에 의식을 잃고 누워(lie unconscious in temperatures as low as 7 degrees Celsius) 있었다. 간간이 의식이 돌아왔지만(slip in and out of consciousness) 꼼짝할 수 없어 저체온증으로 죽을(die of hypothermia) 위기에 처했다.

그러나 다이어는 밤새 살아남을(be kept alive overnight) 수 있었다. 두 마리의 헌신적인 개들(the two dedicated dogs)이 그에게 꼭 붙어 있으며(cuddle up to him) 따뜻하게 지켜준(keep him warm) 덕분이었다. 두 마리의 개가 열여섯 시간 동안 그에게 바짝 다가붙어 있어(snuggle up to him for 16 hours) 저체온증을 피할 수 있게 해줬던(help stave off hypothermia) 던 것이다. 다이어가 발을 헛디뎌 미끄러지고 의식을 잃은(lapse into uncons-ciousness) 이후 밤새 내내 그의 곁에 머물러(stay with him all through the night) 그가 살아남을 수 있도록 몸의 체내 체온을 높게 유지해준(keep his core temperature high to ensure his survival) 결과였다.

영국 언론에 따르면 미키와 보즈는 다이어의 아내 캐서린이 암으로 죽자(die of cancer) 가족들이 다이어의 슬픔을 달래기 위해 선물했던 개들이다. 이후 두 마리의 개는 아내 대신 다이어 인생의 전부가 됐다(become his whole life instead of his wife).

다이어는 이튿날 아침 다른 산책객에 의해 발견(be spotted by another walker next morning)됐다. 연락을 받고 현장에 도착한 긴급구조대(emergency services)는 그를 병원으로 공수(airlift him to hospital)했고, 수술을 받은(undergo surgery) 그는 완전히 건강을 회복(make a full recovery)했다.

현장에 출동했던(attend the scene) 긴급구조대 대원들은 "개들이 그의 생명을 구했다(save his life)"면서 "밤새 그곳에 누워 있었는데도(after lying there all night) 생각보다 체온이 낮지 않았다. 우리가 도착했을 때까지도 두 마리의 개는 그의 몸에 착 달라붙어 체온을 유지해주고 있었다"고 전했다.

Dogs Save Life of Owner who Slipped and Broke his Neck while out Walking them

A man who slipped and broke his neck while walking his dogs was kept alive overnight after his two pets cuddled up to him to keep him warm.

Father-of-two Michael Dyer, 66, fell down a 30ft slope at a remote beauty spot as he exercised Jack Russells, Mickey, three and Boz, five.

He fractured an elbow and broke his neck in the fall and lay unconscious in temperatures as low as 7C (44F).

'Since Michael lost his wife the dogs are his whole life. They are like family to him – his only companion. He loves those dogs and the fact they wouldn't leave him is amazing'

But amazingly, Mr Dyer survived after his two dedicated dogs snuggled up to him for 16 hours and helped stave off hypothermia.

They stayed with him all through the night as he slipped in and out of consciousness and thereby kept his core temperature high to ensure his survival.

The retired lorry driver says at one point he let them off their leads to get help but they refused to leave him.

The brave dogs were given to Mr Dyer by his family after his wife Catherine died of cancer.

Friend Barry Robinson, 48, who is now looking after the dogs said: 'Since Michael lost his wife the dogs are his whole life. They are like family to him – his only companion.

'He loves those dogs and the fact they wouldn't leave him is amazing.'

Mr Dyer was spotted at 9.30am on Friday at Fishcombe Cove in Brixham, Devon, by another walker who thought he had stumbled across a body and called emergency services.

Emergency services airlifted Mr Dyer to hospital where he underwent surgery but is expected to make a full recovering.

Mr Robinson said: 'Michael slipped and fell down a steep bank and broke his wrist and his neck.

'He tried to let the dogs off the lead so they would go and get help but they wouldn't leave him. Instead they stayed with him and cuddled him, keeping him warm.

'He was virtually conscious the whole time, about 16 hours. It must have been horrendous.

'He broke his neck in two places and he is being operated on but he'll be okay. His dogs have saved his life.'

Mr Dyer left his home at 3pm on Thursday and fell down the wooded embankment shortly afterwards.

He was found halfway down the slope and was taken by Devon Air Ambulance to Torbay Hospital in Torquay.

Sgt Jacqui Rees, who attended the scene, said his dogs had saved his life.

She said: 'The man was not as cold as we expected after lying there all night.

'The dogs, who were still with him when we arrived, had cuddled up to him and kept him warm.

'He was very lucky. Once we arrived the shock of what happened started to affect him and he did get quite cold quite quickly.

'It was fortunate that the tree stopped him falling further, although he may have fractured his elbow when it happened.'

✅ 기억하면 좋을 구절!

slip in and out of consciousness 간간이 의식이 돌아오다

Slipping in and out of consciousness, she muttered a few words.
그 여자는 의식이 간간이 돌아올 때면 몇 마디 말을 중얼거렸다.

cuddle(snuggle) up 바싹 다가앉다 / 부둥켜 안다

She *cuddled up* against him.
그녀가 그에게 바싹 몸을 붙였다.

lapse into (부정적인 상태)에 빠지다

He might soon *lapse into* unconsciousness.
그는 의식불명이 될 가능성도 있다.

be spotted by ~에 의해 발견되다

I *was spotted by* him yesterday.
어제 그가 나를 발견했다.

attend the scene (사건) 현장에 출동하다 / 참여하다

A police car *attended the scene*.
경찰차가 현장에 출동했다.

내 인생의 명언 — 아이는 어른의 아버지

▶ 우리가 살아가는 인생의 나날들은 계속
   우리 아이들의 기억 은행에 적립된다.
   찰스 스윈돌 (미국 복음주의학자 · 작가)

> Each day of our lives we make deposits
> in the memory banks of our children.
> Charles Swindoll

▶ 소녀들은 우리 사회의 미래 어머니들이다.
   그들의 건강과 행복에 관심을 집중하는 것이 대단히 중요하다.
   미리엄 마케바 (남아공 가수 · 민권운동가)

> Girls are the future mothers of our society,
> and it is important that we focus on their well-being.
> Miriam Makeba

▶ 10대 아이에게 피할 수 없는 인생의 현실을 이야기해주는 것은
   물고기에게 목욕을 시키는 것과 같다.
   애널드 글래소 (미국 유머작가)

> Telling a teenager the facts of life
> is like giving a fish a bath.
> Arnold Glasow

▶ 아버지가 아이들을 위해 할 수 있는 가장 중요한 일은
   그들의 어머니를 사랑하는 것이다.
   시어도어 히스버러 (미국 성직자 · 교육자)

> The most important thing a father can do
> for his children is to love their mother.

News English

"Prayer for Those Made Redundant"

영국 성공회는 실직의 아픔을 담아 기도문을 만들었다

해고자를 위한 기도

경기침체로 전 세계에 구조조정 바람이 불고 있는 가운데, 급기야 실직자들을 위한 기도문이 나왔다. 직장에 남아 그들을 떠나보내야 하는 동료 직원들을 위한 기도문(prayer for colleagues who remain behind in the workplace)도 만들어졌다.

영국 성공회(聖公會 · Church of England)는 실업 사태로 야기되고 있는 고뇌(the anguish prompted by a wave of job losses)에 위안을 주기(provide comfort) 위해 두 가지 기도문을 만들었다. 하나는 '해고되는 사람들을 위한 기도'(Prayer On Being Made Redundant), 다른 하나는 '남아 있는 사람들을 위한 기도'(Prayer For Those Remaining In The Workplace)이다.

'해고자를 위한 기도'는 최근의 해고 격랑에 휩쓸려(in the wave of recent redundancies) 직장을 잃은 이들의 근심을 말로 표현(put into words the anxieties of those who lose their job)했다.

한 예로 기도문에는 "당혹감에 절규하는 제 말을 들어주시고(Hear me as I cry out in confusion), 또렷하게 생각하며 제 영혼을 진정시킬 수 있도록 도와주소서(help me to think clearly and calm my soul)"라는 표현이 들어 있다.

'남아 있는 사람들을 위한 기도'는 죄책감 및 해고와 관련해 가중된 업무부담에 초점(focus on the guilty conscience and increased workload associated with redundancy)이 맞춰 있다. "이 불확실성 속에서도(in the midst of this uncertainty) 계속 나아가고(keep going) 내 능력의 최선을 다해 일하며(work to the best of my ability) 하루하루를 맞이하게 하소서"라고 기도한다.

두 기도문에 대해 성공회 측은 교회가 언제든지(at all times), 특히 위기에 처했을 때(especially in times of crisis) 사람들과 함께한다는 것을 보여주고자 했다고 취지를 설명한다. 갈수록 늘어나는 실직자들을 위한 새 기도문(a new prayer for the growing ranks of the unemployed)을 제시, 하느님이 늘 그들과 함께한다는 믿음으로 슬픈 감정(the feeling of sadness)과 힘겨운 시간을 헤쳐나갈 수 있도록 돕고자(help them through troubled times) 했다고 밝혔다.

성공회는 두 기도문을 홈페이지에 올리는 한편, 교회에서 나눠주는 전단에도 인쇄해(print the two prayers in a leaflet to be handed out in churches) 신자들이 쉽게 접할 수 있도록 하고 있다.

Church Offers Prayers for Redundant Workers, and those who Stay on

Bishop leads attempt to put into words the anxieties of those losing their jobs and guilt of colleagues left behind.

The Church of England today responded to the economic downturn and growing fears of job losses by issuing prayers for people made redundant and their colleagues remaining in the workplace.

The church said it wanted to provide comfort to people, with the Chartered Institute of Personnel and Development predicting that at least 600,000 workers could lose their jobs this year.

The prayer on being made redundant is an attempt to put into words "the anxieties of those who are losing – or who have already lost – their job in the wave of recent redundancies," the church said. The poem pleads: "As I look to the future, help me to look for fresh opportunities, for new directions."

For those remaining in the workplace, another prayer focuses on the guilt and increased workload associated with redundancy. "Who will be next? How will I cope with the increased pressure of work?" it asks.

The prayers feature in the matter of life and debt section of the Church of England's website, which includes advice for people with financial worries. Other prayers address the current financial situation, wise financial stewardship and people who are worried about debt.

"We need to be on the look-out to support those facing redundancy," said the Right Rev John Packer, the Bishop of Ripon and Leeds and chairman of the church's stewardship committee. "Neighbourliness is so important in crisis situations, whether it's offering people new prayers to God, or by simply being there with a listening ear."

Prayer on Being Made Redundant

"Redundant" – the word says it all –

"useless, unnecessary, without purpose, surplus to requirements."

Thank you, Heavenly Father, that in the middle of the sadness, the anger, the uncertainty, the pain, I can talk to you.

Hear me as I cry out in confusion, help me to think clearly, and calm my soul.

As life carries on,

may I know your presence with me each and every day.

And as I look to the future,

help me to look for fresh opportunities, for new directions.

Guide me by your Spirit, and show me your path,

Through Jesus, the Way, the Truth and the Life.

Amen.

Prayer for Those Remaining in the Workplace

Life has changed:

Colleagues have gone – Redundant, out of work.

Suddenly, what seemed so secure is now so very fragile.

It's hard to know what I feel:

Sadness, certainly,

Guilt, almost, at still having a job to go to,

And fear of the future:

Who will be next?

How will I cope with the increased pressure of work?

Lord Jesus, in the midst of this uncertainty, help me to keep going:

To work to the best of my ability, taking each day at a time,

And taking time each day to walk with you

For you are the Way, the Truth and the Life.

Amen.

☑ 기억하면 좋을 구절!

be made redundant 정리해고 당하다

He *was* recently *made redundant* after 26 years with a company.
그는 최근에 26년간 일했던 회사에서 정리해고되었다.

be prompted by ~에 고무되다 / 자극되다

I *was prompted by* his effort.
나는 그의 노력에 큰 영향을 받았다.

in the midst of ~하는 가운데 / 도중에

My country is *in the midst of* a national crisis.
우리 나라는 현재 국가적 위기 상태이다.

to the beat of one's ability 힘 닿는 데까지 / 할 수 있는 한

I'll help you *to the best of my ability*.
내가 힘 닿는 데까지 너를 도와줄께.

be on the lookout 세심히 살피다 / 지켜보다

You should *be on the lookout* for symptoms of the disease.
그 병의 징후가 나타나는지 세심히 살펴봐야 한다.

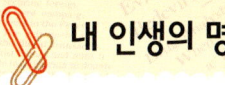

내 인생의 명언 — 천국은 우리 안에 있다

▶ 지구상 모든 사람 인생의 모든 순간과 사건들은
 스스로의 영혼에 무언가를 심는 것이다.
 토마스 머튼 (프랑스 태생 영국 시인·종교작가)

> Every moment and every event of everyman's life
> on earth plants something in his soul.
> Thomas Merton

▶ 씩씩한 영혼은 절대 패배하지 않는다.
 월리스 심슨 (영국 윈저공의 부인)

> For a gallant spirit there can never be defeat.
> Wallis Simpson

▶ 행복은 소유에 존재하는 것이 아니라 영혼에 사는 것이다.
 데모크리투스 (그리스 철학자)

> Happiness resides not in possessions,
> but dwells in the soul.
> Democritus

▶ 당신의 가슴, 마음, 영혼을 당신의 가장 사소한 행동에도 담아라.
 이것이 성공의 비결이다.
 스와미 시바난다 (인도 힌두교 지도자)

> Put your heart, mind, and soul into even
> your smallest acts. This is the secret of success
> Swami Sivananda

"Tragedy of a Couple Following their Son to the Grave"

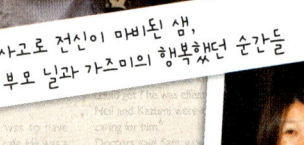

사고로 전신이 마비된 샘,
부모 닐과 가즈미의 행복했던 순간들

아들 따라 죽은 한 부부의 비극

 눈에 넣어도 아프지 않을 외아들이 죽었다. 다섯 살짜리였다. 젊은 아빠와 엄마는 어린 아들을 떠나보내고 도저히 살아갈 자신이 없었다. 두 사람은 아들을 따라가기로 했다. 그래서 높은 절벽을 찾아가 뛰어내렸다. 그들 품에는 아들의 시신을 넣은 가방 하나, 아들의 장난감을 넣은 가방 하나가 안겨 있었다.

 영국 윌트셔 주(州) 웨스트버리에 사는 닐 퍼틱(34세)과 가즈미 퍼틱(44세) 부부는 귀여운 어린 아들 샘을 위해 헌신하며 살았다(live for their adorable young son Sam). 24시간 내내 아들을 돌보기 위해 두 사람 모두 일을 그만뒀다(have both quit their jobs to care for him round the clock). 샘이 교통사고 후(after a car accident) 목 아래 전신이 완전히 마비됐기(be completely paralyzed from the neck down) 때문이다.

 거기에서 끝나지 않았다. 운명은 이 작은 가족에게 또 다른 잔혹한 계략을 숨겨놓고(have another cruel trick in store for this small family) 있었다. 샘이 치명적 뇌질환인 뇌막염까지 걸려(contract the deadly brain bug meningitis) 집에서 숨을 거두고 만 것이다. 자선단체 직원이었던 아빠 닐과 번역사인 엄마 가즈미는 비탄에 잠겼다(be stricken with grief). 어린 아들 없는 인생은 도저히 생각도 할 수 없었다(can not contemplate a life without their young son).

이틀 뒤 이들 부부는 집에서 약 225킬로미터를 운전해(drive 225 kilometers from their home) 악명 높은 자살장소(a notorious suicide spot)인 이스트 서섹스의 비치 헤드라는 절벽(높이 152미터) 위로 올라갔다.

그리고 등산용 가방 하나에는 아들의 시신, 또 다른 가방에는 아들이 제일 좋아했던 노란색 장난감 트랙터를 담아 든 채(with their son's body in one rucksack and his favorite yellow toy tractor in another) 몸을 던져 목숨을 끊었다(leap to their death).

샘은 생후 16개월 때인 2005년 7월 엄마 차를 타고 가다가 정면충돌 사고를 당하면서(be in a head-on collision) 아기용 의자와 함께 차 창문을 통해 튕겨나갔고(be flung through the window of his mother's car), 그 결과 사지가 마비되고(be left quadriplegic) 말았다.

사고로 인해 샘의 척추(spinal cord)는 완전히 절단됐다(be completely severed). 설상가상 병원에서 치료를 받다가(while being treated in hospital) 메티실린 내성황색 포도구균(항생 물질에 내성이 생긴 균 · MRSA · methicillin-resistant staphylococcus aureus)에도 감염됐다.

아빠 닐과 엄마 가즈미는 사고 후 웹사이트를 만들어(set up a website

after the accident) 심한 장애자가 된 아들의 특수장비 구입을 위해 3만 파운드 이상을 모금(raise over £30000 to buy specialist equipment for their severely disabled son)했다. 이후 부부는 샘을 돌보는 데 온갖 헌신을 다했다(be totally devoted to caring for him).

의사들은 샘이 사고 후유증에서 결코 회복될 수 없을(would never recover from his sequelae) 것이라고 말해줬지만, 샘의 부모는 희망을 포기하려 하지 않았다(refuse to give up hope).

샘의 아빠 닐은 아내와 함께 아들의 시신을 안고 투신하기로 결심하기 전 어느 날, 한 온라인 메시지에 이렇게 썼다. "의사들이 틀렸다고 믿는다. 샘은 다시 걷고, 말하고, 숨 쉬게 될(will walk, talk and breathe again) 것이다. 샘이 우리에게 왔을 때(come to us) 그것은 하나의 기적(a miracle)이었고, 사고에서 살아남은(survive the crash) 것도 기적이었다. 샘이 회복하게 되면 또 하나의 기적이 될 것이며, 반드시 샘에게 그 기적은 일어날 것이다."

그러나 샘은 끝내 부모가 지켜보는 가운데 숨을 거뒀다. 아빠와 엄마는 홀로 떠난 어린 아들을 돌봐주기 위해 같은 길을 따라 나섰다.

Devoted Beachy Head Suicide Parents couldn't Live without their Son

They had both quit their jobs to care for him round the clock after a car accident left him completely paralysed from the neck down.

But fate had another cruel trick in store for this small family.

Five-year-old Sam contracted the deadly brain bug meningitis and died at home on Friday.

Stricken with grief, ex-charity worker Neil, 34, and translator Kazumi, 44, could not contemplate a life without their young son.

And so on Sunday they drove 140 miles from their home in Westbury, Wiltshire, to the 500ft Beachy Head suicide spot in East Sussex.

There they leapt to their deaths with their son's body in one rucksack and his favourite yellow toy tractor in another.

Last night stunned friends paid tribute to the tragic young lad and his doting parents.

Sue Capon, 51, who runs a caravan park near their home, said: "To see what they have gone through was awful and I can only assume losing Sam was too much for them. They were a very close family and were 100% dedicated to Sam. He was adorable and always had a smile on his face.

"For him a great treat was to have chocolate cake here in the cafe. He was a lovely child." Sue Hawkins, who lives in a nearby farm, added: "They liked to bring Sam up to see the sheep and cows. He got very excited looking at the animals. He even chose a name for one of our 10-day-old lambs. He called him Sparky.

"Sam could speak quite clearly, and his wheelchair had controls he used to operate. He could move his head but apart from that he was all tubes. His parents just wanted to enjoy their little boy and they loved him. This is absolutely horrible."

Sam was 16 months old when he was left effectively quadriplegic in July 2005. His car seat was flung through the window of his mother's car when it was in a head-on collision at Mere, Somerset, according to former neighbours.

His spinal cord was completely severed in the accident and the boy contracted MRSA while being treated in hospital.

Neil and Kazumi set up a website after his accident and raised over £30,000 to buy specialist equipment for their severely disabled boy.

A grateful Neil wrote: "Being paralysed below the neck and being on a ventilator, his life has health and meaning because of the equipment you have helped provide. I'm a dad who wants to see my son grow healthy and happy."

Friend Jonathan Miall, chief executive of charity Spinal Research, said: "Sam had perhaps the severest form of injury you could get – he was effectively quadriplegic. Neil and Kazumi were totally devoted to caring for him."

Doctors said Sam would never recover from his injuries but his dad refused to give up hope. In one online message Neil wrote: "I believe in my heart the doctors are wrong and he will win. I believe God is with us and Sam will walk, talk and breathe again. He was a miracle when he came to us, it was a miracle he survived the crash and it will be a miracle when he recovers. These things do happen and they will happen to Sam."

☑ 기억하면 좋을 구절!

round the clock 끊임없이, 계속해서 / 24시간 내내 / 밤낮으로

The convenience store opens *round the clock*.
편의점은 24시간 문을 연다.

leap (plunge) to one's death 투신자살하다

He *leapt to his death* from the fifth floor of the building.
그는 5층에서 뛰어내려 자살했다.

be stricken with grief 슬픔에 빠지다 / 비탄에 빠지다

I *was stricken with grief*.
나는 슬픔에 잠겨 있었다.

be left quadriplegic 사지가 마비되다

He *was left quardriplegic* after a horse riding accident.
그는 승마 도중 사고로 사지가 마비됐다.

devote oneself to ~에 헌신하다 / 전념하다

He *devoted himself to* the nourishment of education.
그는 교육 육성에 일신을 바쳤다.

내 인생의 명언 — 성공의 명암

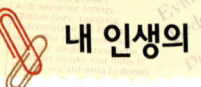

▶ 명성과 성공을 혼돈하지 말라.
에르마 봄벡 (미국 유머작가)

> Don't confuse fame with success
> Erma Bombeck

▶ 우리의 속성이 그렇다.
인간들은 성공은 좋아하면서 성공한 사람들은 미워한다.
캐럿 탑 (미국 코미디언)

> It's our nature: Human beings like success,
> but they hate successful people.
> Carrot Top

▶ 성공은 과학이다. 조건을 갖추면 결과를 얻을 수 있다.
오스카 와일드 (영국 극작가 · 소설가)

> Success is a science; if you have the conditions,
> you get the result.
> Oscar Wilde

▶ 성공은 동료들에 대한 용서받지 못할 죄이다.
앰브로즈 비어스 (미국 언론인 · 작가)

> Success is the one unpardonable sin against our fellows.
> Ambrose Bierce

Favorite famous sayings!

▶ 명예 없는 성공은 양념하지 않은 요리와 같다.
당신의 허기는 만족시킬 수 있을지 모르지만 맛은 없다.
조 패터노 (미국 미식축구 감독)

> Success without honor is an unseasoned dish;
> it will satisfy your hunger, but it won't taste good.
> Joe Paterno

▶ 성공은 천 명의 아버지를 얻게 되고, 실패는 고아가 된다.
앨런 프라이스 (영국 음악가)

> Victory has a thousand fathers,
> but defeat becomes an orphan.
> Alan Price

▶ 어느 것에 성공한 사람이 스스로 행운을 언급하지 않는다면
그건 농담을 하는 거다.
래리 킹 (미국 방송 라이브토크쇼 진행자)

> Who have succeeded at anything and
> don't mention luck are kidding.
> Larry King

▶ 성공한 사람이 되려고 하지 말고, 가치 있는 사람이 되려고 힘쓰라.
앨버트 아인슈타인 (독일 출신 미국 물리학자)

> Try not to become a man of success but
> rather to become a man of value.
> Albert Einstein

*First you take a drink,
then the drink takes a drink,
then the drink takes you.*

Francis Scott Key Fitzgerald

3rd NEWS

Mysterious Science World

신비로운 과학의 세계

News English

"A Newlywed Bride Allergic to her Husband"

A newlywed couple fear they will be unable to have a baby after they discovered the wife was allergic to her husband's semen.

Julie Boyde, 26, discovered the problem when she and husband Mike, 27, had unprotected sexual intercourse for the first time on their wedding night.

The couple had been dating for six when they got married, but had always used protection. As soon as they had unprotected intercourse for the first time she knew something was wrong.

"Before we were always very careful and, you know, used protection, and that time we didn't," Mrs Boyde told ABC News. "So, we figured we were married now, so if we got pregnant, we got pregnant."

Mrs Boyde, from Ambridge, Pennsylvania, added "The pain that I was feeling was inside, kind of like, somebody was sticking needles up inside of me and like a burning, like really painful burning."

Doctors were unable to explain why she experienced pain after intercourse, until a friend of hers suggested she might be allergic to her husband's semen. She was eventually diagnoses with Seminal Plasma Hypersensitivity, which can cause itching and burning.

Dr Andrew Goldstein, from the University of Cincinnati Medical Center said, "The body recognizes semen as a foreign protein just as it would recognize a peanut allergen or pollen." "So you have swelling, you have itching, you have inflammation of the nerve endings."

His colleague Jonathan Bernstein, developed a desensitization treatment similar to receiving an allergy shot. After determining the proteins in the British woman that triggered the allergic reaction, doctors developed a solution to counteract the problem. Although the treatment works for some couples, it did not for the Boydes. They have now started adoption proceedings.

A newlywed couple fear they will be unable to have a baby after they discovered the wife was allergic to her husband's semen.

정액알레르기 환자는 미국 내에만 2만~4만 명에 이른다

새신랑에게 알레르기 반응 보이는 새신부

갓 결혼한 새신랑 새색시가 있다. 그런데 새색시의 몸이 새신랑한테 알레르기를 보인다(be allergic to her husband). 그것도 신랑의 정액에 알레르기 반응을 일으켜(have an allergic reaction to her husband's semen) 아기를 낳을 수 없다고 한다. 이 신혼부부 어쩌야 하나. 미국 펜실바니아 주(州)에 사는 새신부(a newlywed wife) 줄리 보이드(26세)는 고역스러운 첫날밤을 보내야(be given a nasty wedding night) 했다. 관계를 갖던 중 남편의 정액에 알레르기를 일으킨(reject her husband's sperm) 것이다.

그녀와 새신랑(new hubby) 마이크 보이드(27세)는 2년간 사귀었다(go out for two years). 마침내 결혼한(get married) 그들은 그날 밤 처음으로 보호 장구 없이 관계를 갖기로 했다(decide to have unprotected sex for the first time on that evening).

그러나 신부는 그 즉시(almost immediately) 참기 어려운 고통(an

unbearable pain)에 휩싸였다. 그리고 곧 신랑의 정자 때문(because of the bridegroom's sperm)이라는 사실을 알게 됐다. 신부의 몸이 거부 반응을 일으키면서 정자를 파괴하는(reject and destroy the sperm) 것이었다. 두 사람은 임신 계획을 포기할 수밖에 없게(be forced to abandon their plans of conceiving a baby) 됐다.

신혼부부인 줄리와 마이크(the newlyweds Julie and Mike)는 대학 시절 사귀기 시작해(start going out while at university) 2년 뒤 약혼하고(become engaged two years later) 꿈의 결혼식을 올렸다. 앞서 수년간 친구로만 지내다가 마이크가 정식 데이트를 신청하는 용기를 냈다(have the nerve to ask her out).

하지만 결혼식 피로연이 끝나고(after the wedding reception) 공식 결혼한 커플로서 첫날밤을 즐기려던(enjoy their first night as a married couple) 그들은 악몽에 시달려야(be troubled with a nightmare) 했다.

줄리는 "예전엔 늘 굉장히 조심(be always very careful)하면서 꼭 보호장구를 사용했다(use protection)"며 "하지만 첫날밤엔 임신이 되면(get pregnant) 되라 하는 마음에 처음으로 그냥 관계를 가졌다"고 했다. 그런데 고통이 심해지면서 "뭔가 크게 잘못돼 가고 있음을(go badly wrong) 알았다"고 했다.

줄리는 "너무 무서웠다(be really scary)"고 한다. 누군가가 그녀의 몸속을 바늘로 콕콕 찌르는(stick needles up inside of her) 것 같았다고 말한다. 관계를 가질 때마다 고통스러웠고 때로는 수포(the pain, at times blisters)가 생겨 며칠 또는 수 주간 계속되곤(go on for several days or weeks) 했다. 수많은 검사를 받은 끝에(after numerous tests) 받은 진단은 정액 알레르기를 갖고 있다는(suffer from seminal plasma hypersensitivity) 것이었다. "신체가 정자를 이형 단백질로 인식해(recognize the sperm as a foreign protein) 땅콩 알레르기 물질이나 꽃가루(a peanut allergen or a pollen)에 반응하듯 부어오르고(have swelling), 가렵고(have itching), 신경말단 염증이 생긴다는(have inflammation of the nerve endings) 것이다. 다시 말해서 줄리의 신체는 마이크의 정자를 공격해 무력하게 만들고(attack Mike's sperm, making it inactive), 결국엔 난자를 수정시킬 수 없게(be unable to fertilize the egg) 한다는 얘기다.

이 같은 가슴 아픈 진단(this painful diagnosis)은 그들의 임신 계획을 산산조각 내고(shatter their plans to conceive) 말았다. 부모가 되고 싶어 했던 꿈이 조각나(shatter their dream of parenthood)버렸다.

정액알레르기(semen allergy) 환자는 미국 내에만 2만~4만 명이 있는 것으로 추정되고 있다.

마지막 희망이 없지는 않았다. 탈감각(脫感覺) 치료(a desensitization treatment)였다. 알레르기 주사를 맞는 것과 비슷한(be similar to receiving an allergy shot) 것이다. 마이크의 정액에서 아내의 알레르기 반응을 유발하는(trigger his wife's reaction) 세 개의 단백질 성분들을 가려낸 뒤(after determining the three proteins in Mike's semen) 아내를 면역시키는 데 사용되는 백신과 같은(be used almost like a vaccine to immunize his wife) 혈청을 그의 정액으로부터 생성(create a serum from his semen)해냈다.

줄리는 첫 2주 동안엔 일주일에 두 차례씩, 이후엔 일주일에 한 차례씩 그 혈청 주사를 맞았다(receive her serum injections twice a week for the first two weeks and then once a week thereafter). 그러나 불행하게도 다른 부부들에겐 효과를 나타내는(work for other couples) 이 치료법이 줄리에겐 아무 소용이 없었다. 남편의 정액에 대한 알레르기 반응이 계속 일어났고(continue to have a reaction to her husband's semen), 결국엔 주사 맞는 것을 중단하고(stop taking the shots) 말았다.

두 사람은 이 치료가 허사로 돌아간(prove unsuccessful for them) 뒤 입양절차를 밟기 시작(start adoption proceedings)했다고 외신들은 전한다.

Wife is Allergic to her Husband's Sperm

A newlywed couple fear they will be unable to have a baby after they discovered the wife was allergic to her husband's semen.

Julie Boyde, 26, discovered the problem when she and husband Mike, 27, had unprotected sexual intercourse for the first time on their wedding night.

The couple had been dating for two years when they got married, but had always used protection. As soon as they had unprotected intercourse for the first time she knew something was wrong.

"Before we were always very careful and, you know, used protection, and that time we didn't," Mrs Boyde told ABC News. "So, we figured we were married now, so if we got pregnant, we got pregnant."

Mrs Boyde, from Ambridge, Pennsylvania, added: "The pain that I was feeling was inside, kind of like, somebody was sticking needles up inside of me and like a burning, like really painful burning."

Doctors were unable to explain why she experienced pain after intercourse, until a friend of hers suggested she might be allergic to her husband's semen. She was eventually diagnosed with Seminal Plasma Hypersensitivity, which can cause itching and burning.

Dr Andrew Goldstein, from the University of Cincinnati Medical Center said: "The body recognizes semen as a foreign protein just as it would recognize a peanut allergen or pollen." "So you have swelling, you have itching, you have inflammation of the nerve endings."

His colleague Jonathan Bernstein developed a desensitization treatment similar to receiving an allergy shot. After determining the proteins in Mr Boyde's semen that triggered his wife's reaction, he created a serum to counteract the problem. Although the treatment works for some couples, it did not for the Boydes. They have now started adoption proceedings.

✓ 기억하면 좋을 구절!

conceive a baby 아이를 갖다
→ You have to struggle to *conceive a baby*.
아기를 갖기 위해 노력해야 한다.

have the nerve to ~할 용기가 있다
→ She didn't *have the nerve to* say that to him.
그녀는 그에게 말할 용기가 없었다.

go badly wrong 크게 잘못되다
→ It could all *go badly wrong* if we are not careful.
조심하지 않으면 모든 것을 크게 그르칠 가능성이 높다.

have a swelling on ~가 부어오르다 / 혹다
→ This lady *had* a really big *swelling on* her leg.
그 여성은 다리가 정말 심하게 부어올랐다.

have an inflammation in ~에 염증이 생기다
→ I *have an inflammation on* my mouth.
입안에 염증이 생겼습니다.

내 인생의 명언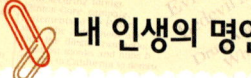

▶ 우리가 사는 것도 꿈꿀 때나 마찬가지다, 혼자이기는.
조셉 콘라드 (영국 작가)

> We live as we dream—alone.
> Joseph Conrad

▶ 자연과 책은 그것을 보는 눈의 것이다.
랠프 에머슨 (미국 평론가·시인·철학자)

> Nature and books belong to the eyes that see them.
> Ralph Waldo Emerson

▶ 모든 이를 사랑하고 몇몇 사람만 신뢰하되,
어느 누구에게도 나쁜 짓은 하지 마라.
윌리엄 셰익스피어 (영국 극작가·시인)

> Love all, trust a few, do wrong to none.
> William Shakespeare

▶ 면전의 아첨꾼과 배후의 험담꾼은 똑같다.
알프레드 테니슨 (영국 계관시인)

> Face-flatterers and back-biters are the same.
> Alfred Lord Tennyson

▶ 진실한 말 한마디는 연설만큼 위력이 있다.
찰스 디킨스 (영국 소설가)

> A word in earnest is as good as a speech.
> Charles Dickens

Favorite famous sayings!

▶ 우리는 인간의 덕행보다는 과오로부터 더 많은 것을 배운다.
헨리 롱펠로우 (미국 시인)

> We may learn more from a man's errors,
> than from his virtues.
> Henry Wadsworth Longfellow

▶ 지상에서 시들지 않는 유일한 꽃은 미덕이다.
그리고 지속되는 유일한 보배는 진실이다.
윌리엄 쿠퍼 (영국 시인)

> The only amaranthine flower on earth is virtue;
> the only lasting treasure, truth
> William Cowper

▶ 처음에는 네가 술을 마시고, 다음에는 술이 술을 마시고,
그다음에는 술이 너를 마신다.
스코트 피츠제럴드 (미국 작가)

> First you take a drink, then the drink takes a drink,
> then the drink takes you.
> Francis Scott Key Fitzgerald

News English

"A Physicist Predicting the Weather Next Year"

Predicting the weather is a notoriously tricky business. For all the new technologies at their disposal -- Doppler, satellite imaging, computer mapping -- weather forecasters can sometimes seem less accurate than grandpa with his bum knee. And that's for tom...
But what about...
or next month or...
On May 29 in Lo...
range weatherm...
news conference...
that in about a m...
United States wer...
for picnicking.
"June 22 to June 2...
said Corbyn, whe...
includes a 20-year...
hold together with...
grade out of a shop...
region, really. Majo...
local floods with de...
very damaging, kille...
would be a fair desc...
as well."
Fast forward three-a...
to today. There's damaging hail in New Jersey. There are tornados in Colorado. A few days earlier than predicted, but just a precursor, Corbyn later explained, to the imminent main event.
By Zeus, Corbyn was just about right.
"We can predict extreme events a year ahead," Corbyn told "Nightline."
"What we can do will help the world."
Watch the full story tonight on...

extreme weather events in the United States, including ice storms Jan. 6-8 in the Northeast and the Midwestern blizzards of Feb. 3-6. Corbyn claims to have been right eight-and-a-half times out of...

내년 날씨를 정확히 예보하는 피어스 코빈 박사

like Geoff Philpot buy Corbyn's forecasts. "It is amazing how accurate he can be on long-range," said Philpot, standing in a field of plump cauliflowers. "He predicted... ...year it was going to be ...oldest part of the winter ...Jan. 6-9.
...to utilize our knowledge ...flower that were at risk ...ut them in advance and ...dy, so the damage was

...his detractors.
...at Corbyn's method ...e probably does have ...grains of truth and ...s," Accuweather.com ...ting operations Ken ...ws.
...concentration on ...predictions does ...said.
...ce are far more

sun shine for a correspondent's family vacation in Cornwall in early June!
"We expect that period, the 6th to 9th or so, to be part of a solar weather impact period around the world, which will see a lot of thundery developments in a lot of places and one of those is very likely to be Cornwall," Corbyn said.
Undaunted, we packed the sunscreen and headed out.
But this time Corbyn was right. Driving to Cornwall June 6, the car's windshield wipers struggled to cope with a deluge. Roads were flooded. The sunscreen was not required.
The weather, it turned out, was dreadful.
Predicting the weather is a notoriously tricky business. For all the new technologies at their disposal -- Doppler, satellite imaging, computer mapping -- weather forecasters can sometimes seem less accurate than grandpa with his bum knee. And that's for tomorrow's weather...
...th -- or next year!
...n London, the maverick long-...enman Piers Corbyn called a ...rence and informed the world ...a month, certain parts of the ...tes were going to be very bad

...o June 24, this is for the U.S.A." ...byn, whose professional kit ...20-year-old calculator, a globe ...the with Scotch tape and a sun ...a shopping bag. "A very wide ...cally major thunderstorms and ...s, with advancing tornados, ...tropical killer hurricanes, I think ...a fair description. Clear, hot

내년 날씨 예보하는 물리학자

"내년 이맘 때 당신의 결혼식 날 날씨가 궁금합니까? 비 옵니다."

영국 런던 임페리얼대학의 천체물리학자 피어스 코빈 박사가 기상 장기 예보 전문가로 명성을 날리고(have renown for a long-range weatherman) 있다. 코빈 박사는 태양에 근거한 비밀기술을 이용해(use a secretive solar-based technique) "자연의 미래를 읽을(read Mother Nature's future) 수 있다"며 1년 후 날씨도 맞힐 수 있다고 장담한다.

날씨를 예보하는(predict the weather) 것은 까다롭기로 악명 높은 일(a notoriously tricky business)이다. 기상예보관들은 모든 첨단기술들을 갖고 있으면서도(for all the new technologies at their disposal) 연약한 무릎을 가진 할아버지보다 정확하지 못할 때가 종종 있다(sometimes seem less accurate than grandpa with his bum knee). 하물며 내일 날씨도 말이다.

그렇다면 다음 주, 내달, 아니면 내년 날씨는 어떤가?(What about the

weather next week or next month or next year?) 2009년 5월 29일 코빈 박사는 기자회견을 열고(call a news conference) "한달 후쯤(in about a month) 미국의 특정 지방들(certain parts of the United States)은 나들이에 아주 좋지 않은 날씨가 될(be going to be very bad for picnicking) 것"이라고 공언했다. 6월 22~24일의 날씨를 전망했던 코빈 박사의 전문장비(his professional kit)는 20년 된 계산기, 셀로판 테이프로 붙여진 지구본, 쇼핑백으로 만든 태양을 포함한(include a 20-year-old calculator, a globe held together with Scotch tape and a sun made out of a shopping bag) 보잘것없는 것들뿐이었다.

그는 "광범위한 지역에서 엄청난 뇌우(雷雨), 강력한 토네이도를 동반한 국지적 홍수, 살인적 토네이도(hellacious thunderstorms, local floods with devastating tornadoes, killer tornadoes)가 일어날 것"이라며 "일부 지역엔 우박도(a hail as well) 예상된다"고 예보했다. 그로부터 3주 반 정도가 지난 후 코빈 박사의 예보는 거의 맞는 것으로(be just about right) 나타났다. 뉴저지 주(州)에 우박이 내렸고, 콜로라도 주에선 토네이도가 기승을 부렸다. 예보했던 것보다 며칠 빨랐지만(a few days earlier than predicted) 곧 일어날 메인 이벤트의 전조(just a precursor to the imminent main event)로 나타난 것이라고 코빈 박사는 설명했다.

그는 미 ABC방송 '나이트라인'과의 인터뷰에서 "극한 자연현상은 1년 전에도 예보가 가능하다(can predict extreme phenomena of nature)"고 단언했다. 코빈 박사는 13개월 동안(over the past 13 months) 미국 내 아홉 건의 극한 기상현상을 예보(predict nine extreme weather events in the United States)했다. 그중에는 동북부의 얼음폭풍(ice storms in the Northeast)과 중서부의 눈보라(the Midwestern blizzards)도 포함돼 있었다. 코빈 박사는 이와 관련, 아홉 차례의 예보 중 8.5개가 적중했다고 주장한다(claim to have been right eight-and-a-half times out of nine). 어떻게 0.5개가 맞았다고 할 수 있느냐는 질문엔 "기후현상은 예보대로 일어났으나 위치가 좀 벗어났기 때문"이라고 응수했다.

코빈 박사는 2007년 11월 영국을 강타했던(thrash Britain in November 2007) 폭풍을 11개월 전 예보하기도 했다. 그는 "특이하고 혁명적인 기술(an unique and revolutionary skill)을 갖고 있다"면서 "표준적인 기상학의 가능성을 완전히 뛰어넘는(be completely beyond the possibility of standard meteorology) 기술"이라고 주장했다. 코빈 박사의 예보 기술에 관한 상세한 내용(the details of Dr. Corbyn's forecasting technique)은 은행 금고에 보관돼(be locked in a bank vault) 있다고 한다. 그는 이른바 '태양 기상 기술'에 대해 핵심은 감춘 채 대체적인 윤곽만 공개하고(offer a broad outline of his so-called Solar Weather Technique)' 있다. 코빈 박사는 태양의 활동과 성층권의 가열 또는 냉각 상태에 주목(look at solar activity, and the heating or cooling of the stratosphere)하며, 그 변화들이 기상 시스템에 어떤 영향을 미칠(what impact those changes will have on weather systems) 것인가를 연구한다고 한다.

또 반복될 수 있는 과거에서 일정한 패턴을 찾아내고(look for certain patterns in history that may repeat themselves), 태양의 자기력 주기와 달의 일식 주기를 연구하는(study the cycle of magnetism on the sun and the eclipse cycle of the moon) 것으로 알려졌다.

코빈 박사는 "날씨는 최근 기상에 벌어진 것에 의해서만 정해지는 것이 아니다(be not driven just by what's happened in the weather recently)"라면서 "태양에서 일어나는 것에 의해, 특히 태양으로부터 오는 하전입자(荷電粒子)에 의해 주도(be driven by what's happening on the sun, especially the charged particles which come from the sun)된다"고 말한다.

직업이 물리학자(a physicist by trade)인 코빈 박사는 20년 전에 첫 기상 예보를 했었다(make his first weather predictions 20 years ago). 자신의 예보에 근거해 내기를 했지만(place bets based on his predictions), 언제나 이기는 쪽은 아니었다(do not always win). 날씨정보 제공 사이트 Accuweather.com의 책임자인 켄 리브스는 "코빈 박사의 방법에 하자가 있다(Corbyn's method is flawed)는 것은 아니지만, 예보를 위해 태양 활동에 집중하는 것(his concentration on solar activity for the predictions)은 비판을 불러올 수(may invite criticism) 있다"고 지적한다. "훨씬 더 많은 환경적 요인들(far more environmental factors)이 있다"는 얘기다. 또 지속적으로 정확한 예보를 낼 수 있는 코빈 박사의 능력에도 의문을 제기(also question Corbyn's ability to consistently produce accurate forecasts)한다. 자신의 방법을 철저히 비밀에 부쳐(be very secretive about his methods) 과학적 정밀조사를 하지 못하게 하는(place them beyond the scrutiny of science) 것도 문제라고 지적한다.

한편 코빈 박사와 인터뷰를 했던 미 abc방송 특파원은 "6월 초에 콘월 지역으로 가족휴가를 갈 예정인데 햇볕이 나겠느냐(would the sun shine for my family vacation in Cornwall in early June)"고 물었다. 코빈 박사는 "그 무렵 숱한 지역에서 천둥이 칠 것(will see a lot of thundery developments in a lot of places)이고, 그 지역 중 하나가 바로 콘월이 될 가능성이 크다(be very likely to be Cornwall)"고 말했다.

특파원 가족들은 이에 개의치 않고 햇볕 차단제를 챙겨 출발(pack the sunscreen and head out)했다. 하지만 콘월로 휴가를 떠난 특파원 가족 차량의 유리창 와이퍼(the car's windshield wipers)는 폭우를 감당하느라 악전고투해야(struggle to cope with a deluge) 했다. 햇볕 차단제는 집에 돌아올 때까지 한 번도 바깥구경을 하지 못했다고 한다.

Will It Rain on Your Wedding Next Year?

Predicting the weather is a notoriously tricky business. For all the new technologies at their disposal—Doppler, satellite imaging, computer mapping—weather forecasters can sometimes seem less accurate than grandpa with his bum knee. And that's for tomorrow's weather.

But what about the weather next week—or next month—or next year?

On May 29 in London, the maverick long-range weatherman Piers Corbyn called a news conference and informed the world that in about a month, certain parts of the United States were going to be very bad for picnicking.

"June 22 to June 24, this is for the U.S.A.," said Corbyn, whose professional kit includes a 20-year-old calculator, a globe held together with Scotch tape and a sun made out of a shopping bag. "A very wide region, really. Major thunderstorms and local floods with devastating tornadoes, very damaging, killer tornadoes, I think would be a fair description. ···Oh yes, hail as well."

Fast forward three-and-a-half weeks—to today. There's damaging hail in New Jersey. There are tornados in Colorado. A few days earlier than predicted, but just a precursor, Corbyn later explained, to the imminent main event.

By Zeus, Corbyn was just about right.

"We can predict extreme events a year ahead," Corbyn told "Nightline." "What we can do will help the world."

Watch the full story tonight on "Nightline" at 11:35 p.m. ET

The "we" is Corbyn and a handful of colleagues who trawl world weather reports from years past, looking for patterns that might be repeated.

Over the past 13 months, Corbyn has predicted nine extreme weather events in the United States, including ice storms Jan. 6-8 in the Northeast and the Midwestern blizzards of Feb. 3-6. Corbyn claims to have been right eight-and-a-half times out of nine.

How do you get half of an event right?

"Well, it's because the event happened but the location was—was a bit out," he said.

Storms that thrashed Britain in November 2007 were predicted by

Corbyn 11 months before they happened.

"We are unique and revolutionary," Corbyn said. "And we have a skill which is completely beyond the possibility of standard meteorology."

Weatherman: 'Charged Particles' From Sun The details of Corbyn's forecasting technique—he calls it the Solar Weather Technique—are locked in a bank vault, he told "Nightline." He did offer a broad outline of his process.

Corbyn looks at solar activity, and the heating or cooling of the stratosphere, and asks what impact those changes will have on weather systems. He looks for patterns in history that may repeat themselves. He studies the cycle of magnetism on the sun and the eclipse cycle of the moon.

"The weather is not driven just by what's happened in the weather recently," Corbyn said. "It's driven by what's happening on the sun. ⋯ Especially the charged particles, which come from the sun."

A physicist by trade, Corbyn made his first weather predictions 20 years ago. He placed bets based on his predictions. He didn't always win.

"We had a June some years ago when we said there was going to be snow in June," he told "Nightline." "Yeah, yeah, yeah, we did say that."

Corbyn has honed his skills over hours spent in his tiny office. Apparently, bookmakers now refuse to take his bets.

"We were making too much money," he said, "so they stopped us."

These days, farmers like Geoff Phillpot buy Corbyn's forecasts.

"It is amazing how accurate he can be on long-range," said Phillpot, standing in a field of plump cauliflowers. "He predicted, for instance, this year it was going to be very cold, the coldest part of the winter was going to be Jan. 6-9.

"We were able to utilize our knowledge and cut our cauliflower that were at risk at that time and cut them in advance and cut them very tightly, so the damage was negligible," he said.

Corbyn does have his detractors.

"I'm not saying that Corbyn's method is flawed. In fact, he probably does have some glimmers or grains of truth and reality in what he says," Accuweather.com director of forecasting operations Ken Reeves told ABC News.

However, Corbyn's concentration on solar activity for his predictions does invite criticism, Reeves said.

"The problem is, there are far more environmental factors that are involved than just one feature," he said.

Reeves also questions Corbyn's ability to consistently produce accurate forecasts.

"Can someone potentially hit a storm, to the day, from 11 months out?" he asked. "Yeah, they could, but realistically, advancement of science isn't at a point where you can do that reliably."

Corbyn is also a global warming denier, automatically qualifying him as a crank to some critics. And he's very secretive about his methods, placing them beyond the scrutiny of science.

That's about to change, he said.

"Later on this year, we're going to reveal key aspects of the Solar Weather Technique—in October, Oct. 28 this year," Corbyn said. "Because we think at some point, the world does have to know."

Weatherman: Should I Plan a Vacation?

When "Nightline" interviewed Corbyn May 29, all we wanted to know was: Would the sun shine for a correspondent's family vacation in Cornwall in early June?

"We expect that period, the 6th to 9th or so, to be part of a solar weather impact period around the world, which will see a lot of thundery developments in a lot of places and one of those is very likely to be Cornwall," Corbyn said.

Undaunted, we packed the sunscreen and headed out.

But this time Corbyn was right. Driving to Cornwall June 6, the car's windshield wipers struggled to cope with a deluge. Roads were flooded. The sunscreen was not required.

The weather, it turned out, was dreadful.

☑ 기억하면 좋을 구절!

have renown for/be renowned for ~로 유명하다 / 명성이 있다
> She *is renowned for* her beauty.
> 그녀는 예쁘기로 유명하다.

notoriously tricky business 힘들기로 악명 높은 일(사업)
> Driving taxi is a *notoriously tricky business*.
> 택시 운전은 힘들기로 유명하다.

call a news conference 기자회견을 열다
> The Prime Minister *called a news conference* to indicate his stance.
> 총리가 자신의 입장 표명을 위해 기자회견을 열었다.

struggle to cope with ~에 맞서느라 악전고투하다
> Farmers are *struggling to cope with* an invasion of slugs.
> 농부들이 민달팽이의 침입에 맞서 싸우느라 고전하고 있다.

invite criticism 비판을 초래하다
> The plan has *invited criticism* from consumer groups.
> 그 계획은 소비자단체들의 비판을 초래했다.

have an impact on ~에 타격을 주다 / 영향을 주다
> Climatic change is also likely to *have an impact on* future food production.
> 기후변화 역시 미래 식량 생산에 영향을 미칠 것이다.

내 인생의 명언 — 현자와 바보 사이

▶ 바보는 자신을 추켜세우고, 현명한 사람은 그 바보를 추켜세워준다.
에드워드 불워 리튼 (영국 정치가 · 시인)

A fool flatters himself, a wise man flatters the fool.
Edward Bulwer Lytton

▶ 주의 깊은 의문은 현명함의 절반이다.
프랜시스 베이컨 (영국 정치가 · 철학자)

A prudent question is one-half of wisdom.
Francis Bacon

▶ 영리함이 현명함은 아니다.
에우리피데스 (그리스 비극 시인)

Cleverness is not wisdom.
Euripides

▶ 무지한 사람들은 현명한 사람들이 천 년 전에 대답한 질문을 이제서야 제기한다.
괴테 (독일 시인)

Ignorant men raise questions that wise men answered a thousand years ago.
Johann Wolfgang von Goethe

Favorite famous sayings!

▶ 당신이 할 수 있는 한 똑똑하라. 그러나 똑똑한 것보다는
현명한 것이 언제나 낫다는 사실을 명심해라.
앨런 앨더 (미국 배우 · 감독 · 극작가)

> Be as smart as you can, but remember
> that it is always better to be wise than to smart.
> Allen Elder

▶ 천재는 품위 있는 상식, 그 이상의 아무것도 아니다.
조쉬 빌링스 (미국 유머작가)

> Genius ain't anything more than
> elegant common sense.
> Josh Billings

▶ 이 세상에는 오로지 두 인종만 있다.
지적인 사람과 어리석은 사람이다.
존 파울스 (영국 소설가 · 수필가)

> There are only two races on this planet—
> the intelligent and the stupid.
> John Fowles

News English

"A Secret Formula for Unstoppable Penalty"

SOCCER aces prone to fluffing penalties no longer have an excuse ? after boffins yesterday unveiled a FORMULA for the perfect spot kick.

University eggheads studied hour after hour of footage to deduce what makes a shot unstoppable.

The SHOT should be 65mph or more. This requires a RUN-UP of five to six paces, commencing from the edge of the 18-yard line ? approaching the ball at an ANGLE of 20 to 30 degrees.

And it must CROSS the goal line at exactly 0.5m below crossbar and 0.5m inside either post.

Researchers say the formula promises 100 per cent success.

Manchester City fans will be gutted the findings emerged too late to prevent £32.5million ace Robinho bungling his penalty against Sunderland on Sunday.

The equation would also have saved Chelsea skipper John Terry from heartbreak at his miss gifting Man United last season's Champions League victory.

A research team at Liverpool John Moores University used Sky Sports high definition cameras installed at the back of goal nets to analyse spot kicks.

Professor Tim Cable, director of sport and exercise sciences, declared: "Many factors make up a 'perfect penalty'. But we've finally nailed the key elements."

페널티킥을 100% 성공시키는 공식이 발견됐다고(?)

244

도저히 막을 수 없는 페널티킥 비법

축구에서 페널티킥을 단 한 차례의 실축도 없이 100% 성공시킬 수 있는 '공식'은 없을까.

걸핏하면(unduly often) 페널티킥을 실축하는 축구 스타선수들(soccer aces prone to fluffing penalties)이 더 이상 변명 거리를 찾을 수 없게(no longer have an excuse) 됐다. 도저히 막을 수 없는 페널티킥 비법(a secret formula for unstoppable penalty)을 전문가들이 발견(?)했기 때문이다.

스포츠·운동과학 전문가인 영국 리버풀 존 무어스 대학교의 팀 케이블 교수 등 연구팀은 오랜 기간 다양한 페널티킥 유형들을 조사, '완벽한 페널티킥을 위한 축구 공식'(a footie formula for perfect penalty)을 찾아냈다.

대학의 지식인들(university eggheads)이 슛을 막을 수 없게 하기 위해(to make a shot unstoppable) 머리를 짜낸 것이어서 얼핏 탁상공론(a desk theory)처럼 비치지만, 현실성 여부를 떠나 타당성(objective validity)이나 설득력(persuasive power)은 있어 보인다.

슛의 속도는 시속 약 105km가 돼야 한다. 이 정도 속도를 내려면 골대에서 16.5m 거리에 있는 골라인 끝에서 5~6 걸음 내달리기(a run-up of five to six paces)를 해야 한다. 공을 향해 달려가는(approach the ball) 각도는 20~30도(at an angle of 20 to 30 degrees)가 적당하다.

킥을 해서 골대 크로스바 밑 50cm, 어느 쪽이든 양쪽 골 포스트 50cm 안쪽으로(50cm below crossbar and 50cm inside either post) 공을 보내면 제아무리 키가 크고 유연성이 뛰어난 골키퍼일지라도 속수무책(be at a loss what to do)이다.

이것만 유념했다면 몸값이 3250만 파운드(약 645억 원)인 맨체스터시티의 호비뉴가 2009년 3월 22일 선덜랜드와의 경기에서 페널티킥을 실축(bungle the penalty)하지 않았을 것이다. 맨체스터시티가 1대 0으로 승리하기는 했지만, 팬들 입장에선 뒤늦게 나온 이번 '발견'(the findings emerged too late)이 안타까울 수밖에 없다. 또 앞서 말한 '방정식'(the equation)대로 공을 찼다면 2008년 5월 첼시의 주장 존 테리가 맨체스터 유나이티드와 승부차기에서 실축해 챔피언스리그 우승컵을 헌납한 뒤, 눈물을 흘리며 사과까지 하는 사태는 벌어지지 않았을 것이다.

이번 연구를 주도한 케이블 교수는 "페널티킥을 분석하기 위해(to analyze spot kicks) 골망 뒤쪽에 설치된 고화질 카메라를 사용해(use the high definition cameras installed at the back of goal nets) 수많은 페널티킥 유형을 반복 조사했다"며 "그 결과 완벽한 페널티킥에 필수적인 주요 요소들을 잡아낼(nail the key elements) 수 있었다"고 밝혔다.

Footie Formula for Perfect Pen

SOCCER aces prone to fluffing penalties no longer have an excuse—after boffins yesterday unveiled a FORMULA for the perfect spot kick.

University eggheads studied hour after hour of footage to deduce what makes a shot unstoppable.

The SHOT should be 65mph or more. This requires a RUN-UP of five to six paces, commencing from the edge of the 18-yard line–approaching the ball at an ANGLE of 20 to 30 degrees.

And it must CROSS the goal line at exactly 0.5m below crossbar and 0.5m inside either post.

Researchers say the formula promises 100% success.

Manchester City fans will be gutted the findings emerged too late to prevent £32.5million ace Robinho bungling his penalty against Sunderland on Sunday.

The equation would also have saved Chelsea skipper John Terry from heartbreak at his miss gifting Man United last season's Champions League victory.

A research team at Liverpool John Moores University used Sky Sports high definition cameras installed at the back of goal nets to analyse spot kicks.

Professor Tim Cable, director of sport and exercise sciences, declared: "Many factors make up a 'perfect penalty'. But we've finally nailed the key elements."

☑ 기억하면 좋을 구절!

persuasive power 설득력

Use your *persuasive powers* if necessary.
필요하면 당신의 설득력을 이용하라.

be prone to ~한 경향이 있는, ~하기 쉬운

I *am prone to* motion sickness.
나는 곧잘 차멀미를 한다.

high definition camera 고화질 카메라

High definition cameras are exported world-wide.
고화질 카메라는 전 세계로 수출된다.

objective validity 객관적인 타당성

The conclusion has no *objective validity*.
그 결론은 객관적인 타당성이 결여되어 있다.

at a loss 어쩔 줄 모르는, 갈팡질팡하는

His comments left me *at a loss* for words.
그의 말에 나는 무슨 말을 해야 할지 몰랐다.

secret formula 비법

This is a sause made by my family's *secret formula*.
이 소스는 우리 집안 전래의 비법으로 만든 것이다.

내 인생의 명언 — 인생은 땀 흘리는 자의 몫

▶ 개천을 다 건너고 난 뒤까지는 악어를 조롱하지 마라.
댄 래더 (미국 기업가 · 작가)

> Don't taunt the alligator until
> after you've crossed the creek.
> Dan Rather

▶ 장애물이란 당신이 당신의 목표에서 눈을 뗐을 때 보이는 무서운 것들이다.
헨리 포드 (미국 자동차왕)

> Obstacles are those frightful things you see
> when you take your eyes off your goal.
> Henry Ford

▶ 발견의 최대 장애물은 무식이 아니라 지식의 환상이다.
대니얼 부스틴 (미국 역사가 · 변호사 · 작가)

> The greatest obstacle to discovery is not ignorance—
> it is the illusion of knowledge.
> Daniel Boostin

▶ 훌륭한 패자가 되는 것은 이기는 방법을 배우는 것이다.
칼 샌드버그 (미국 작가 · 시인)

> To be a good loser is to learn how to win.
> Carl Sandburg

Favorite famous sayings!

▶ 행운은 땀의 배당금이다. 땀을 더 흘릴수록 더 많은 행운을 맞게 된다.
레이 크록 (미국 사업가 · 맥도널드 설립자)

> Luck is a dividend of sweat.
> The more you sweat, the luckier you get.
> Ray Kroc

▶ 목표를 정하는 것은 보이지 않는 것을 보이게 하는 첫번째 단계이다.
토니 로빈스 (미국 작가)

> Setting goals is the first step in turning
> the invisible into the visible.
> Tony Robbins

▶ 내 인생이 끝나 신 앞에 섰을 때
"당신께서 주신 모든 것을 사용했습니다."라고 말할 수 있도록
단 한 조각의 남은 재능도 없기를 바란다.
에르마 봄벡 (미국 유머작가)

> When I stand before God at the end of my life,
> I would hope that I would not have
> a single bit of talent left, and could say,
> "I used everything you gave me."
> Erma Bombeck

News English

"Features that Make a Man Appeal to a Woman"

What makes a woman want to sleep with a man? Is it true that a chap can laugh a woman into bed? Does he need to be tall, dark and handsome to stand any chance at all?

Today, in the second extract from the new book Why Women Have Sex, by psychologists Cindy Meston and David Buss, we reveal the features that make a man appeal to a woman, and why, are far more fascinating and complex than you could imagine...

SIZE MATTERS

What sort of body does a woman find desirable? Perhaps the m[ost] physical characteristic [...] man is height.

Studies consistent[ly] consider tall men [...] genetics of personal [...] women state they w[...] who is 6ft or taller.

Men who indicate in [...] that they are tall have a[...] receive far more respon[...] Other studies show w[...] men as husbands and pu[...] emphasis on height in s[...] partners. Women even p[...] on height when selecting s[...]

Two studies also found [...] average men tend to h[...] number of liveln girlfri[...] children, confirming t[...] for romance and reprod[...]

And, there does see[...] underlying 'logic' in [...] preference for ta[...]

'Western culture[...] to have higher [...]

earn more than 100,000 across a 30-year career than 5ft 5in men.

They also tend to be healthier than shorter men - and if they're police[men,] they get assaulted less than their [...] colleagues, which suggests [...] commands more respect from o[...] What more could a girl want?

THE SCENT OF SEX

According to new scientific [...] a woman will literally sniff o[...] genetic make-up before she d[...] right for her.

A w[...]

complex dissimilar to their own to be the most desirable.

The odours of men who had a complex similar to their own made them recoil in [...]

Women wit[h...] ported more frequent sexual [...] out other men, particularly at the most [...] le phase of their ovulation cycle.

[...] their sexual fantasies about other [...] did not just remain in their heads, [...] y also reported higher rates of sexual [...]ty.

[...] FOR SEX

[...]t is not the only aspect of man's [...] s that excites women.

[...] of mate preferences reveal that [...] desire strong, muscular, athletic [...] long-term partnerships as well as [...] al liaisons.

[...] women also show a distinct [...] ce for a V-shaped torso - broad [...] relating to hips. They are also [...] a least strongly enamoured [...] lar that has muscle-bound [...]

☑ He's 6ft in his socks
☑ Dances like a dervish
☑ Has a voice like a bullfrog
☑ Smells - literally - irresistible
☑ And he likes you because you laugh at his jokes

여성들이 특별히 선호하는 남성들이 있다는데……

they could be easily dominated by other men. Men with a high-shoulder-to-hip ratio begin having sexual intercourse at an early age - 16 or younger.

They report having more sex partners than their slim-shouldered peers. But be [...]ect: they have more affairs while in a [...]ship.

[...]ey report more instances of being [...]h by women who are already in [...]oships for affairs on the side.

[...]fic research, though, has discovered [...]cularity that women find attractive. [...]uming they need to pump iron and [...]t a honed six-pack to be attractive.

[...]ges of muscle-bound men have almost [...]mainly fostered men's misperception of [...]at women find most sexually attractive [...] just as photo spreads of impossibly thin [...] odels have led women to overestimate [...] he degree of thinness that men find most attractive.

One study compared the muscularity of men's bodies in Cosmopolitan magazine (whose readership is 89 per cent women) with Men's Health (whose readership is 85 per cent men).

The level of muscularity in Cosmopolitan was nearly identical to that which women rate as ideal in a sexual partner. Men, in contrast, mistakenly believe women desire a more muscular sex partner, which corresponds more closely with the muscularity of men in Men's Health.

After viewing repeated images of V-shaped bodies, men become more dissatisfied with their own bodies, just as women become more unhappy with their bodies after seeing images of the zero-sized models.

THE FACE OF ATTRACTION

252

여성에게 인기 많은 남성들의 특징

여성이 남성과 잠자리를 같이 하고 싶은 마음이 들게 하는(make a woman to feel like sleeping with a man) 요소는 무엇일까.

남성이 여성에게 어필하는 특징들(the features that make a man appeal to a woman)은 상상보다 훨씬 더 흥미롭고 복잡(be far more fascinating and complex than you could imagine)하다. 여성들이 "와우!" 하는 남성이 있고, "올레!" 하는 남성이 있는데 그 나름의 이유가 있다.

심리학자 신디 메스턴 박사(미국 텍사스대학교)와 데이비드 버스 박사가 저술한 신간《왜 여성들은 성관계를 갖는가》의 발췌본(the extract from the new book 'Why Women Have Sex' by psychologists Dr. Cindy Meston and Dr. David Buss)을 간추려보자.

• 냄새

새로운 과학적 연구에 따르면(according to new scientific researches) 여성은 어떤 남성이 자신에게 맞는지를 결정하기에 앞서(before a woman decides if a man is right for her) 남성의 유전자 구성을 냄새로 알아낸다고(sniff out a man's genetic make-up) 한다.

여성의 후각(a woman's sense of smell)은 임신할 수 있는(can become pregnant) 월경 주기의 중간(during the monthly menstrual cycle) 배란 시기를 전후해 절정에 달하는(reach a peak around the time of her ovulation) 것으로 알려져 있다.

질병을 유발하는 박테리아나 바이러스와 싸우는 유전자들(the genes responsible for fighting off disease-causing bacteria and viruses)은 주요 조직 적합 유전자 복합체(MHC)로 불리는 유전자군(群)에 들어(be found in a group of genes called the major histocompatibility complex, or MHC) 있다.

사람마다 이 유전자의 다양한 변형을 갖고(have various versions of these genes) 있다. 그런데 여성들은 자신들의 그것과 다른 MHC 유전자들을 가진 남성들과 짝을 맺음으로써 두 가지 면에서 이득을 취한다(can benefit in two ways from mating with men whose MHC genes are dissimilar to their own).

그런 짝(such a mate)은 대개 여성 본인과 다른 유전자들을 가진 경우가 많다(be likely to have dissimilar genes in general). 이들 다른 MHC 유전자의 남성과 짝을 지으면, 첫째로 가까운 관계 유전자들의 생식에 따른 여러 선천적 결함 중 많은 것을 방지하는 데 도움을 줄 수(might help to prevent many of the birth defects associated with reproducing with close genetic relatives) 있다.

두 번째로 이점(the second benefit)은 그러한 결합으로 태어난 아이들은 누구나(any children of such a union) 더욱 강한 면역체계를 지니게 된다는(have a more robust immune system) 것이다. 흥미로운 것은 여성들은 냄새로 다른 MHC 유전자를 가진 남성들을 알아낼 수 있다는(be able to sniff out men with dissimilar MHC) 사실이다.

브라질 학자들은 29명의 남성에게 면으로 된 피부 천조각을 5일 동안 걸치도록 해서(ask 29 men to wear cotton skin patches for five days) 땀을, 그리고 체향을 흡수하도록(absorb their sweat and thus their body odors) 했다.

그리고 29명의 표본 여성들(a sample of 29 women)로 하여금 각각의 천조각 냄새를 맡아(smell each cotton patch) 매력적인 것부터 매력적이지 않은 것까지 냄새를 평가하도록(evaluate the odor on a scale from attractive to unattractive) 했다.

과학자들은 이와 함께 혈액 검사를 통해(through blood tests) 각각의 남성과 여성의 특정 MHC 유전자 복합체를 파악(identify the specific MHC complex of each man and woman)했다. 그 결과 여성들은 자신들의 그것과 다른 가장 바람직한 복합체를 가진(have a complex dissimilar to their own to be the most desirable) 남성들의 체향을 짚어냈다.

반면, 자신의 그것과 비슷한 복합체를 가진 남성의 냄새에는 역겨워하며 움찔했다(recoil in disgust). 고도로 발달된 이 후각(this highly developed sense of smell)이 여성들의 성적 관심에 깊은 영향을 미치는(have a profound effect on women's sexuality) 것이다.

진화심리학자(evolutionary psychologist)인 크리스틴 애프가 박사는 48 쌍의 MHC 유사성을 연구한(study MHC similarity in 48 couples) 결과, 각각의 여성과 남성의 유사성 정도(the degree of similarity between each woman and man)가 증가할수록 여성의 남성 상대에 대한 성적인 반응(the woman's sexual responsiveness)은 줄어드는 것으로 나타났다.

또 남성 파트너가 비슷한 유전자를 가졌을 경우 여성은 성관계 갖기를 덜 원하는(want to have sex less often) 것으로 조사됐다. 자신과 비슷한 MHC 남성 파트너를 가진 여성들(women with MHC-similar partners)은 다른 남성들에 대해 더 많은 성적인 환상을 갖는다(have more frequent sexual fantasies about other men).

특히 배란 주기가 가장 왕성할 때(particularly at the most fertile phase of their ovulation cycle) 그런 욕구를 더 느낀다고 한다. 그리고 다른 남성들에 대한 성적인 환상은 단순히 머릿속에 머물지 않고(do not just remain in their heads) 더 높은 비율의 성적 불륜(higher rates of sexual infidelity)으로 이어지는 것으로 조사됐다.

• 키(신장)

여성은 어떤 몸을 바람직하게 생각할까(What sort of body does a woman find desirable?)? 여성이 남성에게 기대하는 가장 분명한 신체적 특징(the most obvious physical characteristic a woman looks for in a man)은 키(height)다.

여성들은 키 큰 남자들을 매력적으로 생각(consider tall men to be attractive)한다. 각종 연구 결과에 따르면, 여성들은 키 큰 남자들을 남편감으로 선호하며(prefer tall men as husbands), 특히 단기적인 섹스 파트너로는 키에 훨씬 더 비중을 높게 두는(put an even greater emphasis on height in shorter-term sex partners) 것으로 나타나고 있다.

실제로 평균보다 키가 큰 남자들(taller-than-average men)은 동거 애인과 자녀가 더 많은(have a greater number of live-in girlfriends and more children) 것으로 조사돼, 연애나 생식 면에서 그들의 인기를 입증하고(confirm their popularity for romance and reproduction) 있다.

키 큰 남성들에 대한 여성들의 선호에는(in women's preference for tall men) 근원적인 논리가 있는 것으로 보인다(there seems to be an underlying logic). 한 예로 서양문화권에서는(in Western cultures) 키 큰 남성들이 작은 남성들보다 더 높은 사회적, 경제적 지위를 갖는(have higher socio-economic status than short men) 경우가 많다.

영국의 경우, 신장이 1인치 더 클 때마다(each added inch of height) 남성의 연봉이 수천 파운드씩 더 증가하는(add several thousand pounds to a man's annual salary) 것으로 조사되고 있다. 평균적으로(on average) 키가 1m 83인 남성은 1m 65인 남성에 비해 30년간의 직장생활 동안 10만 파운드(약 2억 원) 이상을 더 버는(earn more than 100,000 pounds across a 30-year career) 것으로 나타났다.

경찰관인 경우, 키 큰 경찰관들은 작은 키의 동료들보다 공격을 덜 받는다(get assaulted less than their shorter colleagues). 이는 신장이 다른 남성들로부터도 더 많은 존중(more respect from other men)을 받는다는 것을 의미한다. 그러니 이성인 여성들은 어느 쪽을 더 원하겠느냐고(Which one could a woman, the opposite sex, want?) 책의 저자들은 반문한다.

• 체격

키(신장)가 여성들을 자극하는 남성의 신체 사항 중 유일한 것(the only aspect of men's bodies that excites women)은 아니다. 상대 짝 선호도에 대한 연구에 따르면(according to studies of mate preferences) 여성들은 성적인 관계뿐 아니라 장기적 파트너십에 있어서도 힘이 세고, 근육질이며 강건한 남성을 원하는(desire strong, muscular, athletic men for long-term partnerships as well as for sexual liaisons) 것으로 나타나고 있다.

대부분 여성은 엉덩이에 비해 어깨가 넓은 V자형 몸통에 본능적인 선호도(a distinctive preference for a V-shaped torso, broad shoulders relative to hips)를 보인다. 여성들은 또 근육질 상체와 조화를 이룬 날씬한 배에 끌린다고(be attracted to a lean stomach combined with a muscular upper torso) 한다.

그래서인지 엉덩이 대비 어깨가 넓은 남성들(men with a high shoulder-to-hip ratio)은 16세 또는 그 이전의 어린 나이에(at an early age - 16 or younger) 성관계를 갖기 시작하는(begin having sexual intercourse) 것으로 집계되고 있다. 따라서 어깨가 좁은 동료들에 비해 더 많은 섹스 파트너를 갖게(have more sex partners than their slim-shouldered peers) 돼 (한 여성과) 관계를 갖고 있는 도중에도 더 많은 바람을 피우는(have more affairs while in a relationship) 경향이 있다.

그러나 남성들은 여성들이 매력적으로 여기는 근육질의 정도를 너무 과대평가하고(overestimate the degree of muscularity that women find attractive) 있다. 바벨을 들어올리고, 단련된 식스 팩 근육을 과시해야만 하는(need to pump iron and sport a honed six-pack) 것으로 생각한다.

그러나 여성들이 경직된 근육을 지닌 남성 이미지(images of muscle-bound men)를 성적으로 가장 매력적이라고 여기는(find most sexually attractive) 것은 아니다. 마치 불가능할 정도로 여윈 모델들의 사진특집(photo spreads of impossibly thin models)이 여성들로 하여금 남성들이 가장 매력적으로 생각하는 날씬한 정도를 과대평가하게 만드는(lead women to overestimate the degree of thinness that men find most attractive) 것과 같다.

• 얼굴

전통적으로 잘생겼다는 남성과 그보다 덜 매력적인 평범한 남성 중 한 사람을 선택해야 하는 경우가 되면(when it comes to choosing between a conventionally handsome man and an ordinary, less attractive man) 여성들은 그 결정에 어려움을 겪는다(have a difficult choice to make).

여성들은 네모진 턱의 남성적인 얼굴을 평상적인 성적 만남에선 가장 섹시하고 가장 매력적이라고 생각한다(find square-jawed, masculine faces to be the sexiest and the most attractive for a casual sexual encounter). 테스토스테론(남성 호르몬)에 의한 남성적인 얼굴에 대한 여성들의 성적 욕구(women's sexual desires for testosterone-fuelled faces of masculinity)는 여성들의 주기 중 배란 시기 때 특히 강해진다(be especially strong during the fertile window of their cycle).

하지만 여성들은 장기적 관계를 위해서는 어느 정도 덜 남성적인 얼굴이 더 매력적이라고 판단(judge somewhat less masculine faces to be more attractive for a long-term relationship)한다. 여성들은 장기적인 짝을 선택할 때는(when choosing long-term mates) '좋은 아빠'가 될 것 같은 남성들에게 끌린다(be attracted to men who are likely to be 'good dads').

그러나 임신할(become impregnated) 때가 되면 보다 남성적인 얼굴(more masculine faces)이 주는 강건한 건강 신호(the signals of robust health)에 자신도 모르게 끌리게 된다. 남성적 얼굴을 만드는 높은 테스토스테론 생성이 신체의 면역기능을 보장해주기(compromise the body's immune functioning) 때문에 우성을 향한 여성의 본능이 그 쪽으로 기운다는 얘기다.

또 남성적으로 보이는 얼굴(a masculine-looking face)은 남성의 건강(a man's health), 다른 남성들과 경쟁해 성공할 수 있는 능력(his ability to succeed in competing with other men), 보호해줄 수 있는 능력을(his ability to protect) 나타내기 때문이다.

그렇다면 한 가지 수수께끼가 생기게(raise a puzzle) 된다. 여성들은 왜 위험한 관계에서 평생의 사랑에 이르기까지(from dangerous liaisons through to life-long love) 모든 짝짓기 관계에서 매우 남성적인 남성들에게만 끌리지(be attracted to highly masculine males for all mating relationship)는 않는 것일까.

테스토스테론을 더 많이 가진 더 남성적인 남성들(the more masculine men with more testosterone)일수록 성적인 충실도가 적은 경향이 있기(tend to be less sexually faithful) 때문이다. 따라서 대부분 여성들은 '상충성'에 직면하게(face a 'trade-off') 된다.

즉, 덜 남성적인 남성을 선택(choose the less masculine-looking man)하면 보다 좋은 아버지와 성적으로 충실한 짝을 얻게(get a better father and sexually loyal mate) 된다. 반면에 보다 남성적인 남성을 선택하면 건강에 좋은 유전자들을 자식에게 전해줄(endow her children with good genes for health) 수 있지만, 성적인 에너지의 일부를 다른 여성들에게 돌리는(channel some of his sexual energy toward other women) 남성에 대한 대가를 감수해야(must suffer the costs) 하기 때문이다.

• 목소리

목소리의 고저(voice pitch)는 사람의 연설에 있어 가장 인상적인 특징(the most striking feature of human speech)이다. 그중에서도 여성을 성적으로 도취하게 하는 남성의 목소리(male voice that gives women a sexual buzz)가 있다.

사춘기 이전에는(before puberty) 남자와 여자 목소리가 비슷하다. 그러나 사춘기가 되면 현저한 변화가 일어난다(remarkable changes occur). 테스토스테론이 사춘기 소년들에게 변화를 유발(trigger the change in boys at puberty)하는 것이다.

남자아이들은 성대(聲帶) 길이의 급속한 증가를 겪으며(experience a dramatic increase in the length of their vocal cords) 여자아이들의 그것보다 60퍼센트가 더 길어지게(become 60% longer than those of girls) 된다. 더 긴 성대와 성도(聲道)는 더 굵고 공명이 더 큰 목소리가 나게(produce a deeper, more resonant voice) 한다.

최근 연구 결과에 따르면, 여성들이 단기적 관계 또는 장기적 관계의 상대를 선택할 때 남성의 목소리는 결정적 역할을 한다. 굵은 목소리는 여성들의 단기적 또는 장기적 파트너 선택 양쪽에 있어 선호 대상이지만, 오로지 섹스를 위한 단기적 만남 개연성만 놓고 고려할(consider them as prospects for purely sexual, short-term encounters) 경우에는 굵은 목소리 선호도가 훨씬 높다.

특히 배란 주기가 왕성한 단계 때(in the fertile phase of their ovulation cycle)는 굵은 목소리의 남성들에게 가장 성적 매력을 강하게 느끼는(show the strongest sexual attraction to men with deep voices) 것으로 조사됐다.

굵은 목소리는 일반적으로 양호한 건강과 좋은 유전자의 사인으로 받아들여진다(be accepted as a sign of good health and good genes). 그런데 굵은 목소리는 신체의 좌우대칭(the bilateral body symmetry)이 잘 돼 있어야 나오기 때문에 여성들은 자신에게 생길 수 있는 자손을 위해 그 건강한 유전자의 소리(the sound of healthy genes for her possible offspring)를 좇아간다는 것이다.

• 춤과 행동

사람이 춤추는 방식(the way a person dances)은 엄청난 양의 정보를 드러낸다(reveal a huge amount of information). 훌륭한 춤 솜씨(a dancing prowess)는 에너지 수준, 건강 및 생물역학적 효율성 등의 정보를 전달해 준다(convey information about energy level, health and biomechanical efficiency).

한 연구에서는 여성들에게 디지털 처리로 가면을 씌우거나 화소 처리된 춤추는 남성들의 이미지를 보게(have women view digitally masked or pixellated images of men dancing) 했더니, 여성들이 더 크고 더 강렬한 동작들을 보이는 남성에게 끌리는(be attracted to men who display larger and more sweeping movements) 현상을 보였다. 그들을 더 에로틱하게 평가한다는(rate them more erotic) 얘기다.

어떤 여성들은 오로지 춤에 반해서 그 남성들과 성관계를 가지는(have sex with men simply because they are impressed by their dancing) 경우도 있다고 한다. 여성들은 춤 동작들 중에서도 특정 신체의 동작을 다른 것보다 훨씬 매력적인 것으로 느낀다는(find certain body movement to be more attractive than others) 조사 결과도 있다.

남성들 움직임의 다른 행태도 여성들에게 유용한 짝짓기 정보를 제공해(provide women with valuable mating information) 준다. 동성(同性) 간의 쌍방이 아닌 일방적 터치(nonreciprocal same-sex touching)—한 예로 한 남성이 다른 남성의 등에 손을 대는(a man touches another man's back) 것—는 우세를 나타내는 잘 입증된 신호(a well-documented signal of dominance)이다.

여성들은 '손 대는 사람들'이 더 많은 지위를 가진 것으로 여기며(see 'touchers' as having more status), 팔이나 다리를 쭉 펼 때처럼(as when a man stretches his arms or extends his legs) 공간을 최대화하는 동작들(movements that maximize space)을 또 다른 우세 신호(another dominance signal)로 받아들인다고 한다. 또 신체가 열린 자세를 보이는 사람들(those who display open body positioning) - 예를 들어 가슴에 팔짱을 끼지 않은(do not fold their arms across the chest) - 을 더 힘이 있는 쪽으로 판단(be judged to be more potent)한다.

• 개성과 유머

성적 매력(sexual attraction)은 단순히 호환 상대를 찾아 자석처럼 이끌린 육체들의 문제(simply a matter of physical bodies drawn magnetically together in search of compatibility)만이 아니다.

어떤 여성들에게 있어 개성, 특히 뛰어난 유머감각(in particular, a good sense of humor)은 성적인 스파크를 일으키는 데 있어(in generating a sexual spark) 대단히 중요한 역할을 한다. 인터넷 데이트 사이트들 중에 약자로 GSOH(Good Sense Of Humor)가 있다는 것만 봐도 유머가 얼마나 중요한지 알 수 있다.

여성들은 남성의 유머 감각을 단기적, 장기적 관계에 있어 모두 탐나는 특성으로 평가(rate men's sense of humor as a desirable trait)한다. 위트가 있는 남편을 가진(have witty husbands) 여성들은 그렇지 않은 여성들보다 더 결혼생활에 만족해(be more satisfied with their marriages than women who do not)한다.

유머감각이 왜 성적 매력에서 중요한지는(be important in sexual attraction) 과학적 논란의 대상(the subject of scientific debate)이 돼왔다. 유머감각에 관한 남녀 간의 차이는 유머의 생산(남을 웃기는 것)과 유머 감상(남의 농담에 웃어주는 것) 사이에 있다(be between humor production(making others laugh) and humor appreciation(laughing at others' jokes).

유머에 있어서도 남녀 간에 차이가 있다. 남성들은 자신들의 농담에 잘 웃어주는 여성을 유머를 가진 여성으로 규정(define a woman with a good sense of humor as someone who laughs at their jokes)한다. 남성들은 자신들의 유머를 잘 받아주는 여성들(be receptive to their humor)을 좋아하는 것이다.

이와는 대조적으로(in contrast) 여성들은 유머를 구사하는 남성들(men who produce humor)에게 이끌린다. 원 나이트 스탠드부터 평생의 짝짓기까지 모든 유형의 관계에서(for all types of relationships, from one-night stands to lifelong matings) 여성들은 남성들의 유머에 빠져든다.

어쨌든 여성이나 남성 모두 유머감각을 가진 상대를 좋아하는 것은 웃음이 긍정적 분위기를 이끌어내고(elicit a positive mood), 이는 신뢰와 지성의 표시(a sign of confidence and intelligence)로 받아들여지기 때문이다.

What REALLY Makes a Woman Want to Sleep with a Man?

What makes a woman want to sleep with a man? Is it true that a chap can laugh a woman into bed? Does he need to be tall, dark and handsome to stand any chance at all?

Today, in the second extract from the new book Why Women Have Sex, by psychologists Cindy Meston and David Buss, we reveal the features that make a man appeal to a woman, and why, are far more fascinating and complex than you could imagine ···

SIZE MATTERS

What sort of body does a woman find desirable? Perhaps the most obvious physical characteristic she looks for in a man is height.

Studies consistently find that women consider tall men to be attractive.

In analyses of personal ads, 80% of women state they want to meet a man who is 6ft or taller.

Men who indicate in their personal ads that they are tall have also been shown to receive far more responses from women.

Other studies show women prefer tall men as husbands and put an even greater emphasis on height in shorter-term sex partners. Women even place importance on height when selecting sperm donors.

Two studies also found that taller-than-average men tend to have a greater number of live-in girlfriends and more children, confirming their popularity for romance and reproduction.

And there does seem to be an underlying logic in women's preference for tall men. In Western cultures, tall men tend to have higher socio-economic status than short men.

Each added inch of height has been shown to add several thousand pounds to a man's annual salary.

It is estimated that, on average, 6ft men earn more than £100,000 across a 30-year career than 5ft 5in men.

They also tend to be healthier than shorter men – and if they're policemen, they get assaulted less than their shorter colleagues, which suggests height commands more respect from other men. What more could a girl want?

THE SCENT OF SEX

According to new scientific research, a woman will literally sniff out a man's genetic make-up before she decides if he's right for her.

A woman's sense of smell reaches a peak around the time of her ovulation, the 24-hour window -during the monthly menstrual cycle in which she can become pregnant.

The genes responsible for fighting off disease-causing bacteria and viruses are found in a group of genes called the major histocompatibility complex, or MHC.

Different people have various versions of these genes—and it turns out that women can benefit in two ways from mating with men whose MHC genes are dissimilar to their own.

Such a mate is likely to have more dissimilar genes in general, so finding someone dissimilar attractive might help to prevent many of the birth defects associated with reproducing with close genetic relatives. A second benefit is any children of such a union will have a more robust immune system.

The interesting thing is that women seem to be able to sniff out men with dissimilar MHC.

In a revealing study, Brazilian researchers asked 29 men to wear cotton skin patches for five days to absorb their sweat—and thus their body odours.

A sample of 29 women then smelled each cotton patch and evaluated the odour on a scale from attractive to unattractive.

Scientists identified the specific MHC complex of each man and woman through blood tests. Women found the aromas of men who had a complex dissimilar to their own to be the most desirable.

The odours of men who had a complex similar to their own made them recoil in disgust.

This highly developed sense of smell can have a profound effect on women's sexuality.

Evolutionary psychologist Christine Garver-Apgar studied MHC similarity in 48 couples.

They found that as the degree of similarity between each woman and man increased, the woman's sexual responsiveness to her partner decreased.

Women whose partners had similar genes reported wanting to have sex less often. They had less motivation to please their partner sexually compared to the women going out with men with dissimilar genes.

Women with MHC-similar partners also reported more frequent sexual fantasies about other men, particularly at the most fertile phase of their ovulation cycle.

And their sexual fantasies about other men did not just remain in their heads. They also reported higher rates of sexual infidelity.

FIT FOR SEX

Height is not the only aspect of men's bodies that excites women.

Studies of mate preferences reveal that women desire strong, muscular, athletic men for long-term partnerships as well as for sexual liaisons.

Most women also show a distinct preference for a V-shaped torso—broad shoulders relative to hips. They are also attracted to a lean stomach combined with a muscular (but not muscle-bound) upper torso.

In fact, both sexes judge men with a high shoulder-to-hip ratio to be more physically and socially dominant.

This may give a clue to its appeal, since women are not attracted to men who appear as though they could be easily dominated by other men.

Men with a high shoulder-to-hip ratio begin having sexual intercourse at an early age - 16 or younger.

They report having more sex partners than their slim-shouldered peers. But be warned: they have more affairs while in a relationship.

And they report more instances of being chosen by women who are already in relationships for affairs on the side.

Scientific research, though, has discovered that men overestimate the degree of muscularity that women find attractive, assuming they need to pump iron and sport a honed six-pack to be attractive.

Images of muscle-bound men have almost certainly fostered men's misperception of what women find most sexually attractive – just as photo spreads of impossibly thin models have led women to overestimate the degree of thinness that men find most attractive.

One study compared the muscularity of men's bodies in Cosmopolitan magazine (whose readership is 89 percent women) with Men's Health (whose readership is 85% men).

The level of muscularity in Cosmopolitan was nearly identical to that which women rate as ideal in a sexual partner. Men, in contrast, mistakenly believe women desire a more muscular sex partner, which corresponds more closely with the muscularity of men in Men's Health.

After viewing repeated images of V-shaped bodies, men become more dissatisfied with their own bodies, just as women become more unhappy with their bodies after seeing images of size zero models.

THE FACE OF ATTRACTION

When it comes to choosing between a rugged, conventionally handsome man and an ordinary, less attractive partner, women have a difficult choice to make.

In a series of scientific studies, women found square-jawed, masculine faces to be the sexiest and the most attractive for a casual sexual encounter.

But they judged somewhat less masculine faces to be more attractive for a long-term relationship.

Women's sexual desires for testosterone-fuelled facial cues of masculinity were especially strong during the fertile window of their cycle. The most plausible interpretation of these results is that women are attracted to men who are likely to be 'good dads' when choosing long-term mates, but are attracted to the signals of robust health that more masculine faces provide when they are most likely to become impregnated.

Why do more masculine faces signify health? High testosterone production actually compromises the body's immune functioning, leaving men less able to fight off diseases and parasites in adolescence.

Only men who are above average in healthiness during adolescence can 'afford' to produce the high levels of testosterone that masculinise the face.

Less healthy adolescents can't afford to compromise their already precarious immune systems, and so produce lower levels of testosterone at precisely the time when facial bones take their adult form.

So, a masculine-looking face signals a man's health, his ability to succeed in competing with other men and his ability to protect.

This interpretation, however, raises a puzzle: Why wouldn't women be attracted to highly masculine males for all mating relationships, from dangerous liaisons through to life-long love?

The answer lies in the fact that the more masculine men, with more testosterone, tend to be less sexually faithful.

They are more likely to be the risk-taking, womanising bad boys among the male population.

Consequently, most women face a trade- off: if they choose the less masculine-looking man, they are likely to get a better father and sexually loyal mate, but they lose out in the currency of genes for good health.

If they choose the more masculine man, they can endow their children with good genes for health, but must suffer the costs of a man who channels some of his sexual energy toward other women. It's a tricky choice.

A SEXY VOICE

Voice pitch is the most striking feature of human speech and, according to research, there is a definite sound of sexiness—something about male voices that gives women a sexual buzz.

Before puberty, male and female voices are similar. At puberty, however, remarkable changes occur. Boys experience a dramatic increase in the length of their vocal cords, which become 60% longer than those of girls.

Longer vocal cords and tracts produce a deeper, more resonant voice pitch.

Testosterone triggers the change in boys at puberty and high levels of testosterone predict deeper voices among adult men.

Recent investigations show that whether women are looking for a short-term or long-term relationship is critical in how they choose among men's voices.

Evolutionary anthropologist David Puts obtained voice recordings of 30 men attempting to persuade a woman to go out on a romantic date.

Then 142 heterosexual women listened to the recordings and rated each man's attractiveness for a short-term sexual encounter and a long-term committed relationship.

Though women said the deeper voices were more attractive in both mating contexts, they dramatically preferred the deeper voices when considering them as prospects for purely sexual, short-term encounters.

Moreover, women in the fertile phase of their ovulation cycle showed the strongest sexual attraction to men with deep voices.

One hint as to why this is so is found in studies of female frogs. They gravitate towards male bullfrogs with deep, resonant croaks, which are a reliable signal—for frogs—of a mate's size and health.

Research on people has revealed two similar reasons that help to explain why women find some men's voices much more attractive than others.

The first involves bilateral body symmetry (when both sides of the body are symmetrical), which is commonly accepted as a sign of good health and good genes.

Body symmetry is also more likely to produce deep voices.

So when a woman finds the resonance of a man's voice even sexier during her fertile, ovulatory phase, she is attracted to the sound of healthy genes for her possible offspring.

SOMETHING IN THE WAY HE MOVES

The way a person dances reveals a huge amount of information. It broadcasts information about age.

What REALLY makes a woman want to dancing prowess of younger versus older dancers. It also conveys information about energy level, health and biomechanical efficiency.

In fact, in our studies, we found that some women had sex with men simply because they'd been impressed by their dancing. Research reveals that women find certain body movements to be more attractive than others.

One study had women view digitally masked or pixellated images of men dancing. They were more attracted to men who displayed larger and more sweeping movements. They also rated these men more erotic.

Other patterns of men's movements provide women with valuable mating information. Nonreciprocal same-sex touching—when a man touches another man's back, for example—is a well-documented signal of dominance.

Women see 'touchers' as having more status, a key component of a man's mate value. Movements that maximise space, as when a man stretches his arms or extends his legs, are another dominance signal.

Those who display open body positioning—for example, by not folding their arms across the chest—are judged to be more potent and persuasive.

SEXY PERSONALITY

Sexual attraction isn't simply a matter of physical bodies drawn magnetically together in search of compatibility.

For some women, personality—in particular, a good sense of humour—is equally, if not more, important in generating a sexual spark.

One indication of the importance of a good sense of humour in a man is that it is one of the few personality traits that has its own abbreviation in online dating sites: GSOH.

Another is that research shows married women who think their husbands are witty are more satisfied with their marriages than women who do not.

Women rate it as a desirable trait in short-term sexual and long-term romantic relationships.

Why a sense of humour is so important in sexual attraction has been the subject of scientific debate.

One critical distinction is between humour production (making others laugh) and humour appreciation (laughing at others' jokes).

There's a sex difference—men define a woman with a good sense of humour as someone who laughs at their jokes. Men especially like women who are receptive to their humour.

Women, in contrast, are attracted to men who produce humour, and that's true for all types of relationships, from one-night stands to lifelong matings.

The most likely explanation for why women and men alike are attracted to those with a sense of humour is because laughing elicits a positive mood—it's a sign of confidence and intelligence, too.

☑ 기억하면 좋을 구절!

sniff out 냄새로 ~을 알아내다

The dogs are trained to *sniff out* dugs.
그 개들은 냄새로 마약을 찾아내도록 훈련을 받는다.

reach a peak 절정에 이르다 / 피크를 이루다

The beauty of the mountain *reaches a peak* during the fall of the leaf.
그 산의 아름다움은 가을 낙엽질 무렵 절정에 이른다.

recoil in digust 역겨워 움찔하다

These pictures should make any decent human being recoil in disgust.
이 사진들은 어떤 점잖은 사람이라도 역겨워 움찔하게 할 것이다.

lay emphasis on ~을 강조하다 / 중시하다

He *laid emphasis on* practical work.
그는 실제 업무를 중시했다.

at most 기껏해야 / 고작해야

It will take five minutes *at most*.
기껏해야 5분 걸릴 것이다.

be endowed with 재능이 있다 / ~을 타고나다

He *was endowed with* extraordinary talents.
그는 재능이 출중했다.

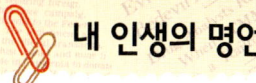

내 인생의 명언 — 꿈은 이루어진다

▶ 꿈을 밀고 나갈 용기만 있다면 모든 꿈은 이루어진다.
월트 디즈니 (미국 만화영화 제작자)

> All your dreams can come true
> if you have the courage to pursue them.
> Walt Disney

▶ 꿈은 한 번에 단 한 명만의 주인 밖에 갖지 않는다.
그래서 꿈을 가진 사람은 외로운 것이다.
에르마 봄벡 (미국 유머작가)

> Dreams have only one owner at a time.
> That's why dreamers are lonely.
> Erma Bombeck

▶ 어머니는 "네가 군인 병사이면 장군이 될 것이다.
수도사이면 교황이 될 것이다"라고 말씀하셨다.
나는 화가였기 때문에 피카소가 됐다.
파블로 피카소 (스페인 입체파 화가)

> My mother said to me, 'If you are a soldier,
> you will become a general. If you are a monk,
> you will become the Pope.'
> Instead, I was a painter, and became Picasso.
> Pablo Picasso

▶ 지금 자면 꿈을 꿀 것이고, 지금 공부하면 꿈을 이룰 것이다.
하버드대학교 명언 30가지 중에서

> If you sleep now, you will have a dream.
> If you study now, your dream will come true.
> An wise saying from Havard University

"Five Scientific Reasons to Serve Parents with Devotion"

자식에게는 어머니의 유전자가 더 강하다고 한다

어머니에게 효도해야 하는 5가지 이유

한국에선 5월 8일이 어버이날이지만, 미국에선 5월 둘째 주 일요일이 '어머니의 날', 6월 셋째 주 일요일이 '아버지의 날'이다.

미국의 과학전문 웹사이트 라이브사이언스(LiveScience.com)가 어머니들이 당연히 대접을 받아야 할 '다섯 가지 과학적 이유'(5 scientific reasons)를 소개했다.

옛날부터 어머니들은 아이들 콧물을 닦아주는(wipe snot off kids' noses) 일부터 집안 청소(cleaning the house), 모든 가족의 재정·사회적 계획까지 챙겨야 하는(handle all the family's finances and social plans) 등 온갖 잡일들을 돌봐야(do all the household chores) 했다. 한마디로(in short) 어머니들은 어려운 생활을 해야(have it tough) 하는 숙명을 타고 난 듯했다.

세상이 많이 달라져 어느 정도(to some extent) 가사일에서 해방됐다(be liberated from doing the houseworks)고는 하지만, 요즘엔 기본적인 집안일을 챙기면서 생업에도 종사하고(work a day job), 일자리를 갖지 않으면 죄책감을 느껴야(feel guilty for not having one) 하는 부담감까지 가지는 신세가 됐다.

• **어머니는 더 많은 고통을 겪는다.**

제대로 된 남자라면 누구나(any man worth his salt) 출산이라는 한 가지 단순한 이유 때문이라도 어머니가 평생 '발 마사지'를 받을 자격이 있다(deserve a lifetime of 'foot massages' for one simple reason: childbirth)고 생각해야 한다.

실제로 아이를 낳는 것은 엄청나게 고통스러운(hurt like hell) 일이다. 하지만 그게 전부가 아니다(that's not all). 여자는 전체적으로 남자보다 더 많은 고통을 겪게(suffer more pain than men across the board) 돼 있다. '달마다 겪는 그때'(that time of the month)만 그런 것이 아니다. 평생의 고통을 말하는(talk about a lifetime of suffering) 것이다.

한 예로 65세 이상 된 미국인들 중에서(among American people over 65) 여성은 같은 나이의 남성보다 2.5배 많은 장애를 겪고 있는(suffer 2.5 times more disabilities than men of the same age) 것으로 조사됐다. 가장 흔한 고질병 중에서도(among the most common chronic conditions) 특히 여성들이 많이 앓는 것은 고통스러운 관절염(painful arthritis)이다.

• **도움 받을 곳이 더 적어졌다**

예전에(in the old days) 어머니들은 아이 양육이나 살림살이에서 많은 도움을 받을(have tremendous help raising kids and keeping house) 수 있었다. 자진해서든 아니든(willingly or otherwise) 할아버지 할머니와 성장한 자녀들이 어린 아이들을 돌보는 여성들을 도와 부담을 덜어주곤(take the load off women burdened with small children) 했다.

오늘날의 어머니는 예전보다도 자녀 양육과 집안 청소에서 훨씬 더 적은 도움 밖에 받지 못하고(have a lot less help with childrearing and housecleaning) 있다. 아버지들이 협조한다고는(pitch in) 하지만, 그 결과가 어떤 식으로 되는지는 당신도 잘 알지 않느냐고(you know well how that goes) 라이브사이언스는 되묻는다. "여보, 게임이 시작됐네(Honey, the game's on). 진공청소기 청소 내일 다 할께(I'll finish the vacuuming tomorrow)"라며 넘어가지 않느냐는 얘기다.

미국의 경우, 1880년에는 학교에 가지 않거나(do not go to school) 집 밖으로 일 나가지 않는(do not go to work outside the house) 10세 이상의 여성과 함께 사는(live with a female aged 10 or older) 어머니의 비율이 24%에 달했지만, 2000년 현재 그 비율은 5%에 불과하다.

• 자식은 어머니에 더 가까운 존재다.

인간의 유전자(the human beings' genes) 절반은 어머니로부터(be half from Mom), 다른 절반은 아버지로부터(be half from Dad) 받는 것으로 알려져 있다. 하지만 최근 연구에 따르면 무슨 이유에서인지(for some reasons) 어머니의 유전자(Mom's genes)가 자녀 형성에 더 큰 영향을 미치는(have a greater effect on what the children become) 것으로 밝혀졌다.

하나의 단적인 예(one stark example)를 들어보자. 태아가 자궁에 있을(be in the uterus) 때 엄마가 매우 스트레스 받는 경험을 할(have a very stressful experience) 경우, 아기는 불안장애를 갖게 될 위험이 더 크다(be at greater risk for anxiety disorders). 임신 중 어머니의 음식 섭취(the mother's diet during pregnancy)가 자녀 유전자에 영향을 미친다는(affect the child's genes) 연구 결과도 발표됐다.

더욱 놀라운 것은(more surprising) 어머니가 어린 시절 먹었던 것과 노출됐던 독소(what the mother ate when she was a child, the toxins she was exposed to), 임신 전과 도중의 다른 경험들(other experiences before and during pregnancy)이 모두 어머니가 자녀에게 전달하는 유전자들이 자녀의 몸속에 실제로 어떻게 나타나는가에 영향을 미친다(affect how the genes the mother passes on to the child actually get expressed in the child's body)는 사실이다.

- **자녀들 때문에 평생 속을 썩인다**

자식 기르는 일은 평생 끝나지 않는다(raising kids never ends). 자녀들이 아무리 좋은 자식이 되려고 노력한다 하더라도(no matter how hard the children try to be a good kid) 자녀들로 인한 고뇌와 실망은 언제까지나 어머니를 따라다닌다(the heartache and frustration caused by the children stick with Mom forever).

최근 한 연구에 따르면 성인이 된 자녀와 부모들 중 94%(94% of adult children and their parents)가 관계에 있어 어느 정도의 불안감을 갖고 있는(have some level of tension in the relationship) 것으로 집계됐다. 부담감을 느끼는(feel the most strain) 것은 대부분 부모 쪽이다. 특히 성장한 자녀들의 가계 형편과 살림살이 능력에 대해(particularly about the household finances and housekeeping prowess of their grown children) 부모들은 끊임없이 애를 태운다.

• 어머니, 휴식이 절실한 나날들

아버지도 마찬가지이지만, 특히 어머니는 몹시 휴식을 필요로 하고(cry out for a break) 있다. 여성들은 남성에 비해 훨씬 적은 자유시간을 가지며(have much less free time), 더 심한 압박감을 느낀다(feel more rushed then men)고 한다.

미국에서 발표된 최신 연구 결과로는 남성은 여성에 비해 매일 40분 더 많은 여유 시간을 갖는(men have 40 minutes more leisure time every day than women) 것으로 나타났다. 지난 2005년 조사에 따르면 근로여성 중 약 20%(nearly 20 percent of working women)는 6년에 한 차례 겨우 휴가를 가며(take a vacation only once every 6 years), 4분의 1가량은 2~5년에 한 번 휴가 시간을 갖는(get a vacation only once every two to five years) 것으로 조사됐다.

그 때문인지 임금이 줄더라도 근무시간을 줄였으면 하는(want to cut back on work hours) 바람을 가진 근로여성들은 남성보다 두 배나 더 많은 수치인(twice as many working women as men)것으로 나타났다. 그만큼 어머니들이 삶에 지쳐 있다는 얘기다.

5 Scientific Reasons Mom Deserves Mother's Day

If you haven't yet planned the brunch or picked out the flowers or at least mailed the card, then consider what follows the only motivation you should need. In short, mothers have it tough.

Changes in American culture have liberated women in many ways. Mom is now free to do all the chores moms have been doing for generations—such as wiping snot off kids' noses, cleaning the house and handling all the family's finances and social plans—and now she can work a day job or feel guilty for not having one, too.

Mom deals with all this, studies show, with less help and as much pain and stress as ever. Consider:

5. Mom Feels More Pain

Any man worth his salt realizes Mom deserves a lifetime of foot rubs for one simple reason: childbirth. She made you. And yeah, it hurt like hell. But that's not all. Women suffer more pain than men across the board, studies find.

And it's not just "that time of the month" pain. We're talking about a lifetime of suffering.

A study out last week found that among people over 65, women suffer 2.5 times more disabilities than men of the same age. Among the most common chronic conditions: painful arthritis.

Even sex, which gloriously led to your conception and which ought to be the ultimate respite, can be painful for women. About 15 percent of women experience recurring genital pain during intercourse. Almost no men do.

4. Mom Gets No Help

In the old days, mothers had tremendous help raising kids and keeping house. It was, literally, a family affair, with grandparents and children working daily, willingly or otherwise, to take the load off women burdened with small children.

Today's mom has a lot less help with childrearing and housecleaning, a study in 2006 found. Sure, fathers are pitching in, but you know how that goes. "Honey, the game's on. I'll finish the vacuuming tomorrow."

In 1880, 24 percent of mothers lived with a female age 10 or older who didn't go to school and didn't work outside the house. By 2000, that number was 5 percent.

3. You Are Mostly Your Mother's Child

Yeah, sure, your genes are half from Mom, half from Dad. But for some reason, scientists recently learned, Mom's genes have a greater effect on what you become.

One stark example: While you were in the uterus, if your mother had a very stressful experience, you'll be at greater risk for anxiety disorders. And a new study on rats, out last month, indicates that your mother's diet during pregnancy affected your genes.

More surprising, studies are showing that what your mother ate when she was a child, the toxins she was exposed to, and other experiences before and during pregnancy affect how the genes she passes on to you actually get expressed in your body.

Another study, reported this year in the journal Child Development, shows a profound impact of nurturing by mothers in the early years, too. A child who has a strong relationship with Mom during preschool years tends to form closer friendships in grade school, the research revealed.

2. You, Child, Are Depressing

Raising kids never ends. And no matter how hard you try to be a good kid, the challenge ? and the heartache and frustration that comes with it ? sticks with Mom forever.

A new study finds **94 percent** of adult children and their parents report some level of tension in the relationship. But it's the parents who feel the most strain, particularly about the finances and housekeeping prowess of their grown children.

Yes, Mom and Dad both stress out to raise their children. Parents have significantly higher levels of depression than child-free adults, and the problem gets worse when the kids move out, according to a 2006 study in the Journal of Health and Social Behavior.

1. Mom Needs a Break

To be fair, Dad takes a beating, too. But the evidence is clear: Mom has it worse. Whether you agree with that or not, here's the No. 1 reason you should do something nice for your mother on Sunday: She's crying out for a break.

Women have less free time and feel more rushed than men, studies have found. A study out just this week found U.S. men report 40 minutes more leisure time every day than women (in Italy, it's an 80-minute spread).

A startling study in 2005 found nearly 20 percent of working women take a vacation only once every 6 years, and nearly a quarter get one only once every two to five years.

In response, twice as many working women as men said in 2007 that they wanted to cut back on work hours, even if it means a pay cut.

☑ 기억하면 좋을 구절!

wipe off 닦다, 없애다, 훔쳐내다
> I will *wipe off* a disgrace.
> 이 불명예를 없앨 것이다.

household chores 허드레 가사일
> She is tied up with *household chores*.
> 그녀는 가사일에 얽매여 있다.

hurt like hell 끔찍하게 아프다
> It will still *hurt like hell*.
> 여전히 무척 아플 것이다.

any one worth one's salt 제 몫을 하는 사람이라면 누구나
> *Everybody* wants a job *worth one's salt*.
> 누구나 자신의 급료에 상응한 일을 하고 싶어 한다.

anxiety disorders 불안 장애, 분리 장애
> Women have a higher rate of *anxiety disorders* to men.
> 남성에 비해 여성이 불안 장애를 보일 확률이 높다.

willingly or otherwise 자진해서든 아니든
> This uncertain world is what most of us find ourselves entering, *willingly or otherwise*.
> 우리 대부분은, 자진해서든 아니든, 이 불확실한 세상에 발을 들여놓는 자신을 발견하게 된다.

내 인생의 명언 — 어머니는 여자보다 위대하다

▶ 여자는 엄마, 아내, 정치인의 역할을 겸비해야 한다.
엠마 보니노 (이탈리아 정치인)

> A woman must combine the role of mother, wife and politician.
> Emma Bonino

▶ 자식은 어머니 인생의 정신적 지주다.
소포클레스 (그리스 비극 시인)

> Sons are the anchors of a mother's life.
> Sophocles

▶ 어머니는 담배를 피웠다. 우리에겐 피우지 않기를 바라셨다.
한번은 헛간에서 나오는 연기를 어머니가 보셨다. 우리는 회초리를 맞았다.
로레타 린 (미국 가수 · 작곡가)

> Mommy smoked but she didn't want us to.
> She saw smoke coming out of the barn one time,
> so we got whipped.
> Loretta Lynn

▶ 어머니는 나에게 우리 모두는 꿈을 이룰 수 있는 힘을 갖고 있다고 가르치셨다. 하지만 나에겐 용기가 없었다.
클레이 에이킨 (미국 가수 · 작곡가)

> My mother taught me that we all have the power
> to achieve our dreams. What I lacked was the courage.
> Clay Aiken

Favorite famous sayings!

▶ 모성의 힘은 때때로 자연의 법칙보다 더 위대하다.
바버러 킹솔버 (미국 소설가 · 시인)

> The strength of motherhood is greater than natural laws.
> Barbara Kingsolver

▶ 엄마의 가슴은 아이의 교실이다.
헨리 비쳐 (미국 성직자)

> The mother's heart is the child's schoolroom.
> Henry Beecher

▶ 어머니가 불러주시곤 했던 노래와 같은 예술은
이 세상에 없다.
빌리 선데이 (미국 복음전도가)

> There is nothing in the world of art like
> the songs mother used to sing.
> William Ashley Sunday

▶ 그래요, 어머니. 어머니에게 결함이 있다는 것을 알았어요.
당신은 그걸 숨기지 않았지요. 그것이 저에겐 가장 위대한 선물이었어요.
앨리스 워커 (미국 작가)

> Yes, Mother. I can see you are flawed.
> You have not hidden it.
> That is your greatest gift to me.
> Alice Walker

News English

"Man-flu"

Imagine for a moment that a member of the U.S. Marine Corps, hardened by four overseas deployments, has endured broken limbs and other serious injuries. Yet, at the first sign of a cold, this trained soldier collapses into a pathetic and helpless pile.

Such a situation is nothing new for Leanne, who preferred that her last name not be disclosed. She said she is amazed by how, at the first sign of a cold, her husband can turn from warrior to what she calls "wimp."

"My husband's been to war five times and a simple head cold takes him down for the count," she said.

She says many women agree that what is regarded as a common cold for women can go simple silent to men. In fact, the ailment has its own name: "man-flu."

An expression popularly coined in the UK, man-flu is a tongue-in-cheek term used to describe any man's experience of getting the common cold.

The phrase, which is gaining popularity among American women, highlights the irony that a man with perhaps the highest level of cold symptoms as a woman, dramatizes his sniffles as if they were a more serious ailment.

"The man-flu is best described as a hangover that's supposed to make you feel bad for him," Leanne said.

Another hallmark of the man-flu is the propensity to bring forth a double standard when it comes to sickness between the sexes. While a man might wish for his may regard it as just right so long out in front of the TV, to become. And sleep for days, perhaps even suggesting on his own even with the proof...

asked of a victim of man-flu likely evokes a perfectly rehearsed sequence of grotesque moans, followed by a dramatic series of short coughs and then a reminder that he has come down with an ailment that has never been seen.

But while some women may...

things that our society has developed is a form of humor that mocks the people that have the power," said Asprinsky. "I think we still live in a society where the sex roles are still divided and...

엄청난 엄살덩어리 남자 감기 환자

paradoxical to make a big thing out of a head cold," he said. "You can wallow in that misery without any serious risk."

And the man-flu is not only a term used between spouses. Leanne said her father and brother also claim to feel so over the top that her mother waits on them hand and foot.

"They just lie in bed with their arms outstretched like death might greet them at any moment," she said.

A Upside to Man-flu?

While there is no evidence suggesting whether or why men suffer worse physical symptoms than women when hit by the cold, Hoban said one of the many benefits of man-flu is that men take the time to rest and fully recover from their ailment while many women may not. Perhaps more women should take note, she said.

"I think it's instinctual for women to be nurturing and caregivers," said Hoban. "I think most women do it willingly, then go downstairs and joke about it."

Rason agreed that while cold symptoms may feel uncomfortable for both men and women, a man may take the advantage of a woman's willingness to care for him while he is sick.

Maybe women shouldn't be so surprised that men are so vulnerable, said Rason. For Leanne, who says she will inevitably endure many more cases of her husband "suck up buttercup"...

남자가 감기에 걸리면?

날씨가 쌀쌀해지면서 부부가 함께 감기에 걸렸다. 남편과 아내, 어느 쪽이 더 심하게 앓을까.

대개는 남편 쪽이다. 미ABC방송 인터넷판이 보도한 예를 보자. 린(Leanne)이라는 여성의 남편은 네 차례 해외 파병을 통해 단련된(be hardened by four overseas deployments) 미 해병대원(a member of the U.S. Marine Corps)이다. 팔다리 골절과 다른 심한 부상도 견뎌낸(endure broken limbs and other serious injuries) 역전의 용사(an experienced warrior)다.

하지만 감기가 들자 이 '용사'는 이내 애처롭고 무력한 존재로 전락하고(collapse into a pathetic and helpless pile) 만다. 아내인 린은 남편이 어쩌다 한 번 감기에 걸리면 갑자기 전사(戰士)에서 겁쟁이로 변모(suddenly turn from a warrior to a wimp)한다며 의아해한다. 단순한 코감기(a simple head cold)가 남편을 완전히 무기력하게 만들어(take him down for the count)버린다고 하소연한다.

여성들에겐 보통의 감기(a common cold for women)인데 남성들에겐 단순한 병이 아닌(be no simple ailment for men) 것처럼 보일 때가 많다는 데 상당수 주부들은 의견을 같이하고 있다. 그래서 주부들 사이에 생겨난 신조어(a newly coined word)가 '남성 감기'(man-flu)다.

'남성 감기'라는 표현이 보통 감기에 걸린 남성들의 경험을 묘사하는 데 사용되는(be used to describe any man's experience of getting the common cold) 비아냥조의 용어(a tongue-in-cheek term)가 되면서 주부들 사이에 인기를 얻고(gain popularity among housewives) 있다는 것이다.

여자와 비슷한 정도의 감기 증상을 겪는 남자(a man with the same level of cold symptoms as a woman)가 마치 훨씬 더 심각한 질병을 앓는 듯(as if he suffers a far more serious ailment) 코 훌쩍거림이나 기침을 극적으로 표현해(dramatize his sniffles and coughs) 여자들이 한심해할 정도라는 얘기다.

'남성 감기'의 또 다른 특징(another hallmark of the man-flu)은 이중적인 기준을 가져오는 경향(a propensity to bring forth a double standard)이 있다는 점이다. 다시 말해(so to speak) 감기에 걸린 남자는 텔레비전 앞에 죽치고 앉아(camp out in front of the television) 있거나 며칠 동안 샤워와 양치질도 하지 않으며(skip shower and toothbrushing) 며칠 동안 잠만 자는 것을 마치 권리처럼 여긴다(regard it as his right).

반면 여자들은 자리에 눕기(be sick in bed)는커녕 이내 감기를 이겨내고(get over the flu) 일상적인 집안일을 하는(be obliged to carry out their daily housework) 것이 당연시 된다는 것이다.

그럼 남자들은 왜 그럴까. 미국 에머리대 의과대학의 찰스 레이슨 박사는 "남자들이 실제로 여자들과 달리 질병의 신체적 영향을 겪는(indeed experience some physical effects of illness differently than women) 것일 수 있다"고 말한다. "남자와 여자가 감기를 겪는 차이를 증명해줄 확실한 증거는(a hard evidence that proves the difference between how men and women experience colds) 없지만, 여자들은 감정적 스트레스 때 의기소침해지는 경우가 많은 데(be more likely to live depression under emotional stress) 비해 남자들은 아플 때 나약해진다(get emasculated when they are sick)"고 한다.

이와 관련해 심리학자인 아몬드 애서린스키 박사는 "남성에 대한 고정관념에서 벗어나려는 의도적 전술(an intentional tactic of dethroning the stereotypical idea of a man)"이라고 지적한다. 그는 "우리는 아직 남녀 성별 역할이 구분돼 있는 사회에 살고(live in a society where the sex roles are still divided) 있다"며 "힘이 세고 강인(be strong and tough)해야 한다는 관념 속에 자라온 남자들이 갑자기(all of a sudden) 아프게 되면 잠시나마 약해질 수 있는 기회를 허락받은(be allowed short opportunity to be vulnerable) 것으로 여긴다"는 것이다. 남자들은 그걸 최대한 이용한다(milk it for all it's worth)는 것이 애서린스키 박사의 주장이다.

남자들은 감기 증상을 알리려는(make their cold symptoms known) 듯 팔을 쭉 늘어뜨리고 침대에 누워(lie in the bed with their arms outstretched)

버린다.

 그러면 본능적인 모성애(instinctive mother's affection)를 가진 아내들은 정성껏 남편을 시중들기(wait on the husband hand and foot) 마련이다. 이를 두고 애서린스키 박사는 "남자들 비겁함의 대단히 재미있는 형태"(a very funny form of men's cowardice)라고 지적했다.

The "Man-Flu"

Imagine for a moment that a member of the U.S. Marine Corps, hardened by four overseas deployments, has endured broken limbs and other serious injuries.

Yet, at the first sign of a cold, this trained soldier collapses into a pathetic and helpless pile.

Such a situation is nothing new for Leanne, who preferred that her last name not be disclosed. She said she is fascinated by how, at the first sign of a cold, her husband can turn from warrior to what she calls "wimp."

"My husband's been to war four times, and a simple head cold takes him down for the count," she said.

She says many women agree that what is regarded as a common cold for women is no simple ailment to men. In fact, it even has its own name:

"man-flu."

An expression popularly coined in Britain, man-flu is a tongue-in-cheek term used to describe any man's experience of getting the common cold.

The phrase, which is gaining popularity among American women, highlights the irony that a man with perhaps the same level of cold symptoms as a woman, will dramatize his sniffles as if they were a far more serious ailment.

"The man-flu is best described as a hangover that's supposed to make you feel bad for him," Leanne said.

Another hallmark of the man-flu is its propensity to bring forth a double standard when it comes to sickness between the sexes. While a man with the flu may regard it as his right to camp out in front of the television and sleep for days—perhaps even skipping showers and the toothbrush—women may be expected to soldier through the flu, carrying out their daily routines.

Worse, any favors asked of a victim of man-flu likely evokes a perfectly rehearsed sequence of grotesque moans, followed by a dramatic series of short coughs and then a reminder that he has come down with an ailment that has never been seen.

But while some women may claim to be able to call their husbands' bluffs, some experts say there may be a bit of truth to the man-flu theory.

Do Men With Colds Feel Worse?

Dr. Charles Raison, clinical director of the Mind/Body Program at Emory University School of Medicine in Atlanta, said that while features used to describe man-flu are at times exaggerated, men may indeed experience some physical effects of illness differently than women.

"There's a lot of evidence to suggest that women are more [emotionally] sensitive than men," said Raison. "But what's interesting is that we see men at one of their most vulnerable moments when sick."

He added that there is no hard evidence that proves a difference between how men and women experience colds. But according to Raison, studies have shown that while women are more likely to experience depression under emotional stress, men are most vulnerable when they are sick.

"There is stronger association between sickness systems in the body and depression in men than women," said Raison. "This may support why men have a rougher time than women."

Getting Even With the Man

There may also be a social basis for the idea of man-flu. Armond Aserinsky, a clinical psychologist who has spent more than a decade focusing on exploring the psychology of partners in marriage, said that however amusing it may be to ridicule a man, man-flu can also be seen as an intentional tactic of dethroning the stereotypical idea of a man.

"I think that one of the things that our society has developed is a form of humor that mocks the people that have the power," said Aserinsky. "I think we still live in a society where the sex roles are still divided and man-flu is a tactic to mock the idea of the head of household."

Dr. Donna Hoban, senior vice president and director of medical services and a family medicine specialist at William Beaumont Hospitals, said man-flu is less about the physical mechanisms and scientific data and more about society's view on gender roles.

"Men have to be strong and tough, that's what our society would say," said Hoban. "And all of a sudden when they're sick, it allows them a short opportunity to be vulnerable."

It's Just a Cold, Honey

Leanne recalled times when both she and her husband, who have been married for six years, had come down with a cold. He stayed in bed, she said, while she took care of their two children. However, Leanne said, her husband refused to take medication or see a doctor when she agreed that his case may be more serious than hers.

"I think my husband doesn't get sick very often," she said. "But when he does get the one or two big colds, he milks it for all it's worth."

According to Aserinsky, even men who are normally tough do not feel threatened by making their cold symptoms known.

"The cold can make you miserable without being threatening, so a man can give into that," Aserinsky said.

Many men may deny larger health concerns out of fear that they may find something more serious, Aserinsky said. So some men view a cold as a safer form of illness.

"It's a very funny form of cowardice, and it's paradoxical to make a big thing out of a head cold," he said. "You can wallow in that misery without any serious risk."

And the man-flu is not only a term used between spouses. Leanne said her father and brother also claim to feel so over the top that her mother waits on them hand and foot.

"They just lie in the bed with their arms outstretched like death might greet them at any moment," she said.

A Upside to Man-Flu?

While there is no evidence suggesting whether or why men suffer worse physical symptoms than women when hit by the cold, Hoban said one of the many benefits of man-flu is that men take the time to rest and fully recover from their ailment while many women may not. Perhaps more women should take note, she said.

"I think it's instinctual for women to be nurturing and caregivers," said

Hoban. "I think most women do it willingly, then go downstairs and joke about it."

Raison agreed that while cold symptoms may feel uncomfortable for both men and women, a man may take the advantage of a woman's willingness to care for him while he is sick.

"Maybe women shouldn't be so surprised that men are so vulnerable," said Raison.

But for Leanne, who says she will inevitably endure many more cases of man-flu, she can't help but wish she could tell her husband, "Buck up, buttercup."

☑ 기억하면 좋을 구절!

collapse into ~에 빠지다 / 참지 못하고 ~하다

Many people *collapse into* a dreary and hysterical depression.
많은 사람들이 음산하고 히스테리적인 의기소침에 빠진다.

a newly coined word 신조어

Those *newly coined words* have gained foothold.
그러한 신조어들이 상용화되게 됐다.

so to speak 말하자면

I was a poor, *so to speak*.
말하자면 나는 가난뱅이였다.

get over 극복하다, 처리하다

She can't *get over* her shyness.
그녀는 부끄러움을 이기지 못했다.

be obliged to 하는 수 없이 ~ 하다

We *were obliged to* obey him.
우리는 그에게 복종하는 수밖에 없었다.

have one's tongue in one's cheek 빈정대며 말하다 / 조롱조로 말하다

We were all disappointed when we found out that the kind man *had* in fact *his tongue in his cheek*.
우리는 그 친절한 남자가 사실은 빈정대며 말하고 있다는 것을 알아내고 모두 실망했다.

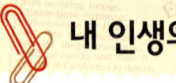

내 인생의 명언 — 역설의 미학

▶ 설명하지 마라. 친구라면 설명할 필요가 없고,
  적이라면 어차피 당신을 믿으려 하지 않을 테니까.
  알버트 하버드 (미국 작가)

> Never explain. Your friends do not need it
> and your enemies will not believe you anyway.
> Albert Havard

▶ 당신의 작품이 스스로 말을 할 때 당신은 끼어들지 마라.
  헨리 카이저 (미국 기업가)

> When your work speaks for itself, don't interrupt.
> Henry John Kaiser

▶ 당신의 가장 위험한 경쟁자들은 당신과 가장 비슷한 사람들이다.
  브루스 헨더슨 (미국 보스턴컨설팅그룹 설립자)

> Your most dangerous competitors are
> those that are most like you.
> Bruce Henderson

▶ 많이 아는 사람일수록 적게 믿는다.
  작자미상

> Who knows much believes the less.
> anonymous

Favorite famous sayings!

▶ 자기에게 덕이 없는 자는 타인의 덕을 시기한다.
작자미상

> A man that has no virtue in himself,
> ever envies virtue in others.
> anonymous

▶ 처음의 큰 웃음보다 마지막 미소가 더 낫다.
작자미상

> Better the last smile than the first laughter.
> anonymous

▶ 모든 세대가 지난 유행을 비웃으면서 새 유행은 종교처럼 따른다.
헨리 소로우 (미국 사상가)

> Every generation laughs at the old fashions,
> but follows religiously the new.
> Henry David Thoreau

▶ 모든 변화가 발전은 아니다.
모든 움직임이 앞으로 가는 것이 아닌 것처럼.
앨런 글래스고 (미국 소설가)

> All change is not growth;
> as all movement is not forward.
> Allen Glasgow

News English

"Medical Common Sense Nobody Questions"

When it comes to our health, there are some facts we just don't question. Like pregnant women are supposed to eat for two, right! And sugar makes children hyperactive, doesn't it? Well, no. They are just two of the countless health myths many believe...

헷갈리는 의학상식에 이러지도 저러지도……

잘못 알려진 의학상식 20가지

건강에 관해 말할 때(when it comes to health) 아무도 이의를 제기하지 않는 것들(some facts that nobody questions)이 있다.

가령 탄수화물을 섭취하면(eat carbohydrates) 살이 찐다(make you fat)든가 윗몸 일으키기(sit-ups)가 똥배를 없애준다(shift a pot belly)든가 하는 것들은 많은 사람들이 맹신하고 있는 수많은 건강 통념들(the countless health myths many give hasty credit) 중 하나다.

영국 일간지 《데일리미러》의 의학 전문기자가 말하는 잘못된 의학상식 20개를 살펴보자.

① 탄수화물이 살찌는 원인이다?

녹말 성분 음식(starchy foods)은 크림이나 마가린과 같은 실제 지방 성분이 더해졌을 때만 살을 찌게 한다(only become fattening when actual fat, such as cream or margarine, is added). 탄수화물은 칼로리가 지방의 절반도 되지 않을(contain less than half the calories of fat) 뿐더러 더 많은 포만감을 줘서(tend to be more filling) 과식을 덜 하게(make you less likely to overeat) 해준다.

② 물을 하루에 8잔은 마셔야(need to drink 8 glasses of water a day) 한다?
지나치게 많은 물(excessive amounts of water)은 실제로는 건강에 위험할 수(can actually be dangerous for health) 있다. 심지어 치명적일(be even fatal) 수도 있다. 대부분의 사람들(most people)에겐 750ml~1000ml 정도만 필요하며(only need 750 milliliters to 1000 milliliters), 이 정도는 쥬스, 차, 커피, 맥주 등을 통해서도 섭취할 수(can get this from juice, tea, coffee, beer and so on) 있다.

③ 독감 예방주사가 오히려 독감에 걸리게 할 수 있다?
독감주사(the flu jab)는 생백신(a live vaccine)이 아니다. 따라서 바이러스 감염을 일으킬 수 없다(can't infect you with the virus). 사람들이 그런 생각을 하게 되는 것은 감기 바이러스에 대비한 예방주사를 일반적으로 가을 절정기에 맞기(be usually given in autumn-peak time for cold viruses) 때문이다. 사소한 감기에 걸려도(get a minor cold) 독감으로 잘못 생각하는(misinterpret it as flu) 것이다.

④ 신진대사가 느려서(have a slow metabolism) 살이 찐다?

미국 시카고대학 연구팀의 연구 결과에 따르면 뚱뚱한 사람들(fat people)이 더 빠른 신진대사를 보이며(have faster metabolism), 호리호리한 사람들보다 에너지로 더 많은 칼로리를 소모하는(burn off more calories as energy than slimmer people) 것으로 나타났다.

⑤ 임신부는 두 사람 분을 먹어야(should eat for two) 한다?

5명의 여성 중 2명은 이런 잘못된 통념을 믿는다고 인정(admit to believing this myth)한다. 사실은 그렇지 않다. 하루에 200칼로리만 추가로 필요할 뿐(only need an extra 200 calories a day)이다. 빵 두 조각 정도에 해당(be equal to two slices of bread)한다. 그것도 임신 마지막 3개월에만(only in the last three months) 하루 200칼로리를 추가 섭취하면 된다.

⑥ 비타민 복용하면 장수할 수(make you live longer) 있다?

덴마크 코펜하겐대학의 연구결과에 따르면, 비타민 A, C, E와 같은 산화방지 비타민을 왕창 먹는(pop antioxidant vitamins such as A, C, E) 것이 생명을 연장시켜(extend the life) 주지는 못하는 것으로 나타났다. 오히려 때이른 죽음을 불러올 수도 있는 것으로 조사됐다. 특히 비타민 A 복용(taking vitamin A in particular)은 사망 위험 16% 증가와 관련돼 있다는(be linked to a 16% rise in risk of death) 연구 결과도 있다.

⑦ 초콜릿을 먹으면 여드름이 생긴다(give you spots)?

여드름은 피부 지방 분비선의 호르몬 영향으로 생긴다(be caused by the

effects of hormones on sebaceous oil glands). 특히 10대에게 영향을 미치는(particularly affect teenagers) 이유, 스트레스에 의해 증가하는(be increased by stress) 이유이다. 초콜릿은 영향을 주지(make a difference) 않는다.

⑧ 설탕은 아이들을 지나치게 활동적으로 만든다?

설탕이 과잉행동 장애를 부르지는(cause a hyperactive behavior) 않는다. 미국 인디애나폴리스의 릴리 아동병원은 열두 건의 실험을 살펴본(review 12 trials) 결과, 어떤 영향도 발견하지 못했다고(be unable to detect any effect) 발표한 바 있다. 상당수 부모들은 아이들이 설탕 성분 음료를 마시면(have a sugary drink) 과잉 행동을 보인다고 여기는 것으로 조사됐다. 그러나 그것은 그저 그렇다고 생각하기 때문(be all in the mind)일 뿐이다.

⑨ 윗몸 일으키기가 똥배를 없애준다?

하루에 100번 윗몸 일으키기를 해도(even 100 sit-ups a day) 배의 지방층을 제거하는 데 아무런 도움이 되지 않는다(do nothing to get rid of the layer of fat on your tummy). 피트니스 전문가인 니콜라 보튼 박사는 "숨이 차도록 하는(get you out of breath) 심장혈관 운동(only cardiovascular exercise)만이 몸속 지방분을 없앨(shift body fat) 수 있다"고 말한다.

⑩ 재채기할 때 심장은 멈춘다?

숨을 들이마시면서 재채기할 때(when you inhale and sneeze) 가슴속 압력(the pressure in your chest)이 증가했다가 숨을 내쉬면서 떨어지는(drop as you exhale) 것은 사실이다. 심박수(the heart rate)가 영향을 받는(be affected) 것도 사실이다. 하지만 심장은 계속 뛰고(keep beating) 있다. 운전 중에 재채기를 해 제어력을 잃으면서 사고를 당하는(have an accident losing control as a result of sneezing while at the wheel) 경우는 많다.

⑪ 계란이 콜레스테롤을 높인다(raise your cholesterol)?
영국심장재단은 일주일에 계란을 세 개 이상 먹지 말 것을 권고하곤(be used to recommend no more than three eggs a week) 했다. 그러나 최근의 연구들에 따라(following recent studies) 이 재단에서도 매일 계란을 먹어도 안전하다(be safe to eat every day)는 입장을 밝히고 있다.

⑫ 건강을 유지하려면 몸속을 해독해야(detox your body to stay healthy) 한다?
영국 임페리얼대학 연구팀은 (몸에 쌓인 독소를 없애는) 디톡스 식이요법(detox diets)이 시간 낭비(a waste of time)일 뿐이라는 결론을 내렸다. 우리 몸의 간과 신장(our livers and kidneys)이 완벽한 해독 장치(the perfect detox machines) 역할을 해주기 때문이다.

⑬ 커피는 건강에 좋지 않다(be bad for your health)?
하루에 두세 잔은 건강에 유익할 수 있다. 미 하버드대 연구팀에 따르면 커피를 마시는 여성들(female coffee drinkers)은 제2형 당뇨 위험이 30% 줄

어드는(cut the risk of type 2 diabetes by 30%) 것으로 조사됐다. 다른 연구 결과에서도 커피는 파킨슨병(Parkinson's disease), 대장암(colon cancer), 간경변(cirrhosis), 담석(gallstone) 위험을 줄인다는 것이 입증됐다.

⑭ 매달 유방 검사(monthly breast examinations) 받으면 암 위험 피할 수 있다?

미 시애틀 암연구센터가 25만 명 이상의 여성들을 조사(a survey of more than a quarter of a million women by the Cancer Research Center in Seattle)한 결과, 유방암 사망률(the death rate from breast cancer)은 유방 검사를 받으라는 권유를 받은 그룹이나 그렇지 않은 사람들이나 같은(be the same in the group taught to check their breasts as those not) 것으로 나타났다.

⑮ 단것을 먹은 뒤 양치질하면(brush the teeth after sweets) 충치를 막을 수(stop decay) 있다?

실제로는 치아에 나쁘다(be actually bad for teeth). 신 것이나 단것(something acidic or sugary)을 먹으면 일시적으로 치아의 법랑질을 약화시킨다(cause a temporary softening of the enamel). 따라서 곧바로 양치질을 하면(by brushing straight away) 보호막을 긁어내는(scrape off the protective coating) 결과를 초래한다. 최소한 한 시간은 기다려야(have to wait at least an hour) 한다.

⑯ 폐암(lung cancer)은 흡연가들의 질병(smoker's disease)이다?

8건 중 1건(one in eight cases)은 흡연과 관련이 없다(be not linked to smoking). 간접 흡연과 암 유발 물질과의 접촉(second-hand smoke and contact with some cancer-causing substances)이 위험을 높인다(increase the risk). 명백한 노출이 없는 사람들에게도 발생할 수(can occur in those with no obvious exposure) 있다.

⑰ 처방받은 항생제를 다 먹지 않아도 된다(do not need to finish the antibiotics)?

의사들은 모든 감염 유발 박테리아(all the infection-causing bacteria)가 박멸되는(be killed off) 데 필요한 만큼 항생제를 처방(prescribe enough antibiotics to ensure it)한다. 따라서 나아졌다 싶더라도(even if you feel better) 끝까지 복용해야 한다. 그러지 않으면 일부 박테리아가 살아남을 수 있으며, 이 박테리아는 항생제에도 저항력을 갖게 된다(become resistant to antibiotics).

⑱ 식사 후 수영(swimming after eating)은 위험하다?

배가 가득 찬 상태에서 하는 운동(exercising on a full stomach)이 심한 복통을 일으켜(cause abdominal cramps) 익사 위험에 처하게(put you at risk of drowning) 할 수 있다는 이론에서 비롯된(stem from the theory) 말이다. 하지만 이를 뒷받침할 의학적 증거(medical evidence)는 없다.

⑲ 가슴 통증이 없으면 심장발작도 없다?

심장병을 심한 가슴 통증과 관련 지어(associate the heart disease with a crushing chest pain) 생각들하지만, 심장발작의 약 40%(around 40% of heart attacks)는 그렇지 않다. 소화불량, 턱·목·어깨 통증(indigestion, jaw, neck or shoulder pain) 등이 모두 의사들이 소리없는 심장발작이라고 부르는 것의 증상이 될 수(can all be symptoms of what doctors dub silent heart attacks) 있다. 계단을 오를 때 과도하게 힘들거나 심한 피로감을 느끼는(feel an extreme exhaustion or excessive exertion on climbing stairs) 것도 증상일 수 있다.

⑳ 애완동물이 아이들에게 알레르기를 일으킬(give kids allergies) 수 있다?

미국의학협회 저널에 실린 연구(a study in the Journal of the American Medical Association)에 따르면 애완동물이 있는 집에서 태어난 아이들(kids born into a pet-owning household)은 오히려 알레르기에 걸리는 경우가 77% 더 낮았다(be 77% less likely to get allergies). 애완동물을 키우면서 접한 박테리아가 자연 백신 역할을 하는 것으로 보인다(seem to act as a natural vaccine).

Get a Healthy Dose of Reality as we Bust 20 Health Myths

When it comes to our health, there are some facts we just don't question.

Like pregnant women are supposed to eat for two, right?

And sugar makes children hyperactive, doesn't it? Well, no.

They are just two of the countless health myths many believe.

Yesterday, new research claimed surgical stockings do nothing to prevent hospital patients suffering deadly deep vein thrombosis.

So what else isn't as it seems? We debunk the top 20 health myths ···

1 MYTH: Eating carbs makes you fat

TRUTH: According to the Food Standards Agency, starchy foods only become fattening when actual fat, such as cream or margarine, is added.

Gram for gram, carbs contain less than half the calories of fat and tend to be more filling—making you less likely to overeat.

2 MYTH: You need to drink eight glasses of water a day

TRUTH: Scientists at the University of Pennsylvania found not a single study to back this up. Excessive amounts of water can actually be dangerous, even fatal. Most people only need 750ml to one litre and can get this from juice, tea, coffee ··· or beer.

3 MYTH: The flu jab can give you flu

TRUTH: The flu jab isn't a live vaccine so it can't infect you with the virus. People make this mistake because the jab is usually given in autumn ?peak time for cold viruses. And if they go on to get a minor cold they misinterpret it as flu.

4 MYTH: I'm fat because I have slow metabolism

TRUTH: A recent study by the University of Chicago revealed that fat people have faster metabolisms and burn off more calories as energy than slimmer people.

5 MYTH: Pregnant women should eat for two

TRUTH: Two out of five women admit to believing this myth, according to SMA Nutrition. But they only need an extra 200 calories a day – equal to two slices of bread – and even then, only in the last three months.

6 MYTH: Vitamins make you live longer

TRUTH: Popping 'antioxidant' vitamins such as C, A and E won't extend your life, concluded one study last year. They may even lead to a premature death. A review of 67 vitamin studies by Copenhagen University. Taking vitamin A in particular was linked to a 16% rise in risk of death.

7 MYTH: Chocolate gives you spots

TRUTH: Acne is caused by the effects of hormones on sebaceous oil glands in the skin. This is why it particularly affects teenagers and can also be increased by stress. So chocolate won't make a difference.

8 MYTH: Sugar makes kids hyperactiv

TRUTH: Sugar does not cause hyperactive behaviour. Riley Hospital for Children in Indianapolis reviewed 12 trials and were unable to detect any effect. Scientists found when parents think their child has had a sugary drink they rate behaviour as hyperactive ? so it may be all in the mind.

9 MYTH: Sit-ups shift a pot belly

TRUTH: "Even 100 sit-ups a day will do nothing to get rid of the layer of fat on your tummy," says fitness expert Nicola Botton, "only cardiovascular exercise ? the type that gets you out of breath—can shift body fat."

10 MYTH: When you sneeze, your heart stops

TRUTH: When you sneeze the pressure in your chest increases as you inhale and drops when you exhale, so your heart rate is affected, but it keeps beating. Yet a survey by Esure(영국 보험 회사) found two million motorists have had an accident, near miss or lost control as a result of sneezing while at the wheel.

11 MYTH: Eggs will raise your cholesterol

TRUTH: The British Heart Foundation used to recommend no more than three a week. But following recent studies, they now say they're safe to eat every day.

12 MYTH: We need to detox our bodies to stay healthy

TRUTH: A study by Imperial College, London, found that detox diets were a waste of time. They concluded that our livers and kidneys are the perfect detox machines already.

13 MYTH: Coffee is bad for your health

TRUTH: Two to three cups a day can be good for health. A Harvard study found female coffee drinkers cut their risk of type 2 diabetes by 30%. Other studies suggest that coffee cuts the risks of Parkinson's disease, colon cancer, cirrhosis and gallstones.

14 MYTH: Monthly breast examinations beat cancer

TRUTH: A survey of more than a quarter of a million women by the Cancer Research Centre in Seattle found the death rate from breast cancer was the same in the group taught to check their breasts as those not.

15 MYTH: Brushing your teeth after sweets stops decay

TRUTH: This is actually bad for teeth. Whenever you eat something acidic or sugary it causes a temporary softening of the enamel. So by brushing straight away, you're scraping off this protective coating. Wait at least an hour.

16 MYTH: Lung cancer is a smoker's disease

TRUTH: One in eight cases are not linked to smoking. Second-hand smoke and contact with some cancer-causing substances will increase the risk, though the disease can occur in those with no obvious exposure.

17 MYTH: If I feel better, I don't need to finish my antibiotics

TRUTH: Doctors prescribe enough antibiotics to ensure all the infection-causing bacteria are killed off. So even if you feel better, you must finish or there's a risk some remain. They can then become resistant to antibiotics.

18 MYTH: Swimming after eating is dangerous

TRUTH: This stems from the theory that exercising on a full stomach causes abdominal cramps, which could put you at risk of drowning. However, there's no medical evidence to support it.

19 MYTH: No chest pain means it's not a heart attack

TRUTH: Although we associate them with a crushing chest pain, around 40% of heart attacks don't present in this way. Indigestion, jaw, neck or shoulder pain can all be symptoms of what doctors sometimes dub silent heart attacks, as can a feeling of extreme exhaustion or excessive exertion on climbing stairs.

20 MYTH: Having a pet can give kids allergies

TRUTH: A study in the Journal of the American Medical Association found kids born into a pet-owning household were 77% less likely to get allergies – their bacteria seems to act as a natural vaccine.

☑ 기억하면 좋을 구절!

when it comes to ~에 대해서라면 / ~에 관한 한
We all could use some help *when it comes to* learning.
배우는 데 있어서 우리 모두에게는 도움이 필요하다.

give credit to 믿다
Public *give credit to* the government.
대중은 정부를 신뢰한다.

have blind faith 맹신하다
One should not *have blind faith* in the science.
과학을 맹신해서는 안 된다.

get rid of ~을 제거하다 / 없애다
Primitive people danced to *get rid of* evil spirits.
원시인들은 악령들을 없애기 위해 춤을 췄다.

be all in the mind 마음가짐에 달려 있다 / 그렇게 생각하기 때문이다
Your happiness *is all in the mind*.
행복은 마음가짐에 달려 있다.

내 인생의 명언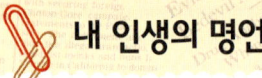

▶ 사람이 우연히 현명할 수는 없다.
세네카 (로마 철학자·극작가·정치가)

　　No man was ever wise by chance.
　　Lucius Annaeus Seneca

▶ 현명함은 당신이 말하고 싶었을 때
상대방을 들어준 일생에 대한 보상이다.
더그 라슨 (미국 언론인)

　　Wisdom is the reward you get for a lifetime
　　of listening when you'd have preferred to talk.
　　Doug Larson

▶ 현명한 사람들은 자신들이 발견하는 것 이상으로
기회를 만들어낸다.
프랜시스 베이컨 (영국 정치가·철학자)

　　Wise men make more opportunities than they find.
　　Francis Bacon

▶ 현명함이란 우리의 시간과 지식을 적절하게 사용하는 힘이다.
토마스 왓슨 (미국 IBM 설립자)

　　Wisdom is the power to put our time and
　　our knowledge to the proper use.
　　Thomas Watson

Favorite famous sayings!

▶ 신념은 지성의 깊이이다.
로버트 윌슨 (미국 작가)

> Belief is the depth of intelligence.
> Robert Wilson

▶ 나는 내가 가진 모든 두뇌뿐 아니라
빌릴 수 있는 두뇌도 모두 사용한다.
우드로 윌슨 (미국 28대 대통령)

> I not only use all the brains that I have,
> but all that I can borrow.
> Woodrow Wilson

▶ 지성은 아내이고, 상상력은 정부(情婦)이며,
기억력은 머슴이다.
빅토르 위고 (프랑스 시인·작가)

> Intelligence is the wife, imagination is
> the mistress, memory is the servant.
> Victor-Marie Hugo

News English

"Mental Power Starting to Dwindle at 27"

Mental powers start to dwindle at 27 after peaking at 22, marking the start of old age, US research suggests.
Professor Timothy Salthouse of the University of Virginia found reasoning, spatial visualisation and speed of thought all decline in our late 20s. Therapies designed to stall or reverse the ageing process may need to start much earlier, he said.
His seven-year study of 2,000 healthy people aged 18-60 is published in the journal Neurobiology of Aging.
To test mental agility, the study participants had to solve puzzles, recall words and story details and spot patterns in letters and symbols. The same tests are already used by doctors to spot signs of dementia. In nine out of 12 tests the average age at which the top performance was achieved was 22. This was the first age at which any marked decline was apparent in brain speed, reasoning and visual puzzle-solving ability.
Things like memory stayed intact until the age of 37, on average, while abilities based on accumulated knowledge, such as performance on tests of vocabulary or general information, increased until the age of 60.
Professor Salthouse said his findings suggested "some aspects of age-related cognitive decline begin in healthy, educated adults when they are in their 20s and 30s."
Rebecca Wood of the Alzheimer's Research Trust agreed, saying: "This research suggests that the natural decline of some of our mental abilities as we age starts much earlier than some of us might expect - in our 20s and 30s.
"Much more research is urgently needed if we are to offer hope to the 700,000 people in the UK who live with dementia, a currently incurable condition."
"The natural decline of some of our mental abilities as we age starts much earlier than some of us might expect".
Rebecca Wood of the Alzheimer's Research Trust
Mental powers start to dwindle at 27 after peaking at 22, marking the start of old age, US research suggests.
Professor Timothy Salthouse...

인간의 두뇌 능력은 영원하지 않다

27세부터 감소하는 사람의 정신 능력

 사람의 정신 능력(mental powers)은 22세쯤 정점에 이르렀다가 27세부터 점차 감소하기 시작(start to dwindle at 27 after peaking at 22)한다는 연구 결과가 나왔다.

 미국 버지니아대학의 티모시 샐도즈 교수는 추리력(reasoning power), 생각의 속도(speed of thought), 공간 시각(spatial visualization) 등이 모두 20대 후반에 쇠퇴한다(decline in our late 20s)는 사실을 발견했다. 샐도즈 교수는 "따라서 노화 과정을 멈추게 하거나 전환시키기 위한 요법들(therapies designed to stall or reverse the aging process)을 지금보다 훨씬 일찍부터 적용할 필요가 있다"고 주장하고 나섰다.

 18~60세 나이의 건강한 사람 2000명을 대상으로 한 이번 7년간의 연구(this seven-year study of 2000 healthy people aged 18~60)는 의학전문지 '노화 신경생물학(Neurobiology of Aging)'에 발표됐다.

연구 참가자들(the study participants)은 정신 유연성을 시험하기(test mental agility) 위해 퍼즐 문제를 풀어보고(solve puzzles) 단어와 이야기 세부 내용을 기억하며(recall words and story details) 문자와 심볼의 양식을 구분하는(spot patterns in letters and symbols) 테스트를 받았다. 이 같은 테스트는 치매 징조를 알아내기 위해(to spot signs of dementia) 사용돼온 것들이다.

그 결과 12건의 테스트 중 9건에서(in nine of 12 tests) 최상의 성과(the top performance)를 나타내는 평균 나이(the average age)는 22세인 것으로 조사됐다. 또 뇌의 속도, 추리 및 시각 퍼즐 해결 능력 테스트에서(in tests of brain speed, reasoning and visual puzzle-solving ability) 눈에 띄리진 쇠퇴(a marked decline)를 보이기 시작하는 첫 연령은 27세로 나타났다.

평균적으로(on average) 기억력 같은 것들은(things like memory) 37세까지 손상되지 않는(stay intact until the age of 37) 것으로 조사됐다. 어휘력이나 일반 상식 테스트 수행과 같은(such as performance on tests of vocabulary or general information) 축적된 지식에 바탕을 둔 능력은(abilities based on accumulated knowledge) 60세까지 증가하는 것으로 나타났다.

샐도즈 교수는 그러나 "문제는 나이에 따른 인식력 감퇴(the age-related cognitive decline)가 20대 때부터 시작된다는 것"이라고 말한다. 사람 정신능력 일부의 자연적 쇠퇴(the natural decline of some of our mental abilities)가 생각보다 훨씬 일찍 시작된다는 것이다.

건강한 뇌가 어떻게 퇴행하는지를 이해하는 것은 알츠하이머와 같은 심각한 질병에 무엇이 잘못되어가는가(what goes wrong in serious diseases like Alzheimer's)를 알아내는 데 대단히 긴요하다.

전문가들은 알츠하이머는 노화의 자연적인 한 부분(a natural part of getting old)이 아니라고 말한다. 뇌세포를 죽이는(kill brain cells) 신체적 질병(a physical disease)으로 봐야 한다는 얘기다.

따라서 현재 불치병(a currently incurable condition)으로 여겨지는 치매를 앓고 있는 수많은 사람들을 구제하기 위해서는 하루빨리 훨씬 더 많은 연구가 이루어져야 한다고 입을 모으고 있다.

'Brain Decline' Begins at Age 27

Mental powers start to dwindle at 27 after peaking at 22, marking the start of old age, US research suggests.

Professor Timothy Salthouse of the University of Virginia found reasoning, spatial visualisation and speed of thought all decline in our late 20s. Therapies designed to stall or reverse the ageing process may need to start much earlier, he said.

His seven-year study of 2,000 healthy people aged 18-60 is published in the journal Neurobiology of Aging.

To test mental agility, the study participants had to solve puzzles, recall words and story details and spot patterns in letters and symbols. The same tests are already used by doctors to spot signs of dementia. In nine out of 12 tests the average age at which the top performance was achieved was 22. The first age at which there was any marked decline was at 27 in tests of brain speed, reasoning and visual puzzle-solving ability.

Things like memory stayed intact until the age of 37, on average, while abilities based on accumulated knowledge, such as performance on tests of vocabulary or general information, increased until the age of 60.

Professor Salthouse said his findings suggested "some aspects of age-related cognitive decline begin in healthy, educated adults when they are in their 20s and 30s."

Rebecca Wood of the Alzheimer's Research Trust agreed, saying: "This research suggests that the natural decline of some of our mental abilities as we age starts much earlier than some of us might expect—in our 20s and 30s.

"Understanding more about how healthy brains decline could help us understand what goes wrong in serious diseases like Alzheimer's.

"Alzheimer's is not a natural part of getting old; it is a physical disease that kills brain cells, affecting tens of thousands of under 65s too.

"Much more research is urgently needed if we are to offer hope to the 700,000 people in the UK who live with dementia, a currently incurable condition."

"The natural decline of some of our mental abilities as we age starts much earlier than some of us might expect"

Rebecca Wood of the Alzheimer's Research Trust

☑ 기억하면 좋을 구절!

spot signs of ~의 징조를 알아내다

Dogs have an ability to *spot signs of* cancer.
개는 암의 징후를 알아내는 능력이 있다.

reasoning power 추리력

His *reasoning power* at the age of 10 is exceptional.
열 살인 그의 추리력은 보통 이상이다.

mental age 정신연령

She is sixteen but has a *mental age* of five.
그녀는 나이가 16세이지만 정신연령은 5세다.

stay intact 온전히 남다 / 손상되지 않고 유지되다

The plane will *stay intact*.
그 비행기는 고스란히 유지될 것이다.

an incurable condition 불치병

He came to be *an incurable condition*.
그는 불치병을 앓게 되었다.

내 인생의 명언 — 사람은 희망으로 산다

▶ 인류에 대한 신념을 잃어서는 안 된다. 인류는 대양과 같은 것이다. 대양의 물 몇 방울이 더럽다 하더라도 대양은 더러워지지 않는다.
마하트마 간디 (인도 정치가 · 민족운동지도자)

> You must not lose faith in humanity.
> Humanity is an ocean;
> if a few drops of the ocean are dirty,
> the ocean does not become dirty.
> Mahatma Gandhi

▶ 희망이 없다면 가슴은 무너지고 말 것이다.
토마스 풀러 (영국 성직자 · 역사가)

> If it were not for hopes, the heart would break.
> Thomas Fuller

▶ 희망은 꽃 없이도 꿀을 만들어내는 유일한 벌이다.
에밀리 디킨슨 (미국 여류시인)

> Hope is the only bee that makes honey
> without flowers.
> Emily Dickinson

▶ 누군가에게서 절대 희망을 빼앗지 말라. 가진 것의 전부일 수도 있으니.
잭슨 브라운 주니어 (미국 작가)

> Never deprive someone of hope;
> it might be all they have
> H. Jackson Brown, Jr.

News English

Our Instinctive 'Fight-or-flight Response'

Bad marriage? Check your feelings about mom and dad By David Code Many couples believe their marriage is fine because they seldom argue. Yet their love life may have dried up, or they may have "married" their kids by making them the center of their lives.

Couples who wo... talk much anymor... their relationship ... It turns out that ... themselves from t... to distance themsel... One of the best thi... marriages ? and-co... more time with our ... Americans may not ... pay for today's trans... beings are social-an... today are more isola... generations. We mi... no longer drop in to ... parents, or meet at ... hole with friends or r... to.

In Europe and develop... three generations of a ... close proximity, divorce ... lower, and mental health ... These nations may env... they don't envy our famil...

Most of us aren't aware that the "flight" part of our instinctive fight-or-flight response may cause us to avoid our parents. We mistakenly believe that distancing from our parents is evidence of our emotional ... owing ? that we're "outgrown our parents." But if we were truly mature, we wouldn't feel ... ... our parents.

actually be our flight-response. Distancing ourselves from our parents seems mature and peaceful on the surface, but our flight instinct is just as primitive and reactive as our fight instinct.

How we leave the nest may have ...

왜 우리는 싸우고 또 도망칠까?

erosion of our relationships. However, there is a third opi... fight or flight mindfulness. Even if our parents inadverte... wired us to create dista... relationships, we don't have to ... as possible. We can renew con... with our parents, and so ... "making" dead turned rese... The rewards are rich ... how to manage our ti... disease as our parents ...

choice. We can react instinctively, or we can respond thoughtfully. Like animals, when humans feel anxious, our fight-or-flight instinct tends to take over, and we overreact.

... the thinking ... ck control of ...
... who make us ...
... o've left our ...
... of our base ...
... s cycle. The ...
... erating on ...
... . The simple ...
... ur thinking ...
... Most of our ...

...t-on-flight ...
... parents, ...
... he hard-...
... learning ...
... ps us to ...
... ake the ...
... reaction ...

personal ? just our fight-or-flight running the show. And it's a bonus that I actually look forward to time with my mom!" Knowledge is power. And God wasn't joking when he commanded us to "Honor thy father and thy mother: that thy days may be long upon the land..."

Honoring our relationship with our parents is not just about spiritual enlightenment. It's a proven means of bettering our own lives ? and the lives of our spouses and kids ? right here and now.

David Code is a family coach, Episcopal priest, and author of "To Raise Happy Kids, Put Your Marriage First."

Bad marriage? Check your feelings about mom and dad
By David Code

Many couples believe their marriage is fine because they seldom argue. Yet their love life may have dried up, or they may have "married" their kids by making them the center of their lives.

Couples who wonder why they don't talk much anymore might take a look at ... ip with their own parents. ... hat people who distance ... from their parents also ... ce themselves from their ...

ext things we can do for our ... nd our children ? is to spend ... with our parents.

... may not realize the phone we ... ay's transient lifestyle. Human ... e social animals, but couples ... e isolated than in previous ... We move often, and can ... drop in to say "hello" to our ... eet at a ... watering ... iends or relatives like our ...

'투쟁'과 '도전'은 우리의 본능

"결혼생활이 불행합니까. 그럼 당신이 당신 부모에게 어떤 감정을 갖고 있는지 체크해보세요. 분명히 관련이 있습니다."

미국의 가정문제 지도사이자 성공회 목사이며 '행복한 아이들을 키우려면 당신의 결혼생활을 가장 중시하라'는 책의 저자(a family coach, Episcopal priest and author of 'To Raise Happy Kids, Put Your Marriage First')인 데이비드 코드 박사가 하는 말이다.

많은 부부들은 좀처럼 다투지 않는다(seldom argue)는 이유만으로 자신들의 결혼생활이 원만하다고 생각한다(believe their marriage is fine). 그러나 그들의 애정 생활(their love life)은 말라비틀어졌을지(may have dried up) 모른다. 아니면 아이들을 자신들 삶의 중심으로 만들어놓고 아이들과 '결혼'한(may have 'married' their kids by making them the center of their lives) 것처럼 사는 경우도 있다.

왜 더 이상 많은 대화를 나누지 않을까 스스로 의아해하는 부부들(couples who wonder why they don't talk much anymore)은 자신들의 부모와의 관계를 살펴볼(take a look at their relationship with their own parents) 필요가 있다. 부모들과 거리를 두는 사람들(people who distance themselves from their parents)은 자신들의 배우자와도 거리를 두는 경향이 있다(also tend to distance themselves from their spouses).

우리의 결혼생활과 아이들을 위해 할 수 있는 최상의 것(the best things we can do for our marriages and our children)은 우리의 부모와 더 많은 시간을 보내는(spend more time with our parents) 것이다. 미국인들은 오늘날의 무상한 생활방식을 위해 치르는 대가를 자각하지 못하1(do not realize the price they pay for today's transient lifestyle) 있다. 인간은 사회적 동물이다(human beings are social animals). 하지만 오늘날의 부부들은 전 세대들보다 더 단절돼(be more isolated than in previous generations) 살고 있다.

부모에게 문안 인사차 들러보지도 않고(do not drop in to say hello to their parents), 지역 사교장에서 친구나 친척들을 만나보려(meet at the local watering hole with friends or relatives) 하지도 않는다.

가족 3세대(three generations of a family)가 가까운 이웃에 몰려 사는(live in close proximity) 경우가 많은 유럽이나 개발도상국들에선(in Europe and developing countries) 이혼과 중독 비율이 더 낮고(divorce and addictions are lower), 정신건강(mental health)은 높다. 그 국가들이 미국의 풍요로움은 부러워할지 몰라도(may envy Americans' wealth) 미국의 가족생활은 부러워하지 않는다(do not envy their family lives).

우리 대부분은 우리의 본능적인 '투쟁 또는 도주 반응' 중 '도주' 부분(the 'flight' part of our instinctive 'fight-or-flight response')이 우리로 하여금 부모를 피하게 만든다는(cause us to avoid our parents) 사실을 잘 모르고 있다. 부모와 거리를 두는(distance ourselves from our parents) 것이 감정적 성숙의 증거(evidence of our emotional maturity)에 따른 것이라고 잘못 생각한다(mistakenly believe).

하지만 정말 성숙했다면(be truly mature) 부모와 투쟁하거나 부모로부터 도주할 필요가 없을(wouldn't have to fight-or-flee our parents) 것이다. 부모와 다툴(argue with our parents) 때는 우리의 투쟁 반응을 쉽게 알아챌(be easy to spot our fight-response) 수 있다. 그러나 부모를 피하는(avoid our parents) 것이 우리의 도주 반응(the flight-response)에 따른 것이라는 사실은 잘 깨닫지 못한다.

우리가 둥지를 어떻게 떠나느냐 하는 것(how we leave the nest)은 장래 우리의 행복에 우리가 자각하는 것보다 더 큰 영향을 미친다(have a bigger impact on our future happiness than we realize). 우리 중 다수는 부모와 감정적으로 너무 얽매여 부모 주변에 머무는 것이 화가 나기 때문에(be so emotionally enmeshed with our parents that being around them drives us crazy) 아버지와 어머니를 피하기 시작한다(begin to avoid our mom and dad).

그러면 두 가지 선택 밖에 없다. 하나는 부모의 행동을 바꾸기 위해 투쟁하는(fight to change our parents) 것이고, 다른 하나는 그들 존재의 불편함으로부터 도주하는(flee the discomfort of their presence) 것이다.

문제는 도망가는(run away) 것이 어떤 문제도 해결하지 못한다는(do not solve anything) 점이다. 부모와는 다르게 살겠다는 결심에도 불구하고(despite our determination to be different from our parents) 우리는 나이가 들어가면서(as we grow older) 매일 그들을 점점 더 닮아간다(become more like them every day).

자신이 태어난 가족 사이에서 행동하던 행태(the way we act in our families of origin)는 성인이 된 후 행동하는 행태로 이어지는 경향이 있다(tend to become the way we act in our adult relationships). 어린 시절 불쾌한 이슈들을 피함으로써 '평화를 지키는' 것에 길들여진(be conditioned as children to 'keep the peace' by avoiding unpleasant issues) 부부는 결국 부부 간의 대화도 줄어들고 소원해지는(end up talking to each other less and drifting apart) 경우가 많다.

따라서 도주 반응(flight-response)은 투쟁보다 훨씬 더 많은 대가를 치르게(be even more costly than fighting) 된다. 자각하지 못하는 사이에 천천히 관계의 침식을 야기하기(cause the slow and unconscious erosion of our relationships) 때문이다.

투쟁 또는 도주 외에 제3의 선택(a third option besides fight or flight)이 있기는 하다. 주의하는 것(be mindful)이다. 부모가 무심코 우리로 하여금 관계에 거리감을 만들게 하더라도(even if our parents inadvertently hardwire us to create distance in our relationships) 그것을 숙명처럼 받아들여서는 안 된다(don't have to accept that as destiny). 부모와의 관계를 새롭게 만들 수 있고(can renew our relationships with our parents), 그 과정에

서(in the process) 그러한 유해한 경향을 바꿔놓을(rewire those harmful tendencies) 수 있다.

그 보상은 값어치가 있다(the rewards are rich). 부모와의 관계에서 도주 본능을 관리하는 법을 배우면(learn how to manage our flight-instinct in relation to our parents) 그 변화는 다른 관계들을 통해서도 파급 효과가 나타난다(have a ripple effect through our other relationships). 우리 자신과 배우자, 우리 아이들에게 모두 원-윈 결과가 된다(that's win-win for us, our spouses and our children).

이러한 치유의 길에서 첫 걸음(the first step on this healing path)은 우리 행동의 근간을 이해하는(understand the basis of our behavior) 것이다. 동물들은 순전히 본능에 따라 행동한다(animals act purely on instinct). 하지만 인간은 선택을 할(have a choice) 줄 안다.

인간은 본능적으로 반응할 수도(can react instinctively) 있지만, 심사숙고해서 반응할(react thoughtfully) 수도 있다. 동물처럼 인간도 불안감을 느끼게 되면(feel anxious) 투쟁 또는 도주 본능이 우세해지면서(our fight-or-flight instinct tends to take over) 과잉 반응을 보이게(overreact) 된다.

하지만 인간은 동물과 다르게(unlike animals) 두뇌의 사유하는 부분을 이용해(use the thinking part of our brains) 우리 행동에 대한 제어 능력을 되찾을(take back control of our behavior) 수 있다.

자기 인식(self-awareness)이야말로 악순환 고리를 끊을(break the vicious cycle) 수 있는 수단이다. 자동 조정 장치에 의해 움직이고 있다는(be operating on autopilot) 것을 인식하기만 해도 그 자체가 승리(a victory in itself)다. 기본적 본능의 자동 조정 장치를 꺼버릴 수 있는 사유 능력 스위치가 있음을 아는(notice switches on our thinking mind) 것이 중요하다.

　본능을 주시하는 법을 배우면(learn to observe our instinct) 행동하기 전에 생각하는 데 큰 도움이 된다. 무릎반사와 같은 반사적 반응과 사려 깊은 반응 사이의 차이를 만들어(make the difference between a knee-jerk reaction and a thoughtful response) 낼 수 있다.

　다른 사람이 뭐가 잘못됐는지에 초점을 맞추는 대신(instead of focusing on what is wrong with somebody else) 내 자신이 언제 투쟁 또는 도주 상태에 있었는지에 초점을 맞추게(focus on noticing when I was in fight-or-flight mode) 된다.

　아는 게 힘이다(Knowledge is power). 성경에 "네 아버지와 어머니를 공경하라(Honor thy father and thy mother)"고 한 것은 농담이 아니다. 부모와의 관계를 존중하는 것(honoring our relationship with our parents)은 영적인 교화에 그치지 않는다(be not just about spiritual enlightenment). 우리 자신의 삶과 우리 배우자와 아이들의 삶을 더 나아지게 하는 방법(means of bettering our own lives and the lives of our spouses and kids)이다.

Bad Marriage? Check Your Feelings about Mom and Dad

Many couples believe their marriage is fine because they seldom argue. Yet their love life may have dried up, or they may have "married" their kids by making them the center of their lives.

Couples who wonder why they don't talk much anymore might take a look at their relationship with their own parents. It turns out that people who distance themselves from their parents also tend to distance themselves from their spouses.

One of the best things we can do for our marriages—and our children—is to spend more time with our parents.

Americans may not realize the price we pay for today's transient lifestyle. Human beings are social animals, but couples today are more isolated than in previous generations. We move often, and can no longer drop in to say "hello" to our parents, or meet at the local watering hole with friends or relatives, as we used to.

In Europe and developing nations, where three generations of a family often live in close proximity, divorce and addictions are lower, and mental health is higher.

These nations may envy our wealth, but they don't envy our family life.

Most of us aren't aware that the "flight" part of our instinctive fight-or-flight response may cause us to avoid our parents. We mistakenly believe that distancing from our parents is evidence of our emotional maturity —that we've "out-grown our parents." But if we were truly mature, we wouldn't have to fight-or-flee our parents.

It's easy to spot our fight-response—when we argue with our parents, for example. But we don't realize that avoiding our parents could actually be our flight-response. Distancing ourselves from our parents seems mature and peaceful on the surface, but our flight instinct is just as primitive and reactive as our fight instinct.

How we leave the nest may have a bigger impact on our future happiness than we realize. Many of us begin to avoid our mom and dad because we are so emotionally enmeshed with them that being around our parents drives us crazy. We may see only two options: 1. Fighting to change our parents' behavior, or 2. Fleeing the discomfort of their presence.

The problem is, running away doesn't solve anything, and what we resist persists. As we grow older, many of us notice that, despite our determination to be different from our parents, we become more like them every day—sometimes in ways we're not proud of.

The way we act in our families of origin tends to become the way we act in our adult relationships. Couples who were already conditioned as children to "keep the peace" by avoiding unpleasant issues may end up talking to each other less, and drifting apart. That's why our flight-response can be even more costly than fighting, if it causes the slow, unconscious erosion of our relationships.

However, there is a third option besides fight or flight: mindfulness.

Even if our parents inadvertently "hard-wired" us to create distance in our relationships, we don't have to accept that as destiny. We can renew our relationships with our parents, and in the process, "rewire" those harmful tendencies.

The rewards are rich, because if we learn how to manage our flight-instinct in relation to our parents, the change will have a ripple effect through our other relationships. That's win-win for us, our spouses, and our children.

The first step on this healing path is to understand the basis of our behavior. Animals act purely on instinct. Humans, though, have a choice. We can react instinctively, or we can respond thoughtfully. Like animals, when humans feel anxious, our fight-or-flight instinct tends to take over, and we overreact.

But, unlike animals, we can use the thinking part of our brains to take back control of our behavior.

When we are with people who make us anxious, we don't realize we've left our brains on the "auto-pilot" of our base instincts.

Self-awareness can break this cycle. The recognition that we're operating on autopilot is a victory in itself. The simple act of noticing switches on our thinking mind, which turns off the autopilot of our base instincts.

Every time we observe our fight-or-flight instincts as we interact with our parents, we are re-wiring some of the hard-wiring we received as kids. So, learning to observe our instincts helps us to think before we act, which can make the difference between a knee-jerk reaction and a thoughtful response.

As a family coach, I've witnessed the power of mindfulness to restore damaged relationships.

Take James and Gail (not their real names). "It's like, before, my tombstone could have read, 'My life was my husband's fault,'" Gail says. "But then I noticed that in my relationship with my parents, I was polite but distant—often just going-through-the-motions with them. And I realized I was doing the same thing with James."

"I felt tremendous relief, because now I knew I didn't have to put my kids and myself through the hell of a divorce," Gail remembers. "Instead of focusing on what was wrong with James, I focused on noticing when I was in fight-or-flight mode. Now, we make up much more quickly after an argument, and I don't carry all that bitterness because I know it's nothing personal—just our fight-or-flight running the show. And it's a bonus that I actually look forward to time with my mom!"

Knowledge is power. And God wasn't joking when he commanded us to "Honor thy father and thy mother: that thy days may be long upon the land···."

Honoring our relationship with our parents is not just about spiritual enlightenment. It's a proven means of bettering our own lives—and the lives of our spouses and kids—right here and now.

David Code is a family coach, Episcopal priest, and author of "To Raise Happy Kids, Put Your Marriage First."

☑ 기억하면 좋을 구절!

take a look at ~을 보다

Let me *take a look at* it.
어디 좀 봅시다.

distance oneself from ~로부터 거리를 두다

You'd better *distance yourself from* the guy.
그 남자와 거리를 두는 것이 좋을 것이다.

drop in ~에 잠깐 들르다

Let *'s drop in* somewhere to fill up our empty stomach.
어디 들러서 빈 속이나 채웁시다.

ripple effect 파급효과

His resignation will have a *ripple effect* on the whole department.
그의 사직은 부서 전체에 영향을 미칠 것이다.

drift apart 사이가 멀어지다

As a result, he says, they *drifted apart*.
그 결과, 그는 그들의 관계가 멀어졌다고 말했다.

be mindful 주의하다 / 유념하다

Be mindful only of your own interest.
네 일에만 집중하도록 하라.

내 인생의 명언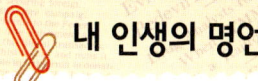

▶ 행동을 수반하지 않는 생각은 뇌세포 크기보다 결코 더 커질 수 없다.
애널드 글래소우 (미국 작가)

> An idea not coupled with action will never get any bigger than the brain cell it occupied.
> Arnold Glasow

▶ 아첨하는 방법을 아는 사람이 중상모략 하는 방법도 안다.
나폴레옹 (프랑스 군인 · 제1통령 · 황제)

> He who knows how to flatter also knows how to slander.
> Napoleon

▶ 신념은 실제의 사실을 만들어낸다.
윌리엄 제임스 (미국 실용철학자 · 심리학자)

> Belief creates the actual fact.
> William James

▶ 행동하는 사람처럼 생각하고, 생각하는 사람처럼 행동하라.
작자미상

> Think like a man of action, act like a man of thought.
> anonymous

News English

" The Best Way to Load the Airplane "

"Zone 4 is now boarding." With that announcement, one lines up, walks past the ticket-taker, down the ramp, and eventually enters the plane to witness a few people valiantly crunching their ungainly carry-on bags into the overhead compartments and most others impatiently waiting in the aisles to do the same. Those already in the aisle seats are casting a wary eye on the next backpack threatening to attack them when its owner unthinkingly pivots in the aisle. Is the standard boarding method really the best way to load an airplane? There are variations, but almost all methods currently in use board by seat or zone number so that those whose seats are near the back of the plane board first and hence don't block passengers boarding after them. That's the theory, at least. Alas, since the people in a single row can't all stow their bags simultaneously, there are always people blocking the aisle as they try to stow their bags. Moreover, those sitting in the aisle seats are not only dodging passing luggage, but must rise and let later-arriving passengers sitting in the window and middle seats enter their row. It's a time-consuming, spirit-sapping mess. Better Boarding Procedures: Separating Passengers

Enter Jason Steffen, an astrophysicist at Fermi Lab near Chicago. Using computer simulations, he has examined different plane boarding strategies with an eye toward their speed and efficiency. For simplicity, his model assumes a plane with 120 passengers seated in 40 rows, each row having three seats to the right of the aisle. He assumes that each of the 120 passengers has an assigned seat, carries luggage, and that they move ...

비행기 타는 순서에도 요령이 있다는데……

they move forward if and only if no one is directly in front of them. So, given these reasonable assumptions, what's the best way to board? It seems intuitive that the worst way is to load those ... they can step into the ... someone seated further back ... pass. After these passengers ha... passengers to even-numbered ... seats in the middle of the ... and they are followed by ... numbered window seats ... of the plane. Next, the same ... followed for those in the e... middle side and then for ... even-numbered aisle seats ... Finally, after the e...

It appears that the reason the protocol is faster is that it allows multiple passengers to simultaneously stow their baggage, the most ...

348

천체물리학자가 발견한 최상의 비행기 탑승순서

비행기 탑승 때 누구나 치르는 곤욕이 있다. 자리를 찾아 안으로 들어가려는 승객과 이미 자리를 찾아 짐칸에 짐을 올리려는 승객들이 뒤엉켜 진땀을 뺀다. 항공사들은 이런 혼란을 피하기 위해 오래 전부터 뒷자리 승객들을 먼저 타게 하고 있다.

그러나 한 천체물리학자의 컴퓨터 시뮬레이션(an astrophysicist's computer simulation) 결과, 기존의 표준적인 탑승 방법(the standard boarding method)은 비행기 적재에 최상의 방식(the best way to load the airplane)이 아닌 것으로 밝혀졌다.

기존의 방식은 이렇다. 기내 뒤쪽 좌석 승객들에게 먼저 탑승하라는 안내방송이 나간다. 그러면 승객들은 줄을 지어(line up) 검표직원들을 거친(walk past the ticket-taker) 뒤 진입로를 따라 내려가(down the ramp) 마침내 비행기 안으로 들어선다(eventually enter the plane).

먼저 탑승한 승객들은 다루기 힘든 휴대 가방들을 머리 위 짐칸에 구겨 넣느라(crunch their ungainly carry-on bags into the overhead compartments) 끙끙대고, 대부분의 다른 사람들은 똑같은 일을 하기 위해 기내 복도에서 조바심을 내며 기다린다(most others impatiently wait in the aisles to do the same).

복도 쪽 좌석에 이미 앉은 사람들(those already in the aisle seats)은 다음에 올려지는 짐이 행여나 자신들을 덮치지 않을까 걱정스러운 눈으로 쳐다보고(cast a wary eye on the next backpack threatening to attack them) 있어야 한다.

현재 사용 중인 대부분의 방식들(almost all methods currently in use)은 비행기 뒤쪽에 가까운 좌석의 사람들(those whose seats are near the back of the plane)을 먼저 탑승시켜 그들 뒤에 탑승하는 승객들을 막지 않도록(don't block passengers boarding after them) 하고 있다.

문제는 일렬로 들어간 승객들이 모두 동시에 짐을 짐칸에 집어넣지 못한다(can't all stow their bags simultaneously)는 데 있다. 짐을 올려 넣느라 복도를 가로막는 사람들이 꼭 있기 마련(there are always people blocking the aisle as they try to stow their bags)이다.

게다가(moreover) 복도 쪽 좌석들에 앉은 사람들(those sitting in the aisle seats)은 지나가는 짐을 피해야 할 뿐 아니라(not only dodge passing luggage) 나중에 도착하는 같은 줄의 창가 또는 가운데 좌석 승객들이 들어갈 수 있도록 자리에서 일어서야(must rise and let later-arriving passengers sitting in the window and middle seats enter their row) 한다. 시간 낭

비(time-consuming)에 기운 빠지게 하는 혼잡(spirit-sapping mess)이 반복될 수밖에 없다.

이와 관련, 미국 시카고대학 페르미연구소의 천체물리학자인 제이슨 스테펀 박사는 "보다 나은 탑승 절차"(better boarding procedures)가 있다고 말한다. 컴퓨터 시뮬레이션을 통해 속도와 효율성 측면에서 여러 가지의 비행기 탑승 전략을 관찰(examine different plane boarding strategies with an eye toward the speed and efficiency)한 결과, 최상의 탑승순서 묘수를 발견했다는 것이다.

스테펀 박사는 120명의 승객이 탑승할 수 있는 40개 열(列)의 비행기 좌석들을 모델로 삼았다. 각 열은 가운데 복도를 중심으로 왼쪽과 오른쪽에 각각 3개씩의 좌석이 있는(each row with a central aisle having three seats to the left and three seats to the right of it) 것으로 했다. 또 120명의 승객은 각자 부여된 좌석 번호(an assigned seat number)가 있고, 휴대하고 있는 짐(carry-on baggage)을 들고 있는 것으로 가정했다.

지금까지는 뒷줄을 먼저 태우고 점차 앞 쪽에 가까운 줄을 태우는(load the back rows first and then gradually rows nearer the front) 것이 탑승에 가장 좋은 방법 중 하나(be among the best ways to board)인 것으로 생각돼왔다.

하지만 스테펀 박사의 시뮬레이션에 따르면 이는 앞좌석부터 태우는 것에 이어 속도가 두 번째로 느린 방식(second-slowest way)인 것으로 나타났다. 심지어 무작위 탑승이 더 빠른(even random boarding is faster) 것으로 조사됐다.

승객들 변수와 짐칸에 짐 올리는 시간들을 여러 조합으로 묶이 시뮬레이션을 실시(carry out the simulations allowing for different sets of passenger quirks and luggage-stowing times) 해본 결과, 최상의 선택은 기내 뒷부분에 가까운 짝수 열들의 창가 좌석 승객들을 가장 먼저 탑승하도록(let the passengers in even-numbered window seats near the back of the plane to board first) 하는 것으로 나타났다.

머리 위 짐칸에 휴대물품들을 들어올리는 승객들(passengers hefting their carry-ons into the overhead compartments)은 그들 사이 중간에 빈 줄(an empty row between them)이 있어서 각자의 움직임에 덜 얽히게(be less likely to get in each other's way) 된다.

또 더 뒤쪽에 앉는 사람이 지나갈 필요가 있더라도(if someone seated further back needs to pass) 중간에 서 있는 승객은 빈 줄로 피해 들어갈(step into the empty row) 수 있다.

다음엔 기내 중간 부분 짝수 열의 창가 좌석, 이어서 기내 앞부분 짝수 열의 창가 좌석 승객들을 탑승시킨다. 그다음엔 다시 기내 뒷부분부터 앞부분으로 짝수 열의 가운데 좌석 승객들, 이어 복도 쪽 좌석 승객들을 '입장'하도록 한다.

그리고 짝수 열 승객들이 모두 탑승한 다음엔 똑같은 절차(the same procedure)를 홀수 열 승객들(passengers in the odd-numbered seats)에 적용해 순서대로 타도록 한다.

이 같은 방식이 기존 방법들에 비해 속도가 빠른 것은 다수의 승객들이 동시에 짐을 짐칸에 올려 넣을 수 있기(allow multiple passengers to simultaneously stow their baggage) 때문이다. 탑승절차에서 가장 시간 낭비가 많은 부분(the most time-consuming component of the boarding process)을 해소한 결과다.

시뮬레이션 결과에 따르면, 새 방식은 탑승시간을 보통 절차에 소요되는 시간의 6분의 1로 줄일(reduce boarding time to 1/6th of that required by the standard procedure) 수 있는 것으로 분석됐다.

하지만 이 방식은 승객들이 숙지하기에 너무 복잡해 보일 수(may seem too complicated for passengers to master) 있다. 그러나 승객들은 이런 착석 순서 연산법을 기억할(remember the seating order algorithm) 필요가 없다. 항공사들이 승객 각자에게 해당되는 지역을 할당(assign a zone consistent with it)해 현재 하고 있는 것처럼 지역 순서에 따라 들어가게 하면 된다.

그렇다고 아무 문제가 없는 것은 아니다. 나란히 앉는 커플이나 가족들(couples or families being seated together)이 탑승 때 잠시나마 '이별'해야 하는 문제는 어떻게 할 것인가. 스테펀 박사는 "그런 문제는 항공사들이 이론적 결론들을 경험적 연구로 보완(supplement the theoretical conclusions with empirical investigations)하면 쉽게 해결할 수 있을 것"이라고 자신했다.

The Optimal Way to Board Plane Passengers

"Zone 4 is now boarding."

With that announcement, one lines up, walks past the ticket-taker, down the ramp, and eventually enters the plane to witness a few people valiantly crunching their ungainly carry-on bags into the overhead compartments and most others impatiently waiting in the aisles to do the same. Those already in the aisle seats are casting a wary eye on the next backpack threatening to attack them when its owner unthinkingly pivots in the aisle.

Is the standard boarding method really the best way to load an airplane? There are variations, but almost all methods currently in use board by seat or zone number so that those whose seats are near the back of the plane board first and hence don't block passengers boarding after them. That's the theory, at least. Alas, since the people in a single row can't all stow their bags simultaneously, there are always people blocking the aisle as they try to stow their bags. Moreover, those sitting in the aisle seats are not only dodging passing luggage, but must rise and let later-arriving passengers sitting in the window and middle seats enter their row. It's a time-consuming, spirit-sapping mess.

Better Boarding Procedures: Separating Passengers

Enter Jason Steffen, an astrophysicist at Fermi Lab near Chicago. Using computer simulations, he has examined different plane boarding strategies with an eye toward their speed and efficiency. For simplicity, his model assumes a plane with 120 passengers seated in 40 rows, each with a central aisle having three seats to the left and three seats to the right of it. It also assumes that each of the 120 passengers has an assigned seat number and carry-on baggage and that they move forward if and only if no one is directly in front of them. So, given these reasonable assumptions, what's the best way to board? It seems intuitive that the worst way is to load those passengers seated in the front of the plane first and then those a bit further back and so on. And this is, in fact, the worst way to board passengers. So, it might seem almost as intuitive that the standard way—loading the back rows first and then gradually rows nearer the front—should be among the best ways to board, but Steffen's simulations indicate that this is the second-slowest way. Even random boarding is faster.

The Algorithm

After many simulations allowing for different sets of passenger quirks and luggage-stowing times, it turns out that the best method (one of several more or less equivalent methods) calls for passengers in even-numbered window seats near the back of the plane to board first.

Passengers hefting their carry-ons into the overhead compartments are less likely to get in each other's way if there's an empty row between them. Moreover, they can step into the empty row if someone seated further back needs to pass. After these passengers have boarded, passengers in even-numbered window seats in the middle of the plane board, and they are followed by those in even-numbered window seats near the front of the plane. Next, the same procedure is followed for those in the even-numbered middle seats and then for those in the even-numbered aisle seats.

Finally, after the even-numbered passengers have boarded, the same procedure (window, middle, aisle from back to front) is followed for passengers in the odd-numbered seats. These passengers may not always have an empty row to step into, but they will still be separated from entering passengers by a row of already seated even-numbered passengers.

It appears that the reason the protocol is faster is that it allows multiple passengers to simultaneously stow their baggage, the most time-consuming component of the boarding process. This and other similar schemes Steffen discusses may seem too complicated for passengers to master, but passengers needn't remember the seating order algorithm. They can each be assigned a zone consistent with it and enter by zones, as they presently do.

The outcome is fairly robust in the sense that it's relatively insensitive to deviations from it, say, because of couples or families being seated together. Airlines should, of course, supplement these theoretical conclusions with empirical investigations. The simulations suggest that using something like the above protocol would reduce boarding time to 1/6th of that required by the standard procedure! Multiply the average number of passengers per plane trip by the approximate number of trips by the number of minutes saved per boarding, and the number of man hours saved would be more than considerable.

There must be faster, more rational ways to go through security, as well, but, alas, "Zone 4 is now boarding."

John Allen Paulos, a professor of mathematics at Temple University, is the author of the best-sellers "Innumeracy" and "A Mathematician Reads the Newspaper," as well as of the just-released "Irreligion: A Mathematician Explains Why The Arguments for God Just Don't Add Up." His "Who's Counting?" column on ABCNews.com appears the first weekend of every month.

☑ 기억하면 좋을 구절!

time-consuming 시간 낭비인, 시간이 많이 소요되는

➥ This is *time consuming* and obviously inefficient.
이것은 시간낭비에 분명 비효율적이다.

keep a wary eye on 경계의 눈으로 주시하다

➥ The police *keeps a wary on* this area of town.
경찰은 도시 이 지역을 경계의 눈으로 주시하고 있다.

odd number 홀수
even number 짝수

➥ This elevator only stops on *even number* floors.
이 엘리베이터는 짝수 층에만 선다.

aisle seat 통로 쪽 좌석

➥ Would you prefer a window seat or an *aisle seat*?
창가 쪽 좌석으로 드릴까요, 통로 쪽으로 드릴까요?

get in the way 방해되다

➥ Tell him not to *get in the way*.
그에게 방해하지 말라고 말해라.

내 인생의 명언 — 아름다움은 순간이다

▶ 아름다움은 깨지기 쉬운 선물이다.
오비디우스 (로마 시인)

> Beauty is a fragile gift.
> Publius Ovidius Naso

▶ 아름다움은 보는 사람의 가슴속에 있다.
H. G. 웰스 (영국 작가)

> Beauty is in the heart of the beholder.
> H. G. Wells

▶ 아름다움의 문제는 부자로 태어났다가 점점 가난해지는 것과 같다는 사실이다.
조안 콜린스 (영국 작가 · 여배우 · 칼럼니스트)

> The problem with beauty is that it's like being born rich and getting poorer.
> Joan Collins

▶ 위대한 예술은 영원 속에서 붙잡힌 한순간이다.
작자미상

> Great art is an instant arrested in eternity.
> anonymous

News English

"Various Remedies for Hangover in the World"

PARIS (AFP) ! The French call it "la gueule de bois," or wooden mouth. For Germans, it's "Kater," or a tomcat. Japanese know it as "futsukayoi," or "two-days drunk."
But whatever the language and wherever it takes place, a hangover is the same: headache, nausea, shaking, blurred vision, biliousness, dry ... long.

Just as length... for alcohol a... over the cent... In Roman time... raw owls' eggs... In Elizabetha... suffocated in wo... Green frogs wer... for those who w... In the 19th cen... sweeps would ... teaspoon of soot... Look around to... has unleashed an ... hangover fixes, fro... hair of the dog to ... derived from plant e... For those who wake ... head and a mouth li... parrot's cage, the cho... saver − as long as they overlook the fact that the "cures" are underpinned more by hope than the approval of science.

From aspirin and bananas to Vegemite and water, Internet searches present seemingly endless options for preventing or treating alcohol hangovers, say US paediatricians...
Rachel Vreeman and Aaron Carroll.

and the Netherlands reviewed the only trials of hangover cures that had been conducted to objective criteria.
The eight remedies tested were three drugs and four dietary supplements, as well as the fruit sugar f...

...moderation and have water ... dehydration, as well as some ... Whoever finds a cure for ... clearly on the fast track to ... In 2004, alcohol-related ab... work due in part to hango... up to 1.8 billion pounds (... 1.39 billion annual ... as estimate by 10... but the figure does ... costs such as the impact of wo... performance from hangovers ...

It comprises symptoms affecting different parts of the body, varies according to the individual and the circumstances in which the drinking occurred (for instance, a ... eadache could be exacerbated ... in a smoky, noisy nightclub).

...al pathways – metabolic, ... id so on – in which genetic ... also play a role.

...ors together, apart it is most ... a single, one-off cure is ...

...s your body telling you a ... abuse me," he told AFP ...noof cure for hangovers, ... me included," would ... a bit less over the last ...

French call it "la gueule ... rymouth. For Germans, ... ncat. Japanese know it ... -days drunk."

가장 훌륭한 숙취 해소법은 적당한 음주!

wake up with a throbbing head and a mouth like the bottom of a parrot's cage, the choice seems like a life-saver − as long as they overlook the fact that the "cures" are underpinned more by hope than the approval of science.
"From aspirin and bananas to Vegemite and water, Internet searches present seemingly endless options for preventing or treating alcohol hangovers," say US paediatricians Rachel Vreeman and Aaron Carroll.
"No scientific evidence, however, supports any cure or effective prevention," they write in the latest issue of the British Medical Journal (BMJ).
In a 2005 study, doctors in Britain and the Netherlands reviewed the only trials of hangover cures that had been conducted to objective criteria.
The eight remedies tested were three drugs and four dietary supplements. The drugs comprised tolfenamic acid, a painkiller; a beta-blocking drug called propranolol and ... nausea and vertigo ... ments were derived ... from a flower called ... officinalis); the globe ... (cynara) and prickly ... indica).

...chosen randomly and ... two groups, with one ... supposed remedy and ... placebo.

...tent and the tolfenamic ... tive symptoms in a ... ... olunteers, and a prescribed ... tichoke had no ... tivity. "No ... tion for hangover ... ... her to be found to date," ... ose effects are affected so greatly ...

360

세계의 다양한 숙취(宿醉) 해소법

영어로는 'hangover', 불어로는 'la gueule de bois', 독어로는 'kater', 일어로는 '후츠카요이(ふつかよい)'······.

술에 쩔어 깨어나지 못하는 '숙취'(宿醉)를 뜻하는 말들이다. 어느 나라가 됐든, 표현이야 어찌됐든 숙취 증상은 똑같다. 두통, 메스꺼움, 몸 떨림, 흐릿해지는 시각, 담즙 분비 과다, 바싹 마른 입(headache, nausea, shaking, blurred vision, biliousness, dry mouth) 등등.

숙취 증상이 하나 둘이 아닌 것처럼 수 세기에 걸쳐 권유된 과음 치유법들의 면면(the roster of remedies for the intemperance in drinking) 역시 적지 않다. 로마시대엔(in Roman times) 올빼미 알이 술독(alcohol poisoning)을 없애는 데 최고라고 했고, 영국에선 옛날부터 와인에 빠트린 뱀장어 두 마리(a pair of eels suffocated in wine)보다 좋은 것이 없다고 했다. 뱀장어가 없는 사람들에겐(for those who are out of eels) 청개구리(green frog)도

대용물이 될 수(may be an acceptable substitute) 있다고 했다. 19세기 들어 숙취 해소법(hangover chimney sweep)으로 널리 알려진 것은 그을음 한 찻숟가락을 탄 따뜻한 우유를 마시는(sip warm milk with a teaspoon of soot added) 것이었다. 외몽고에선 소금·식초에 절여 토마토 주스에 넣은 양(羊)의 눈알(pickled sheep eyeballs in tomato juice), 미국 서부시대 때는 토끼 똥을 우려낸 차(tea brewed from rabbit dung), 러시아에선 큰 컵 안의 기름진 소시지 위에 보드카를 부어(drip vodka over fatty sausage into a tumbler) 마셨다.

그렇다면 요즘엔 어떤 '비법'들이 있을까. AFP통신은 요즘 인터넷에 숙취 해소법이라고 소개되는 것들이 엄청나게 쏟아지고(unleash an explosion in proposed hangover fixes) 있다고 전한다. 개딜부터 식물 추출물에서 뽑아낸 값비싼 처방약에 이르기까지(from the hair of the dog to expensive formula derived from plant extracts) 한둘이 아니다.

그렇다면 아침에 일어났을 때 지끈거리는 머리와 깔깔한 입안(a throbbing head and a mouth like the bottom of a parrot's cage)에 과연 특효약(a sovereign remedy)은 있는 것일까.

아스피린, 바나나, 양배추 수프, 보리 싹 등 숙취 예방 또는 해소에 수많은 선택들을 제시(present endless options for preventing or treating alcohol hangovers)하지만 그 어느 것도 과학적 근거(scientific evidence)가 있는 것은 아니라고 영국의학저널(British Medical Journal)은 지적한다.

한 예로 영국과 네덜란드 의학자들이 약물 세 종류와 식이보충제(dietary supplement) 네 종류를 실험한 결과를 보자. 약물 세 종류는 진통제인 톨페

나믹 산(tolfenamic acid), 베타 차단 약품(beta-blocking drug)인 프로프라놀롤, 메스꺼움과 어지러움에 사용되는(used for nausea and vertigo) 트로피세트론 등이었다. 네 종류의 식이보충제는 말린 누룩, 서양지치로 불리는 꽃, 솜엉겅퀴, (부채선인장의 일종인) 프리클리 페어에서 추출된(be derived from dried yeast, a flower called borage, the globe artichoke and prickly pear) 것들이었다. 의학자들은 자원자들을 두 그룹으로 나눈 뒤 한 그룹에는 약물 또는 식이보충제, 다른 그룹에는 유효성분이 없는 위약(僞藥)인 플라시보(placebo)를 복용토록 했다. 그 결과 약물 또는 식이보충제를 먹은 상당수 자원자들은 일부 증상에서 완화되는 느낌을 받았다고 밝혔다. 그러나 의학자들은 숙취 예방이나 치유에 설득력 있는 증거(compelling evidence)는 없는 것으로 조사됐다고 말한다. 완화되는 느낌을 받았을 뿐 실제 과학적으로 그런 효과가 입증되지는 못했다는 얘기다.

쉽게 말해서(in plain language) 숙취의 수많은 증상 중 두통 등 일부에 일시적 효과는 나타날 수 있지만, 숙취 증상들을 모두 말끔히 없애주는 약이나 식품은 없다는 것이다. 숙취는 신체의 여러 부위에 영향을 미치는 복잡한 증상들(complex symptoms affecting different parts of the body)로 나타나고, 유전적 차이(genetic variations) 또는 음주 환경에 따라 증상들도 달라지기 때문이다. 따라서 숙취를 한 방에 날려주는 치유법(one-off cure)을 발견하는 사람은 금세 백만장자가 될(be on the fast track to a millionaire) 것이라고 의학자들은 입을 모은다. 다시 말해(in other words) 숙취를 겪지 않으려면 아예 술을 마시지 않거나 적당히 마셔야(drink in moderation) 하며, 차선책이 있다면 각자가 효험이 있다고 믿는 요법을 쓰는 것뿐이라는 얘기다.

Hungover? Take Two Eels and Call me in the Morning

The French call it "la gueule de bois," or wooden mouth. For Germans, it's "Kater," or a tomcat. Japanese know it as "futsukayoi," or "two-days drunk."

But whatever the language and wherever it takes place, a hangover is the same: headache, nausea, shaking, blurred vision, biliousness, dry mouth ⋯ the list of evils is long.

Just as lengthy is the roster of remedies for alcohol abuse that have been touted over the centuries.

In Roman times, Pliny the Elder swore by raw owls' eggs.

In Elizabethan England, a pair of eels suffocated in wine was touted as the trick. Green frogs were an acceptable substitute for those who were out of eels.

In the 19th century, hungover chimney sweeps would sip warm milk with a teaspoon of soot added.

Look around today, and the Internet has unleashed an explosion in proposed hangover fixes, from fried food and the hair of the dog to expensive formulae derived from plant extracts.

For those who wake up with a throbbing head and a mouth like the bottom of a parrot's cage, the choice seems like a life-saver—as long as they overlook the fact the "cures" are underpinned more by hope than the approval of science.

"From aspirin and bananas to Vegemite and water, Internet searches present seemingly endless options for preventing or treating alcohol hangovers," say US paediatricians Rachel Vreeman and Aaron Carroll.

"No scientific evidence, however, supports any cure or effective prevention," they write in the latest issue of the British Medical Journal (BMJ).

In a 2005 study, doctors in Britain and the Netherlands reviewed the only trials of hangover cures that had been conducted to objective criteria.

The eight remedies tested were three drugs and four dietary supplements, as well as the fruit sugar fructose. The drugs comprised tolfenamic acid, a painkiller; a beta-blocking drug called propranolol and tropisetron, used for nausea and vertigo.

The dietary supplements were derived from dried yeast; from a flower called borage (Borago officinalis); the globe artichoke (Cynara scolymus); and prickly pear (Opuntia ficus-indica).

Volunteers were chosen randomly and were divided into two groups, with one group taking the supposed remedy and the other taking a placebo.

The borage, the yeast and the tolfenamic acid did ease some symptoms in a number of volunteers, and a previous study found the prickly pear also made a difference. Apart from that, "no compelling evidence" could be found to describe any of these products as effective in treating or preventing a hangover.

In plain language, say experts, to avoid a hangover, do not drink or drink only in moderation and have water too, to avoid dehydration, as well as some food.

Whoever finds a cure for hangovers is clearly on the fast track to millions.

In 2004, alcohol-related absenteeism from work, due in part to hangover, cost Britain up to 1.8 billion pounds (2.7 billion dollars, 1.89 billion euros), per year, according to an estimate by 10 Downing Street. But this figure does not include indirect costs such as the impact of worker performance from hangovers.

But can a cure ever be found? And—here's an intriguing question—

should we even look for one?

Edzard Ernst, a professor of complementary medicine at the Peninsula Medical School at Britain's University of Exeter, who took part in the 2005 study, says a hangover is a simple word for a complex thing.

It comprises symptoms affecting different parts of the body, varies according to the individual and the circumstances in which the drinking occurred (for instance, a hangover headache could be exacerbated after a night in a smoky, noisy nightclub).

All this means there are many different pathological pathways—metabolic, hormonal and so on—in which genetic variations will also play a role.

Put these factors together, and it is most unlikely that a single, one-off cure is available, suggests Ernst.

"A hangover is your body telling you a message: 'Don't abuse me'," he told AFP.

"If we had a foolproof cure for hangovers, we would drink more. Those of us who like their tipple, me included, would probably hesitate a bit less over the last glass."

✅ 기억하면 좋을 구절!

hangover [hǽŋoʊvər] n. 숙취

She woke up with a terrible *hangover*.
그녀는 끔찍한 숙취와 함께 일어났다.

be brewed from ~로 양조한 / ~로 빚은

Beer *is brewed from* barley.
맥주는 보리로 양조한다.

be derived from ~에서 유래하다 / 나오다 / 파생하다

The information *derived from* them is available worldwide.
그들로부터 입수된 정보는 전세계적으로 유용하다.

throbbing head 지끈거리는 머리 / 두통

Take the medicine to avoid a runny nose and *throbbing head*.
콧물과 지끈거리는 두통을 피하도록 약을 먹어라.

dietary supplements 영양 보충제

Most *dietary supplements* are not subject to drug regulations.
대부분의 영양보충제는 제약 규정에 따르지 않는다.

in plain language 쉽게 말해서

Please explain it *in plain language*.
쉬운 말로 설명해주세요.

내 인생의 명언 — 세상의 어머니는 하나

▶ 여러 나라 엄마들이 함께 만난다면 전쟁은 더 이상 없을 것이다.
E. M. 포스터 (영국 소설가·수필가)

> If the mothers of various nations could meet,
> there would be no more wars.
> E. M. Forster

▶ 남자의 가정은 그 아내의 성이다.
알렉산더 체이스 (미국 언론인)

> A man's home is his wife's castle.
> Alexander Chase

▶ 가정을 꾸려나가는 데 있어 문제점들을 이해하는 여성은
국가를 경영하는 문제점들을 거의 이해한다고 해도 과언이 아니다.
마가릿 대처 (영국 최초 여총리)

> Any woman who understands the problems of
> running a home will be nearer to understanding
> the problems of running a country.
> Margaret Thatcher

▶ 교황청은 대리모에 반대한다. 다행인 것은 예수님이 태어났을 때는
교황청에 그런 원칙이 없었다는 것이다.
엘레인 부슬러 (미국 코미디언)

> The Vatican is against surrogate mothers.
> Good thing they didn't have that rule
> when Jesus was born.
> Elayne Boosler

*There are two ways of
spreading light:
to be the candle or
the mirror that reflects it.*

Edith Wharton

4th NEWS

We are the Global Village

지구촌 이모저모 신기한 세상

News English

"A Blonde in her 20s and her Octogenarian Husband"

WHEN a blonde in her 20s weds an 84-year-old billionaire most people would think her life wouldn't be more demanding than fetching him the odd glass of hot milk.

But then Joe Hardy is hardly your average octogenarian. And now fed-up wife Kristin and Joe have divo... three months together... insatiable demands for ro... sex.

"He wanted sex almost a... I'm just not that sort of gir... of her Viagra-loving husband... And Joe used to get very f... had so keep saying no to him... "I just could not believe wha... me to do. He'd lean over wh... watching TV and grope me...

"That's not how married coupl... But then Joe had always been ... exactly what he expected fro... wife...and even drew up a list... He required her to let him have... s*** when he wanted and par... the house in sexy underwear...

Kristin, who has a four-year-old s... a former relationship, says she... Joe had puts into wives working... luxury hotel in Pyeongsan, Transy... Was two private jets, homes in ... and a mansion at the Nanual Isla...

...husband, Resort. Joe were ... ...children from pre-pr... wildness...as a sui... ...figure in those... sum...

EUR827-a month at the resort and still lived with her mum, was flattered by the attention he showed her.

Self-made Joe, who owns the third biggest DIY chain in the US, 84 Lumber, clearly has an eye for blondes. He own... ...Ch...

told I found it hard to keep up.
"He was always flying off on his private jet. It was so exhausting."

Less than a month after their first date Joe proposed ... ...ed ...id ... ...

22세인 크리스틴과 83세인 조 하디 부부의 한때

just two, and Joe hated that. He also disliked me wearing pyjamas- he called them my army fatigues.

"He wanted me always to wear sexy lingerie to bed and dress in a quite provocative way. And when we went out I had to look a million dollars. I now realise I was his trophy wife."

Kristin, who as Joe's wife had a chauffeur and housekeeper, says her husband's badgering for sex caused her so much stress that she took up smoking.

She claims her hair then began to fall out as she got rashes all over her body. She says: "That just made Joe even more angry as I was ill and he could not touch me."

The final straw came when Joe allegedly demanded that she let a nanny look after her soft, full-time.

Kristin immediately moved back in with her mum. But the next day her husband sent her a sexual contract, listing what she would have to do if she came back. Joe said, "I never allowed him a feel of a s*** our sex life was 'non-existent' and at would all have to change.

But the breaking point was him spending 2pm than a nanny look after rothov so I could spend more tim... k him. My solu...ppa more to be that wishing...

...es later be filed for divorce on the ...ds of irreconcilable differences ... ...ing of the pre-nup. Kristin the for... ...accept – but was awarded an op... ...settle...

...e has happily resettled in 38...
... Seoul. "I am thrilled..."

372

85세와 이혼한 24세 여성, 위자료 한 푼 못 받은 사연

22세 미국 여성이 83세 억만장자와 결혼했다. 근무하던 직장의 사장이었다. 돈 때문은 아니었다. 워낙 잘 대해주는 데 감동해 사랑하게 됐다고 한다. 하지만 결혼 3개월 만에 이혼했다. 그는 24시간 내내 잠시도 놓아주지 않는 섹스광이었다. 친정으로 도망갔다. 무단 가출이라고 했다. 이혼 소송을 당했다. 위자료는 한 푼도 받지 못했다. 그녀에겐 네 살 연상인 새 애인이 생겼다. 행복하다고 한다.

20대 나이의 금발여성 크리스틴(Kristine, a blonde in her 20s)이 83세 억만장자와 결혼한다고(marry an 83-year-old billionaire) 할 때 대부분 사람들은 "이따금 따뜻한 우유나 갖다 주는 것 이상 힘들 일이 없을(wouldn't be more demanding fetching him the odd glass of hot milk) 것"이라고 수군거렸다(talk in whispers).

그러나 61세 연상의 남편 조 하디는 평범한 80대 노인이 아니었다(be

hardly your average octogenarian). 진절머리가 난 크리스틴(the fed-up wife Kristine)은 3개월 만에 이혼하기로 했다. 24시간 섹스를 원하는, 만족시킬 수 없는 83세 남편 하디 때문(because of the 83-year-old Hardy's insatiable demands for round-the-clock sex)이었다.

크리스틴은 "그는 거의 항상 섹스를 원했어요(want sex almost all the time). 난 그런 여자가 아닌데(be not that sort of girl) 말이에요"라고 비아그라를 좋아하는 남편에 대해 털어놓았다(say of her Viaga-loving husband).

83세 남편은 크리스틴이 계속 싫다고 하는(keep saying no to him) 데 대해 크게 실망하곤(used to get very frustrated) 했다. 함께 TV를 볼 때도(even while watching TV together) 크리스틴에게 기댄 채 몸을 더듬어(lean over and grope her)냈다. 심지어 크리스틴에게 해주기를 원하는 항목을 분명히 해서(be clear about exactly what he expects from his third wife Kristine) 목록을 작성하기까지(even draw up a list) 했다.

그는 원할 때마다 크리스틴이 만족시켜주기를 원하며, 언제나 프렌치 키스를 하고(Fench-kiss him constantly), 섹시한 속옷을 입고 집 안을 돌아다니라고(parade around the house in sexy underwear) 종용했다.

다른 사람과의 과거 관계에서 얻은 네 살짜리 아들이 있는 크리스틴은 2년 전 하디와 사랑에 빠졌다고(fall for Hardy two years ago) 한다. 펜실바니아 주(州) 파밍턴 소재 그의 소유 호화 호텔에서 일하고 있을(work at his luxury hotel in Farmington, Pennsylvania) 때였다.

두 대의 개인용 제트기(two private jets), 플로리다 주에 있는 여러 채의 집, 5성급 네마콜린 우드랜즈 리조트의 맨션(a mansion at the five-star

Nemacolin Woodlands Resort) 등을 소유하고 있는 하디는 과거 두 차례 결혼에서 낳은 일곱 명의 자녀가 있으며(have seven children from two previous marriages) 주변 지역에선 내로라 하는 유명 인사(a well-known figure)이다.

호텔 근무로 1170달러(약 140만원)의 월급을 받으며 어머니와 함께 살던 크리스틴은 처음에 하디가 그녀에게 보이는 관심을 받게(be flattered by the attention he shows her) 된다. 자수성가한 하디(self-made Hardy)는 미국 내 3대 주택건축자재업체인 84 럼버의 소유주로 크리스틴에게 물불 안 가리고 정면 돌파를 시도했다(make a beeline for Kristine).

걸핏하면 크리스틴에게 100달러 팁을 쥐어주곤 하던 하디는 어느날 크리스틴에게 전화번호를 알려달라고(ask for her phone number) 했다. 크리스틴은 일과 관련된 일 때문(because of something to do with work)이려니 하고 번호를 알려줬다.

이튿날 전화를 걸어온 하디는 크리스틴에게 어디를 가고 싶은지, 뭘 하고 싶은지, 여권은 갖고 있는지, 함께 여행을 갈 수 있는지 묻기 시작했다. 결국 크리스틴은 점심식사를 같이 하기로 했고(agree to meet him for lunch), 곧이어 물 쓰듯 하는 쇼핑이 이어졌다(shopping spree soon followed).

약 2주 후쯤 하디는 크리스틴을 가까운 포르쉐 대리점에 데려가더니(take her to a nearby Porsche dealership) 8만 4000달러(약 1억 300만 원)짜리 신형 스포츠카의 열쇠를 건네주었다(hand over the keys to a new silver $84000 sports car). 부활절 선물(an Easter present)이라고 했다.

뿐만 아니었다. 쇼핑을 함께 가서 크리스틴이 핸드백이나 구두를 쳐다보

노라면 그 자리에서 두세 개씩 사서 손에 쥐어줬다. 하디와 가까이 지낸다는 사실은 금세 소문이 났고, 크리스틴은 혹독한 비아냥에 직면(be subject to cruel taunts)하게 됐다.

"주위 사람들이 나를 보고 '돈 많은 남자를 우려먹는 여자'라고 한다는(call me a gold-digger) 걸 알고 있었다. 하지만 전혀 그런 것이 아니었다. 하디는 나이는 80대이지만 40대 젊은 사람 같은 힘을 갖고 있는(have the energy of someone 40 years younger) 남자였다. 우정과 재미로 시작됐던 것(what started out as a friendship and some fun)이 좀 더 깊이 발전됐을(develop into something more deep) 뿐"이라고 크리스틴은 말한다.

첫 데이트 후 3개월도 안 된(less than a month after their first date) 2007년 4월, 하디는 3.5 캐럿 다이아몬드를 선물하며 프로포즈를 해왔다(propose and present Kristin with a three-and-half carat diamond). 로맨틱할 것도 없었다고 했다. 반지를 건네주면서(hand her the ring) 그냥 "여기 있어"라고 말했을(say 'here y'are) 뿐이라고 한다.

결국 혼전계약에 서명한(sign a pre-nuptial agreement) 크리스틴은 "하디를 사랑한 것이지 그의 돈을 사랑했던 것이 아니다(be in love with Hardy, not his money)"고 극구 강조한다. 돈 때문에 결혼했다는(marry him for his money) 주위 사람들의 말은 얼토당토않은(couldn't be further from the truth) 소리라고 일축한다.

두 사람은 2007년 5월 5일 라스베이거스의 호화스러운 윈호텔에서 성대하게 결혼식을 올렸다(wed in a lavish ceremony at the luxury Wynn hotel in Las Vegas). 신혼여행은 유럽으로 갔다(spend their honeymoon in

Europe). 하지만 두 사람에게 딱히 로맨틱한 휴가는 아니었다(be not exactly a romantic break for two).

하디가 일곱 자녀 중 둘과 여러 명의 친구들을 데리고 왔기(bring along two of his seven children and several friends) 때문이다. 크리스틴은 "나는 주변에 사람들이 많은 것을 좋아한다(like a big group around me). 그의 자녀들과도 정말 잘 지냈다(get on really well with his children)"며 "가장 친한 내 친구도 같이 가서(my best friend come along too) 유럽을 누루 돌아다니며 좋은 시간을 가졌다(have a great time going all over Europe)"고 했다.

크리스틴은 하디의 사치스러운 제트족(제트여객기로 세계를 돌아다니는 상류계급) 생활양식에 몹시 놀랐다(be bowled over Hardy's extravagant jet-set lifestyle)고 한다. 자신은 실제로 시골 여자에 불과하고(be just a simple country girl at heart) "웨딩드레스도 124달러(약 15만 원)짜리였다"며, 그러나 하디는 출신 배경이 다른 사람이었다(be cut from a different cloth)고 했다.

파리에선 어느날 아침 옷 구입 비용으로만 11만 7000달러(약 1억 4300만 원)를 썼고, 하룻밤 호텔비로 1170달러(약 143만 원)의 룸서비스 비용을 포함해 5만 달러(약 6100만 원)를 냈다.

집으로 돌아온 뒤 그들의 로맨스는 하디의 '특이한' 요구로 삐그러지기 시작(start to sour as Hardy's 'unusual' demands)했다. 힘센 남자임을 입증이라도 해보이려는(prove himself as some sort of stud) 듯 거의 매일 밤 관계를 요구(want sex almost every night)했다. 이를 위해 그는 약도 복용(there are pills involved on his part)했다.

크리스틴이 밤중에 일어나 다른 방에 있던 두 살배기 아기를 보러 가는 것도 싫어했고, 파자마를 입는 것은 질색(dislike her wearing pajamas)했다. 파자마 속옷을 입으면 전투복 같다며(call them her army fatigues) 당장 벗으라고 호통을 쳤다.

그는 그녀에게 늘 섹시한 속옷을 입도록 했다(oblige her always to wear sexy lingerie to bed). 평상시 옷도 아주 도발적인 스타일로 입도록(dress in a quite provocative way) 했다. 특히 외출할 때면 아주 매력적으로 꾸며야(have to look a million dollar) 했다. 전형적인 (부자가 얻은) 미녀 아내(be a trophy wife) 신분이었던 것이다.

크리스틴에게는 개인 전용 운전기사와 가정부가 딸려(have a full-time chauffeur and housekeeper) 있었다. 하지만 남편의 성적인 괴롭힘(her husband's badgering for sex)이 워낙 큰 스트레스를 줘(cause her so much stress) 담배까지 피우게(take up smoking) 됐다.

스트레스가 어찌나 심했던지 온몸에 발진이 생기고(develop rashes all over her body) 머리털이 빠지기 시작(begin to fall out)했다. 몸이 아파서 그녀의 몸을 만지지 못하게 되면서 남편은 더욱 신경질적이 됐다.

결정적으로 한계를 넘어서는 일(the final straw)은, 하디가 크리스틴의 두 살짜리 아들을 하루 종일 보모에게 맡기라고 요구(demand her to let a nanny look after her son, full-time)하면서 벌어졌다.

크리스틴은 즉시 어머니 집으로 돌아와 버렸지만(immediately move back in with her mom), 남편 하디는 다음 날 그녀가 귀가하면 해야 할 것들의 목록을 적은(listing what she would have to do after coming back home) 섹스 계약서를 보내왔다(send her a sexual contract).

게다가 자신과 더 많은 시간을 보내야 한다며 아들을 보모에 맡기라고 또 다시 요구했다. 하지만 크리스틴에게 아들은 그 무엇보다 소중한 존재(be more to be than anything)였다. 디자이너 명품 의상과 핸드백, 구두 등 그 모든 것들을 가질 수(keep all the designer handbags, shoes and dresses) 있다는 것도 그녀에겐 아무 의미가 없었다. 곧바로 돌아가지 않겠다며 거절하는(refuse to go back) 메시지를 보냈다.

수 주가 지난 뒤 하디는 극복할 수 없는 성격 차이를 이유로 이혼소송을 접수(file for divorce on the grounds of irreconcilable differences)시켰다. 크리스틴은 혼전 계약 내용을 어겼다는 이유로 한 푼의 위자료도 받지 못했다(do not get any consolation money). 결혼 전 선물받은 포르쉐 차 한 대는 그냥 가져도 좋다는 소리를 들었다.

크리스틴은 현재 28세의 한 IT 컨설턴트와 약혼한(now happily engaged to a 28-year-old It consultant) 상태다. "아무런 후회도 없다(have no regrets)"고 한다. 하디가 1만 달러(약 1200만 원)짜리 핸드백을 사주곤(be bought handbags that cost $10000) 했지만, 할인매장에서 물건을 사는(shop at a thrift shop) 지금이 훨씬 더 행복하다"고 말했다.

HE'S SEX-MAD; Single Mum, 22 Ditches her Billionaire Husband, 84 After Only 3 Months' Marriage Because......

WHEN a blonde in her 20s weds an 84-year-old billionaire most people would think her life wouldn't be more demanding than fetching him the odd glass of hot milk.

But then Joe Hardy is hardly your average octogenarian. And now fed-up wife Kristin and Joe have divorced after just three months together··· because of his insatiable demands for round-the-clock sex.

"He wanted sex almost all the time, but I'm just not that sort of girl," says Kristin of her Viagra-loving husband.

"And Joe used to get very frustrated as I had to keep saying no to him.

"I just could not believe what he wanted me to do. He'd lean over while we were watching TV and grope me.

"That's not how married couples behave."

But then Joe had always been clear about exactly what he expected from his third wife … and even drew up a list.

He required her to let him have a "feel of t*t" when he wanted and parade around the house in sexy underwear.

Kristin, who has a four-year-old son from a former relationship, says she fell for Joe two years ago while working at his luxury hotel in Farmington, Pennsylvania. With two private jets, homes in Florida and a mansion at the fivestar Nemacolin Woodlands Resort, Joe—with seven children from two previous marriages—was a wellknown figure in their small town.

Kristin, who earned just EUR827-amonth at the resort and still lived with her mum,was flattered by the attention he showed her.

Self-made Joe, who owns the third biggest DIY chain in the US, 84 Lumber, clearly has an eye for blondes. He even paid singer Christine Aguilera to serenade him on his 84th birthday.

And he made a beeline for pretty Kristin after she gave him a manicure.

"He was my boss," she says. "And he was a big tipper. He left me a $100 tip, the biggest I ever got.

"I hardly knew him but he asked me for my number. I really thought it was something to do with work.

"The next day he called and started asking me about where I would like to go, what I wanted to do. He wanted to know if I had a passport and could I travel with him."

Kristin agreed to meet Joe for lunch and shopping sprees soon followed. Two weeks later he took her to a nearby Porsche dealership where he handed over the keys to a silver EUR30,000 sports car.

"It was my Easter present. I couldn't believe it, but Joe was always so generous.

"Like anyone around the town I knew he was very rich, but money has never really interested me.

"When we'd go shopping and I'd see a handbag or pair of shoes he'd tell me to buy two or three." As news of her friendship with Joe spread round town Kristin was subjected to cruel taunts.

"I knew people were calling me a gold-digger, but it wasn't like that," she says. "Joe might have been in his 80s but he had the energy of someone 40 years younger. What started out as a friendship and some fun developed into something more deep.

"But although I was more than 60 years younger than him, truth be told I found it hard to keep up.

"He was always flying off on his private jet. It was so exhausting."

Less than a month after their first date Joe proposed in April 2007 and presented Kristin with a threeand-half carat emerald cut diamond. She moans: "But it wasn't romantic. He just handed me the ring and said 'here y'are'."

Kristin, who signed a pre-nuptial agreement, is adamant that she was in love with Hardy, now 85, not his money.

The 24-year-old added: "People were calling me a gold-digger but that could not be further from the truth. I married for love and it is as simple as that."

The couple wed in a lavish ceremony at the luxury Wynn Hotel in Las Vegas on May 5, 2007.

They spent their honeymoon in Europe, but it wasn't exactly a romantic break for two, since Joe brought along two of his seven children and several friends.

But Kristen did not object. "I liked having a big group around me and I got on really well with his children.

"My best friend came along too so I had a great time going all over Europe." Kristin was bowled over by her extravagant jet-set lifestyle.

"I'm just a simple country girl at heart and I was proud that my wedding dress cost just EUR88," she says. "But Joe is cut from a different cloth. One morning in Paris we spent more than EUR80,000 on clothes.

"And the hotel bill for one night at the Ritz was more than EUR35,000."

But when they returned home, the romance soon started to sour as Joe's "unusual" demands dominated their life.

"He wanted sex almost every night but I wasn't having any of that," says Kristin. "Yes, there were pills involved on his part but they did not always work. I think he was trying prove himself as some sort of stud.

"There were nights when I would have to get up and go and see to my son who was then just two, and Joe hated that. He also disliked me wearing pyjamas- he called them my army fatigues.

"He wanted me always to wear sexy lingerie to bed and dress in a quite provocative way. And when we went out I had to look a million dollars. I now realise I was his trophy wife."

Kristin, who as Joe's wife had a chauffeur and housekeeper, says her husband's badgering for sex caused her so much stress that she took up smoking.

She claims her hair then began to fall out as she got rashes all over her body. She says: "That just made Joe even more angry as I was ill and he could not touch me."

The final straw came when Joe allegedly demanded that she let a nanny look after her son, full-time.

Kristin immediately moved back in with her mum. But the next day her husband sent her a sexual contract, listing what she would have to do if she came back.

"Joe said I never allowed him a 'feel of a t*t', our sex life was 'non-existent' and that would all have to change.

"But the breaking point was him demanding again that a nanny look after Matthew so I could spend more time with him. My son meant more to be than anything."

Weeks later Joe filed for divorce on the grounds of irreconcilable differences. Because of the pre-nup, Kristin did not get a payout - but was allowed to keep her Porsche.

But, now happily engaged to 28year-old IT consultant Tony Lizza, she has no regrets.

"Sitting in a private jet drinking champagne was fun, and Joe was very generous," she says.

"But, to be honest, the money, designer clothes and private jet meant nothing to me."

✅ 기억하면 좋을 구절!

octogenarian [ɑ́:ktədʒəˈneriən] a. 나이가 80대인 사람

 Most of them are *octogenarians*.
그들 대부분은 나이가 80대인 사람들이다.

talk in whispers 수군대다

 They *talked in whispers* among them-selves when they saw me.
그들은 나를 보더니 수군거렸다.

insatiable [ɪnséɪʃəbl] a. 채울 수 없는, 만족 못하는

 Suddenly he has an *insatiable* taste for reading.
그는 갑자기 끊임없이 책을 읽고 싶어졌다.

a well-known figure 유명인사

 He was once *a well-known figure*.
그는 예전에는 유명인사였다.

make a beeline for (사람, 물건)을 향해 직행하다, 돌진하다

 I will *make a beeline for* her.
나는 그녀를 향해 직행하겠다.

couldn't be further from the truth 사실무근이다

 The rumor *couldn't be further from the truth*.
그 소문은 사실과는 전혀 다르다.

내 인생의 명언 — 나눔은 나를 위한 것

▶ 빛을 퍼뜨리는 두 가지 방법이 있다.
촛불이 되거나 촛불을 반사하는 거울이 되는 것이다.
이디스 워튼 (미국 소설가)

> There are two ways of spreading light:
> to be the candle or the mirror that reflects it.
> Edith Wharton

▶ 자선을 베푸는 모든 행동은 천국을 향한 디딤돌을 놓는 것과 같다.
헨리 비처 (미국 목사 · 저술가)

> Every charitable act is a stepping stone towards heaven.
> Henry Beecher

▶ 누구나 모두를 도와줄 수는 없다.
그러나 모두 누군가를 도와줄 수는 있다.
로널드 레이건 (미국 40대 대통령)

> We can't help everyone, but everyone can help someone.
> Ronald Reagan

▶ 당신의 현재 상황은 당신이 갈 수 있는 곳을 결정하는 것이 아니다.
단지 당신이 출발하는 곳을 결정할 뿐이다.
니도 큐베인 (미국 컨설팅사업가)

> Your present circumstances don't determine where
> you can go; they merely determine where you start.
> Nido Qubein

▶ 숨겨진 숭고한 행위가 가장 존경받는다.
블레즈 파스칼 (프랑스 수학자 · 물리학자 · 철학자 · 종교사상가)

> Noble deeds that are concealed are most esteemed.
> Blaise Pascal

News English

"A Girl Resuscitated Singing 'Mamma Mia'"

Parents say final goodbye, then coma girl wakes up singing Abba

A toddler expected to die from meningitis stunned her family by waking up from a coma singing the Abba song Mamma Mia!

Layla Towsey suffered a heart attack after being struck down with the potentially fatal brain bug.

Her parents kissed the three-year-old goodbye and watched helplessly as the boy unconscious for five days.

But miraculously the little fighter pulled through and came round singing her favourite song from the hit musical.

Mum Katy Towsey, 23, said: "We'd been preparing ourselves for bad news as the life support machine was keeping her alive. Even when doctors took her off support and reduced the drugs she was on, we didn't know how badly disabled she would be.

"But on the Sunday morning I could hear her singing Mamma Mia! quietly. I could believe it.

"I knew immediately she was going to be OK."

Layla, from Gidea Park, Essex, fell ill last month and suffered a heart attack just two hours after being admitted to hospital with a rash.

She was transferred to St Mary's Hospital in Paddington, West London, and put on life support. Katy, who was joined by Layla's dad Jay Malik, 28, said: "Before they put her in the ambulance we were told to give her a kiss goodbye, it was an awful moment."

Layla, who was diagnosed with meningitis B and meningococcal septicaemia, is a huge fan of hit movie Mamma Mia!

Katy said: "That's definitely one of her favourite songs, she's seen the film and she loves it."

Layla has now made a good recovery but has some scarring on her legs from the blood poisoning.

Steve Dayman of charity Meningitis UK, said: "Layla is a very lucky little girl."

Parents say final goodbye, then coma girl wakes up singing Abba

A toddler expected to die from meningitis stunned her family by waking up from a coma singing the Abba song Mamma Mia!

Layla Towsey suffered a heart attack after being struck down with the potentially fatal brain bug.

Her parents kissed the three-year-old goodbye and watched helplessly as the boy unconscious for five days.

But miraculously the little fighter pulled through and came round singing her favourite song from the hit musical.

Mum Katy Towsey, 23, said: "We'd been preparing ourselves for bad news as the life support machine was keeping her alive. Even when doctors took her off support and reduced the drugs she was on, we didn't know how badly disabled she would be."

기적적으로 다시 살아난 레일라 타우시

'맘마 미아' 노래 부르며 되살아난 소녀

  뇌막염으로 죽어가던(be dying from meningitis) 3세 여아가 갑자기 '맘마 미아' 노래를 부르며 혼수상태에서 깨어나 가족들을 놀라게(stun her family by waking up from a coma singing the song 'Mamma Mia') 했다.

  영국 남부 에섹스 주(州)에 사는 레일라 타우시라는 세 살배기 여자아이는 2009년 4월 치명적인 뇌질환으로 쓰러진 뒤(after being struck down with the fatal brain bug) 심장발작을 일으켰다(suffer a heart attack). 부모들은 회생 가망성이 없다는 의사들의 말에 세 살짜리 딸에게 작별 키스를 하고(kiss the three-year-old daughter goodbye), 생명유지장치에 의지해 의식 없이 누워 있는(lie unconscious on life support) 모습을 망연자실 지켜볼 수밖에 없었다. 하지만 그 어린 투병 환자(the little fighter against the disease) 레일라는 기적적으로 생명의 위기를 이겨내고 자기가 가장 좋아하는 히트 뮤지컬의 노래를 부르며 소생해 살아났다(miraculously pull through and come round singing her favorite song from the hit musical). 레일라의 엄마 케이티(23세)는 "아이가 생명유지장치에 의지하고 있었기 때문에 나쁜 소식을 각오하고(be preparing oneself for bad news) 있었다"며 "의사들이 생명유지장치를 떼어내고(take her off life support) 복용 중이던 약도 줄인 상태였다"고 말했다. 그런데 기적 같은 일이 일어났다. 엄마 케이티는 딸 아이가 나지막한 목소리로 맘마 미아를 부르는 소리를 들었다(hear her daughter singing Mamma Mia in a low voice). 환청이 아니었다(be not an auditory hallucination). 믿을 수 없는 일이었다. 그 순간 아이가 괜찮아질 것(be going to be OK)이라는 생각이 불현듯 들었다.

　레일라는 병세를 느껴(fall ill last month) 병원에 입원한 지 두 시간 만에(just two hours after being admitted to hospital with a rush) 심장 발작을 일으켰다. 레일라는 즉각 런던의 세인트 메리 병원으로 후송돼 생명유지장치 아래 응급 조치에 들어갔다. 레일라의 부모는 "레일라를 앰뷸런스에 태우기 전에 작별 키스를 하라는 말을 들었다(be told to give her a kiss goodbye)"며 "정말 끔찍한 순간(be an awful moment)이었다"고 회상했다. 뇌막염 B와 수막구균성 패혈증 진단을 받은(be diagnosed with meningitis B and meningococcal septicemia) 레일라는 영화 히트작 맘마 미아의 열렬한 팬(a huge fan of hit movie Mamma Mia)이었다. 엄마 케이티는 레일라가 영화 '맘마 미아'를 보고 너무나 좋아했고, 가장 좋아하는 노래도 '맘마 미아'였다며, 아이가 그 노래를 부르며 깨어나 완연한 회복세를 보이기(make a good recovery) 시작한 것이 너무나 놀랍고 신기하다고 말했다.

Meningitis Toddler Wakes from Coma Singing Mamma Mia!

Parents say final goodbye..then coma girl wakes up singing Abba.

A toddler expected to die from meningitis stunned her family by waking up from a coma singing the Abba song Mamma Mia!

Layla Towsey suffered a heart attack after being struck down with the potentially fatal brain bug.

Her parents kissed the three-year-old goodbye and watched helplessly as she lay unconscious for five days.

But miraculously the little fighter pulled through and came round singing her favourite song from the hit musical.

Mum Katy Towsey, 23, said: "We'd been preparing ourselves for bad news as the life support machine was keeping her alive. Even when doctors took her off life support and reduced the drugs she was on, we didn't know how badly disabled she would be.

"But on the Sunday morning I could hear her singing Mamma Mia! quietly. I couldn't believe it.

"I knew immediately she was going to be OK."

Layla, from Gidea Park, Essex, fell ill last month and suffered a heart attack just two hours after being admitted to hospital with a rash.

She was transferred to St Mary's Hospital in Paddington, West London, and put on life support. Katy, who was joined by Layla's dad Jay Malik, 28, said: "Before they put her in the ambulance we were told to give her a kiss goodbye, it was an awful moment."

Layla, who was diagnosed with meningitis B and meningococcal septicaemia, is a huge fan of hit movie Mamma Mia!

Katy said: "That's definitely one of her favourite songs, she's seen the film and she loves it."

Layla has now made a good recovery but has some scarring on her legs from the blood poisoning.

Steve Dayman, of charity Meningitis UK, said: "Layla is a very lucky little girl."

☑ 기억하면 좋을 구절!

be on life support 생명유지장치를 달고 있다

He *is on life support* after suffering lung damage and other complications.
그는 폐 손상과 합병증 들을 겪고 생명유지장치에 의지하고 있다.

an auditory hallucination 환청

I've developed *auditory hallucinations*.
내게 환청이 생겼다.

fall ill 병에 걸리다

It is not until we *fall ill* that we fully appreciate our good health.
병에 걸린 뒤에야 건강의 소중함을 깨닫게 된다.

pull through (심한 병·수술 뒤에) 회복하다

The doctors think she will *pull through*.
의사들은 그녀가 회복할 것으로 생각한다.

prepare oneself for (to do) ~의 준비를 하다 / 각오하다

The armed forces *prepared themselves for* warfare or military conflict.
군은 전쟁 또는 군사적 충돌 대비에 들어갔다.

내 인생의 명언 — 권력의 재미난 속성

▶ 권력의 유일한 이점은 더 많은 선을 행할 수 있다는 것이다.
발타사르 그라시안 (스페인 예수회 신부 · 작가)

> The sole advantage of power is that you can do more good.
> Baltasar Gracian

▶ 권력의 고통을 알려면 권력 있는 자들에게 가야 한다.
권력의 기쁨을 알려면 권력을 추구하는 자들에게 가야 한다.
찰스 콜튼 (영국 성직자 · 작가)

> To know the pains of power, we must go to
> those who have it; to know its pleasures,
> we must go to those who are seeking it.
> Charles Caleb Colton

▶ 권력을 가진 자는 어느 누구도 믿을 수 없다.
뉴트 깅리치 (미국 정치인)

> You can't trust anybody with power.
> Newt Gingrich

▶ 원칙보다 특권을 더 중시하는 사람은 곧 둘 다 모두를 잃게 된다.
아이젠하워 (미국 34대 대통령)

> A people that values its privileges above
> its principles soon loses both.
> Dwight D. Eisenhower

Favorite famous sayings!

▶ 권력은 부패하기 쉽다. 절대권력은 절대적으로 부패한다.
액톤 (영국 정치인 · 역사가 · 작가)

Power tends to corrupt and absolute power corrupts absolutely.
John Acton

▶ 정치가는 자신이 한 말을 믿지 않기 때문에
다른 사람들이 자신을 믿으면 놀란다.
샤를 드골 (프랑스 정치가)

Since a politician never believes what he says, he is surprised when others believe him.
Charles de Gaulle

▶ 정치인은 인류를 두 부류로 나눈다. 도구와 적으로.
프리드리히 니체 (독일 철학자)

A politician divides mankind into two classes; tools and enemies.
Friedrich Wilhelm Nietzsche

News English

"A Rapist Arrested by an Elderly Woman of Sagacity"

A rapist who posed as a policeman to get into his 89-year-old victim's home was snared because she copied a scene from CSI and scratched his face for DNA. Bouncer Mauro Lopes, 31, who weighs 20 stone, raped the frail seven-stone widow twice after tricking his way into her home in Leeds, West Yorkshire.

In the midst of her horrific ordeal she had the presence of mind to remember an episode of the cult U.S. forensics drama and clawed his face knowing police would be able to retrieve his DNA from under her fingernails.

It allowed [police] to catch Lopes just two days [after] the attack on March 14 because he was already on the national database after a drink-driving offence in 2005.

Lopes, who won asylum after coming to the UK from Angola on a false passport seven years ago, was jailed for nine years at Leeds Crown Court, yesterday.

Prosecutor Felicity Davis said the attack [on the elderly] woman's face [was so violent that she] had to be [taken] to hospital with heavy bleeding.

But the widow told police, 'I have been watching CSI so I scratched his face so you could get DNA from my fingernails.'

'I live alone now so I [was] terrified... [I am] trying to find strength [to be] identified for legal reasons.'

Anne Dixon, defending, told the court that Lopes was remorseful and, in his own words, 'had fallen out of his personality with drink'.

He carried out the attack following a visit to a lapdancing club after discovering his girlfriend was cheating on him.

[Lopes admitted] his offences [and faces deportation.]

Judge Sally Cahill QC told him at Leeds Crown Court: 'Due Sept Steve Payne of West Yorkshire Police, who led the investigation, said: 'I paid to the pay the respect to the victim in this case who acted with incredible bravery despite the terrible ordeal she went through to bring this man to justice.'

A rapist who posed as a policeman to get into his 89-year-old victim's home was snared because she copied a scene from CSI and scratched his face for DNA. Bouncer Mauro Lopes, 31, who weighs 20 stone, raped the frail seven-stone widow twice after tricking his way into her home in Leeds, West Yorkshire.

In [the midst of] her horrific ordeal she [had the presence] of mind to remember [an episode of] the cult U.S. forensics [drama and cla]wed his face knowing [police would be ab]le to retrieve his DNA [from under her fi]ngernails.

[It allo]wed [polic]es to catch Lopes just [two days after] the attack on March 14 [because he was] already on the national [database after a] drink-driving offence in [2005.]

[Lopes, who won] asylum after coming to [the UK from] Angola on a false passport, [seven years ago,] was jailed for nine years [at Leeds] Crown Court yesterday.

[Prosecutor] Felicity Davis said the attack [on the elderly woman's face] was so violent that she [had to be ta]ken to hospital with heavy [bleeding.]

[But the widow], of 20 years [managed to] [tell police:] 'I have been watching CSI so I [scratched] his face so you could get DNA [from my fi]ngernails.'

'I [live now to live alone this is a rare] case [and] had trouble sleeping. She [launched for legal reasons.]

Anne Dixon, defending, told the court that Lopes was remorseful and, in his own words, 'had fallen out of his personality with drink'.

할머니를 성폭행한 바운서 로프스와 인기 드라마 CSI의 한 장면

할머니 총명함에 붙잡힌 성폭행범

7년 전 위조여권으로 앙골라에서 영국으로 건너온(come to the UK from Angola on a false passport) 바운서 로프스는 9년형을 선고받고 수감(be jailed for nine years)됐다. 그는 2009년 3월 14일 경찰관을 가장해 웨스트 요크셔 주(州) 리즈 소재 89세 피해자의 집에 들어가(pose as a policeman to get into the 89-year-old victim's home) 성폭행한 혐의로 9년의 실형을 선고 받았다(be sentenced to nine years' imprisonment).

체중이 127kg나 나가는(weigh 127kg) 로프스는 44kg 밖에 안 되는 연약한 과부 할머니를 두 차례나 범하는(rape the frail 44kg widow twice) 만행을 저질렀다(commit the act of brutality).

하지만 범인은 할머니가 미국 과학수사드라마 CSI의 한 장면을 모방해(copy a scene from the U.S. forensics drama CSI) DNA를 확보하기 위해 손톱으로 얼굴을 긁어놓는(scratch the rapist's face for DNA) 바람에 걸

려들었다(be snared).

끔찍한 시련 와중에도(in the midst of her horrific ordeal) 할머니는 냉정을 잃지 않고(have the presence of mind) CSI의 내용을 기억해내(remember an episode of CSI) 성폭행범의 얼굴을 손톱으로 할퀴었다(claw his face). 나중에 경찰이 자신의 손톱 밑에서 범인의 DNA를 확보할 수 있을(be able to retrieve his DNA from under her fingernails) 것으로 생각했던 것이다.

할머니는 경찰에 성폭행 피해 사실을 신고하면서 자신의 손톱 밑에서 범인의 DNA 추출이 가능하다고(can get DNA from her fingernails) 밝혔고, 덕분에 형사들은 로프스를 성폭행 사건 이틀 만에 체포할(catch Lopes just two days after the sexual assault) 수 있었다. 로프스가 과거 세 차례의 성폭행과 음주운전으로 검거돼 전국 DNA데이터베이스에 올라 있었기(be on the national DNA database after a drink-driving offence and three counts of rape and sexual assaults) 때문에 잡아들이는 것은 시간문제였다.

범인 로프스가 커다란 베개를 할머니의 얼굴에 덮은(put a large pillow over the woman's face) 뒤 어찌나 포악하게 폭행했던지 할머니는 심한 출혈로 병원에 실려가야만(have to be taken to hospital with heavy bleeding) 했다.

혼자 살기 어렵게 된(be unable to live alone) 할머니는 현재 요양시설에 들어가 있으나 지금도 잠을 제대로 이루지 못하고(have trouble sleeping) 있다고 한다. 할머니의 신원은 법적인 이유 때문에 공개할 수 없는(cannot be identified for legal reasons) 상태.

경찰과 검찰은 "그런 끔찍한 상황에도 불구하고(despite the terrifying

ordeal) 믿기지 않는 용감함으로(with incredible bravery) 대처해 범인 검거를 도와준 할머니에게 경의를 표한다(pay respect to the victim)"면서, "그 덕분에 성폭행범이 정의의 심판을 받게(bring the rapist to justice) 할 수 있었다"고 말했다.

Rapist Caught After Victim, 89, Traps him with Trick from CSI

A rapist who posed as a policeman to get into his 89-year-old victim's home was snared because she copied a scene from CSI and scratched his face for DNA.

Bouncer Mauro Lopes, 31, who weighs 20 stone, raped the frail seven-stone widow twice after tricking his way into her home in Leeds, West Yorkshire.

In the midst of her horrific ordeal she had the presence of mind to remember an episode of the cult U.S. forensics drama – and clawed his face knowing police would be able to retrieve his DNA from under her fingernails.

It allowed detectives to catch Lopes just two days after the attack on March 14 because he was already on the national database after a drink-driving offence in 2005.

Lopes, who won asylum after coming to the UK from Angola on a false passport seven years ago, was jailed for nine years at Leeds Crown Court yesterday.

Prosecuting, Felicity Davis said the attack – after Lopes put a large pillow over the woman's face – was so violent that she had to be taken to hospital with heavy bleeding.

But the widow of 20 years managed to tell police: 'I have been watching CSI so I scratched his face so you could get DNA from my fingernails.'

Unable now to live alone, she is in a care home but still has trouble sleeping. She cannot be identified for legal reasons.

Anne Dixon, defending, told the court that Lopes was remorseful and, in his own words, 'had fallen out of his personality with drink'.

He carried out the attack following a visit to a lapdancing club after discovering his girlfriend was cheating on him.

Judge Peter Collier QC said his offences were 'vile and extreme' and added: 'He is a 31-year-old man with all his faculties and his desires. He got drunk and did something unspeakable.'

Lopes had previously pleaded guilty to two counts of rape and one count of sexual assault. It is thought he will be deported at the end of his sentence.

Outside court Det Supt Steve Payne of West Yorkshire Police, who led the investigation, said: 'I would like to pay my respect to the victim in this case who has acted with incredibly bravery despite the terrifying ordeal she suffered.

'During the incident itself she even managed to scratch Lopes which helped us significantly with the investigation.

'Lopes⋯ had his DNA taken for a minor offence in 2005 and as such he was placed on the national DNA database which assisted my investigation greatly in bringing this man to justice.'

✓ 기억하면 좋을 구절!

pose as   ~인 체하다 / ~행세를 하다

➡ He *posed as* a millionaire.
그는 백만장자 행세를 했다.

commit an act of brutality   만행을 저지르다

➡ They are more likely to *commit acts of brutality*.
그들이 만행을 저지를 가능성이 더 크다.

lay a snare   함정을 파놓다 / 덫을 놓다

➡ The teacher always *lays a snare* on the tests to embarrass his students.
선생님은 학생들을 당황하게 만들기 위해 시험에 항상 함정을 파놓는다.

pay respect to   ~에 경의를 표하다

➡ I *pay* my *respect to* your efforts.
나는 당신의 노력에 경의를 표한다.

have the presence of mind   평정을 유지하다 / 차분히 대처하고 응하다

➡ The boy *had the presence of mind* to turn off the electricity.
소년은 침착하게 대처하며 전원을 껐다.

trick one's way into   속이고 ~안으로 들어가다

➡ He *tricked his way into* her office.
그는 속임수를 써서 그녀의 사무실로 들어갔다.

내 인생의 명언 — 나이 듦의 아름다움

▶ 나이가 들어도 아이스크림 덩어리가 콘에서 떨어질 때의
극한 실망감이 덜해지지는 않는다.
짐 피빅 (미국 시인·작가)

> Age does not diminish the extreme disappointment
> of having a scoop of ice cream fall from the cone.
> Jim Fiebig

▶ 나이는 성숙에 대한 값비싼 대가이다.
톰 스토파드 (영국 극작가)

> Age is a very high price to pay for maturity.
> Tom Stoppard

▶ 일정한 나이 이후 모든 사람은 자신의 얼굴에 책임져야 한다.
알베르 카뮈 (프랑스 소설가·극작가)

> After a certain age, every man is responsible
> for his own face.
> Albert Camus

▶ 고고학자는 여자에게 최고의 남편감이다.
아내가 나이가 들면 들수록 더 아내에게 관심을 갖기 때문이다.
아가사 크리스티 (영국 추리소설 작가)

> An archeologist is the best husband
> any woman can have; the older she gets,
> the more interested he is in her.
> Agatha Christie

Favorite famous sayings!

▶ 나는 결코 노인이 되지 않을 것이다. 나에게 있어 노령은
언제나 나보다 열다섯 살 더 많은 나이를 말한다.
프랜시스 베이컨 (영국 정치인·철학자)

> I will never be an old man. To me,
> old age is always 15 years older than I am.
> Francis Bacon

▶ 젊은 시절엔 하루는 짧고 한 해는 길다.
늙어서는 한 해는 짧은데 하루는 길다.
교황 바오로 6세

> In youth the days are short and the years are long.
> In old age the years are short and day's long.
> Papa Paolo VI

▶ 젊음이 가버렸다는 것을 알게 되는 어떤 특정한 시점이 있다.
그러나 세월이 흐른 뒤에 보면 그것은 훨씬 나중 일임을 알게 된다.
미뇽 머클로플린 (미국 언론인·작가)

> There is always some specific moment
> when we become aware that our youth is gone;
> but, years after, we know it was much later.
> Mignon McLaughlin

▶ 주름살은 미소가 머물렀던 곳을 나타내주는 것일 뿐이다.
마크 트웨인 (미국 소설가·작가)

> Wrinkles should merely indicate where smiles have been.
> Mark Twain

News English

"A Tongue more Expensive than Parton's Breast"

A leading coffee company in United Kingdom has insured its chief coffee taster for a record amount of $10 million ($13.95m). The company says he is vital for their growth.

Costa Coffee's Gennaro Pelliccia, Costa's chief taste tester, is so invaluable to the company, they insured him for a record amount with Lloyd's of London insurance giant.

In the highly competitive coffee industry, especially against Starbucks, Costa Coffee needs a solid person like Pelliccia behind them to fight against competition, they claim.

It is no wonder Costa Coffee is one of the few companies that have posted positive sales growth this year. They have an annual sales of more than $216 million ($304.71 million) and has opened 100 more coffee shops in a recession year.

Compare this performance to Starbucks, which has closed many stores worldwide and has been making lot of changes at its stores.

Pelliccia has been working for 18 years with the company. He told Telegraph, why his insurance is important.

"In my profession, my taste buds and sensory skills are crucial. My 18 years of experience enable me to distinguish between thousands of flavors. My taste buds also allow me to distinguish any defects which enables me to protect and guarantee Costa's unique Mocha Italia blend. Pelliccia's insurance policy is even more than the insurance of the highest wine taste tester; Ilja Gort, a Bordeaux wine maker, took a $3.9 million ($5.5 billion) policy in order to protect his nose. The policy however, lags behind the David Beckham's legs and Dolly Parton's breasts (the pair). A leading coffee company in United Kingdom has insured its chief coffee taster for a record amount of $10 million ($13.95m). The company says he is vital for their growth.

Costa Coffee's Gennaro Pelliccia, Costa's chief taste tester, is so invaluable to the company, they insured him for a record amount with Lloyd's of London insurance giant.

In the highly competitive coffee industry, especially against Starbucks, Costa Coffee needs a solid person like Pelliccia behind them to fight against competition, they claim.

It is no wonder Costa Coffee is one of the few companies that have posted positive sales growth this year. They have an annual sales of more than $216 million ($304.71 million) and has opened 100 more coffee shops in a recession year.

Compare this performance to Starbucks, which has closed many stores worldwide and has been making lot of changes at its stores.

Pelliccia has been working for 18 years with the company. He told Telegraph, why his insurance is important.

"In my profession, my taste buds and sensory skills are crucial. My 18 years of experience enable me to distinguish between thousands of flavors. My taste buds also allow me to distinguish any defects which enables me to protect and guarantee Costa's unique Mocha Italia

맛 감별사 젠나로 펠리치아와 돌리 파튼

돌리 파튼 가슴보다 더 비싼 혓바닥

세계 최고의 가슴을 가졌다는 미국 여가수 돌리 파튼의 가슴 보험금은 양쪽 합해서 35만 파운드(약 7억 2000만 원)다. 그런데 혀 보험금이 자그마치 1000만 파운드(약 210억 원)인 사람이 있다.

세계적인 커피숍 체인 '코스타 커피'의 수석 맛 감별사(a chief taste tester) 젠나로 펠리치아가 그 주인공이다. 회사가 1000만 파운드 보험을 들어준 혀를 가지고(have a tongue insured by his company for 10 million pounds) 있다.

펠리치아는 코스타 커피 제품을 시음하는(sample products for Costa Coffee) 일을 한다. 원두를 볶고 혼합해 만든 각종 커피 제품들을 일선 체인점들에 내보내기에 앞서 일일이 맛을 보며 완성도를 체크한다.

미각 기관인 혀의 미뢰(味蕾)를 보호하기 위해(to protect the taste buds of the tongue in this way) 보험증서를 신청한(apply for an insurance policy)

경우가 이번이 처음은 아니다. 영국의 유명 음식 평론가 에곤 로네이가 지난 1993년 자신의 맛 감식력에 25만 파운드 보험을 들었다(insure his palate for £250000). 그는 보험 가입 이유로 "내게 이 '자산'이 없으면(without this 'asset') 나는 손을 잃은 조각가(a sculptor shorn of hands)나 마찬가지이기 때문"이라고 말했었다.

로네이의 40배 가치에 달하는 펠리치아의 보험 증권(Pelliccia's policy worth forty times Ronay's)은 지난 15년간(in the last 15 years) 보험 인플레이션의 방증(a testament to insurance inflation)이기도 하지만, 길거리 커피 체인점들이 국가 경제에 미치는 중요성(the importance of high street coffee chains to the national economy)을 단적으로 보여주는 것이다.

한 해 동안 1800만 잔의 커피를 판매해 2억 1600만 파운드(약 4440억 원)를 넘는 연간 매출규모(with an annual turnover of more than £216 million)를 자랑하는 코스타 커피는 세계 각국에 커피숍 100개를 추가 오픈할 계획이다. 펠리치아에게 혀 보험을 들어준 것은 경기침체 돌파를 시도(attempt to buck the recession)하겠다는 코스타 커피의 방침에 따른 것이다.

전 세계 매장 수백 개를 폐점해야 했던(be forced to shut hundreds of its stores around the world) 스타벅스와 달리 코스타 커피는 지금까지 세계적인 소비자 위축 현상을 잘 피해(have so far shrugged off the global consumer downturn) 왔다.

대부분의 경쟁사에 비해 가격이 싼(be cheaper than most of its rivals) 것을 강점으로 내세우고 있는 코스타 커피는 매출 신장을 공표한(report positive sales growth) 몇 안 되는 길거리 프랜차이즈 중 하나(one of the few high street franchises)다.

한편 펠리치아는 "나의 18년 경험(my 18 years of experience)이 수천 가지 맛을 구분할 수 있게 해줬다(enable me to distinguish between thousands of flavours)"며 "직업상 미각세포와 감별기술(the taste buds and sensory skills)은 코스타 커피 고유 혼합방식의 어떠한 결함도 구분해 낼 수 있도록 해주기(allow me to distinguish any defects of Costa's unique blend) 때문에 매우 중요하다(be very crucial)"고 말한다.

보험증권 대비 일람표에 따르면(according to the league table of insurance policies) 펠리치아의 혀 보험 가입액은 신체 부위 세계 최고액을 기록 중인 축구선수 데이비드 베컴의 두 다리(4000만 파운드)보다는 적다(come behind David Beckham's legs).

하지만 미국 록 음악계의 대부 브루스 스프링스틴의 목소리(350만 파운드) 보다는 더 많은(come ahead of Bruce Springsteen's voice) 액수다.

또 미국 여배우 아메리카 페레라의 미소(500만 파운드), 배우 켄 도드의 치아(400만 파운드), 독일 출신 모델 하이디 클럼의 다리(115만 파운드), 영화배우 베티 그레이블의 다리(50만~100만 파운드), 돌리 파튼의 가슴(35만 파운드), 전 크리켓 호주대표팀 선수 머브 휴즈의 팔자 수염(20만 파운드) 등 다른 유명인들의 신체 보험보다는 훨씬 큰 액수다.

Coffee Taster's Tongue Insured for £10 Million with Lloyd's

A leading coffee company in United Kingdom has insured its chief coffee taster for a record amount of $10 million ($13.95m). The company says he is vital for their growth.

Costa Coffee's Gennaro Pelliccia, Costa's chief taste tester, is so invaluable to the company, they insured him for a record amount with Lloyd's of London insurance giant.

In the highly competitive coffee industry especially against Starbucks, Costa Coffee needs a solid person like Pelliccia behind them to fight against competition, they claim.

It is no wonder Costa Coffee is one of the few companies that have posted positive sales growth this year. They have an annual sales of more than $216 million ($304.71 million) and has opened 100 more coffee shops in a recession year.

Compare this performance to Starbucks, which has closed many stores worldwide and has been making lot of changes at its stores.

Pelliccia has been working for 18 years with the company. He told Telegraph, why this insurance is important.

"In my profession, my taste buds and sensory skills are crucial. My 18 years of experience enable me to distinguish between thousands of flavors. My taste buds also allow me to distinguish any defects, which enables me to protect and guarantee Costa's unique Mocha Italia blend."

Pelliccia's insurance policy is even more than the insurance of the highest wine taste tester. Ilja Gort, a Bordeaux wine maker, took a $3.9 million ($5.5 million) policy in order to protect his nose.

Pelliccia's policy however lags behind the insurance policy for David Beckham's legs, which was insured for $40 million ($56.43 million).

The Costa Coffee policy was placed through Glencairn, a Lloyd's broker. Glencairn spokesman told Telegraph:

"The taste buds of a Master of Coffee are as important as the vocal chords of a singer or the legs of a top model, and this is one of the biggest single insurance policies taken out for one person. It shows how valuable Gennaro's tongue is to the Costa brand."

Other famous body part insurance policies are the following:

- $25m ($35.27m) Michael Flatley's legs
- $5m ($7.05m) America Ferrera's smile
- $3.5m ($4.94m) Bruce Springsteen's voice
- $1.15m ($1.62m) Heidi Klum's legs (the pair)
- $350,000 ($493,745) Dolly Parton's breasts (the pair)

☑ 기억하면 좋을 구절!

be shorn of ~을 빼앗기다 / 박탈 당하다

➥ *Shorn of* his power, the doposed king went into exile.
권력을 빼앗기고 폐위된 그 왕은 망명길에 올랐다.

win a come-from-behind victory 역전승하다

➥ We *came from behind* to *win* the final match.
우리는 결전승에서 역전승을 거뒀다.

an annual turnover 연간 매출규모

➥ The firm has *an annual turnover* of ten million.
그 회사는 연매출 천만 달러에 이른다.

attempt to ~하려고 시도하다

➥ The football player *attempted to* attack down the wings.
그 축구선수는 측면돌파를 시도했다.

shrug off 대수롭지 않게 취급하다 / 떨쳐내다

➥ He *shrugged off* the criticism.
그는 그러한 비판 정도는 무시했다.

distinguish between ~와 ~를 구별하다

➥ We need to *distinguish between* myth and reality.
우리는 신화와 현실을 구별해야 한다.

내 인생의 명언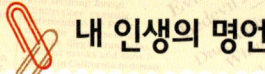

▶ 성공한 사람은 다른 사람들이 자신을 향해 던진 벽돌들로
탄탄한 토대를 쌓을 수 있는 사람이다.
데이비드 브링클리 (미국 방송인)

> A successful man is one who can lay a firm foundation with
> the bricks others have thrown at him.
> David Brinkley

▶ 실패는 최악의 실패가 아니다. 시도조차 해보지 않은 것이 진짜 실패다.
조지 우드버리 (미국 시인·비평가)

> Defeat is not the worst of failures.
> Not to have tried is the true failure.
> George Woodbury

▶ 좌절감과 실패는 성공을 향한 가장 확실한 두 개의 디딤돌이다.
데일 카네기 (미국 교육자)

> Discouragement and failure are two of
> the surest stepping stones to success.
> Dale Carnegie

▶ 실패도 거기서 무언가를 배운다면 성공이다.
말콤 포브스 (미국 경제전문지 포브스 전 발행인)

> Failure is success if we learn from it.
> Malcolm Forbes

Favorite famous sayings!

▶ 성공하기 위해서는 성공에 대한 욕구가
실패에 대한 두려움보다 더 커야 한다.
빌 코스비 (미국 코미디언 배우 · 작가 · 교육자)

> In order to succeed, your desire for success
> should be greater than your fear of failure.
> Bill Cosby

▶ 성공은 아홉 번 쓰러지고 열 번 일어나는 것이다.
존 본조비 (미국 록밴드 멤버)

> Success is falling nine times and getting up ten.
> John Francis Bongiovi

▶ 성공은 옳은 방향으로 잘못 발을 짚었다가
얻은 결과일 때가 종종 있다.
알 번스타인 (미국 스포츠캐스터 작가)

> Success is often the result of taking
> a misstep in the right direction.
> Al Bernstein

News English

"Accursed Children, So-called 'Boche Babies'"

One of the last World War II taboos is being lifted in France.

So-called "Boche babies" - the illegitimate offspring of occupying enemy troops - are speaking openly for the first time about their family secret and hunting for long-lost German fathers.

Spurred by a 2004 investigative book, Enfants Maudits (Accursed Children), and a television documentary that came out at the same time, hundreds of men and women in their 60s have contacted the army archives department in Berlin to find out more about their lost parents.

"Everyone tells the same tale. They say: 'There's a hole in my life. Something is missing,'" said Jean-Paul Picaper, co-author of Enfants Maudits, which helped found the Association of War Children. The association is following a trail blazed by "enfants de la Wehrmacht" - the Association for War Losses, Germany (WASt), where index cards on five million German soldiers are stored.

Today, ANEG (French association) has helped more than 60 children of German paternity find relatives. Though no one has ever found figures, it is estimated that 200,000 French children were born between 1940 and Liberation in 1944. The figure is almost certainly higher.

impossible to verify. 'Shocking blow'

Ms Nivoix-Sevestre's own story is typical. In 1941, her mother was 16 and working in a shop-bar in the Normandy village of Cambes-en-Plaine, when she met a young German soldier called Werner.

Ms Nivoix-Sevestre was born in 1942. Two years later, her mother was killed in the Allied bombardment of Caen.

"My mother's family spurned me because of what had happened, and I was brought up by a foster mother," she says.

"I discovered the truth when I was 13. I asked a friend who..." ...said he... ...

...several were forced into hiding. Cambes-en-Plaine in 1941. Several were forced into hiding... enough photographs of their eastern... Sometimes Picard always referring to some...

ministry on the Place de la Concorde. Willi Schober took the bold step of moving into her flat at once...

arrested and taken away to another locality, not knowing that his lover was pregnant.

"I often asked my mother who my father was, but she refused to tell me. It was a taboo subject," says Ms Trincal.

"Finally, in 2001, I persuaded her to give me his name. I sent out letters to about 30 people in the Leipzig region who could have been him. Then one day, I got a letter back. It was him!"

Ms Trincal met her father for the first time in 2002, and now sees him regularly. "It was a huge surprise for him. He had no idea I existed. But he took one look at me and said - 'Well, I can't deny it: you're obviously my daughter.'"

Ms Trincal's mother had written to Otto at his new place... ...46. But the farm-owner was... ...tions not to pass on any...

...ters later, Otto still wondered ...had failed to contact him ...to Ms Trincal. "He said that ...affair was not just a fling. He ...married her if she had come...

...of the enduring generosity of ...stories that Ms Trincal refuses ...her father's full name and will ...photographs to be shown. ...paintful telling but I regard it as ...courageous for the future - for our ...children, she says.

...of the war babies' childhood ...ned a cost.

...the ravages of being shorn of ...

아버지의 옛 사진을 들고 있는 펭정

2차 대전 당시 프랑스 여인과 사랑에 빠진 독일인 쇼버(펭정의 아버지)

저주받은 아이들, 이른바 '독일놈의 자식들'

 프랑스에서 제2차 세계대전의 마지막 금기(禁忌) 중 하나(one of the last World War II taboos)가 깨지고(be being lifted) 있다.

 이른바 '독일놈 자식들'(so-called 'Boche babies') 즉 점령군의 사생아들(the illegitimate offspring of occupying enemy troops)이 가족 비밀에 대해 처음 공개적으로 밝히는가(speak openly for the first time about their family secret) 하면 오랫동안 행방불명이었던 독일 아버지들을 찾아(hunt for long-lost German fathers) 나서고 있다.

 2004년에 나온 탐사서적 《저주 받은 아이들》에 자극받고(be spurred by a 2004 investigative book 'Accursed Children'), 같은 시기에 나온 TV 다큐멘타리에 용기를 얻어(be encouraged by a television documentary put on air at the same time) 이제 60대 나이에 접어든 수백 명의 '독일놈 자식들'(hundreds of boche babies in their 60s)이 잃어버린 아버지들에 대해 더

알아내고자(find out more about their lost fathers) 독일 베를린의 군사기록 보관소와 접촉(contact the army archives in Berlin) 하고 있다. 이들은 모두들 같은 이야기를 한다(everyone tells the same tale). "내 인생엔 빈자리가 있다(a hole in my life). 나의 반쪽(half of me)이 빠져 있다(be missing)"고 들 말한다.

'전쟁 고아'들 중 일부는 지난 2005년 제2차 세계대전 중 독일군 병사들에 관한 약 1800만 건의 색인카드(some 18million index cards on World War II German soldiers)가 보관돼 있는(be stored) 독일군 문서보관소를 방문하고 온 뒤 전국전쟁피해아동협회(ANEG)를 설립했다.

현재 이 협회는 335명의 회원을 갖고 있으며, 130명 이상의 회원들이 독일 내 아버지 가족들을 찾을 수 있도록 도왔다(help more than 130 of the members locate paternal families in Germany). 소수(a handful)이기는 하지만 아직 살아 있는(be still alive) 아버지를 만난 사람들도 있다.

프랑스에서는 1940년 5월~1944년 12월 독일군 점령기간 중(during the German occupation between May 1940 and December 1944) 대략 20만명의 프랑스 아기들(as many as 200,000 French babies)이 '부정한 관계'에서 태어난(be born to illicit liaisons) 것으로 추산되고 있다. 물론 입증은 불가능한(be impossible to verify) 수치다.

한 예로 ANEG 회장인 니봐 세베스트르의 사연은 '독일놈 자식'의 전형적 이야기다(be a typical story). 1941년 그녀의 엄마 나이 16세였을 때다. 노르망디의 한 바에서 일하던 그녀의 엄마는 베르너라는 젊은 독일 병사(a young German soldier called Werner)를 만났다.

니봐 세베스트르는 이듬해인 1942년 태어났다. 그리고 2년 뒤 그녀의 엄마는 연합군 폭격에 목숨을 잃었다(be killed in the Allied bombardment). 엄마 가족들은 과거에 일어났던 일 때문에 그녀를 내쫓았고(spurn her because of what have happened), 그녀는 수양 어머니에 의해 키워졌다(be brought up by a foster mother).

그녀가 사실을 알게 된 것은 13세 때. 친구에게 "내 신분증에는 왜 '아버지 미상'(father unknown)으로 적혀 있느냐"고 물었고, 친구는 "네 아버지는 독일인"이라고 말해줬다. 그녀를 제외한 마을 사람들은 모두 알고 있었던(everyone knows in the village except her) 것이다.

충격적인 쇼크(a shocking blow)였다. 나중에 엄마 친구로부터 들은 이야기로는 아버지가 오스트리아인이었으며, 금발에 키는 그다지 크지 않았다고 한다. 외향적인 성향을 가진 사람으로(something of an extrovert) 하모니카를 불 줄(play the harmonica and walk on his hands) 알고 물구나무서서 걷기를 할 수 있던 남자였다.

그녀는 2003년 독일군 문서보관서를 접촉한 첫 사람들 중 한 명(be among the first to contact the German army archives)이었다. 이후 1941년 자신이 태어난 지역에 주둔했던 독일군 병사들의 자취를 추적하기 시작해(set out to trace German soldiers) 몇몇을 찾아냈다. 일부는 다른 병사들과 함께 찍은 사진을 간직하고 있기도 했다. 그러나 유감스럽게도 누구도 꼭 필요한 것을 주지는 못했다(sadly none fits the bill). 동부전선에서 사망했을 것이라는 것 외엔 찾아낼 수 없었다.

마리 크리스틴느 펭정이라는 여성은 운이 조금 더 좋았던 편이다. 그녀의 어머니는 해군성에서 근무하는 빌리 쇼버라는 독일인과 사랑에 빠졌고(fall in love with a German working at the navy ministry), 1943년 두 사람 사이에 펭정이 태어났다. 그녀의 아버지 쇼버는 대담하게도 펭정의 어머니 집으로 이사를 해(take the bold step of moving into Pengeon's mother), 상관들의 빈축을 샀다(be frowned on by his superios).

1944년 생말로(Saint-Malo) 항구에 배치됐던 쇼버는 자신의 아기가 아프다는 사실을 전해 듣게 된다. 그는 휴가 허가증을 위조해(forge a permit of leave) 파리로 갔고, 결국 체포돼 독일로 보내져 처벌받게(be caught and sent for punishment in Germany) 된다. 이후 펭정 모녀는 다시는 그를 볼 수 없었다(never see him again).

펭정은 어려서부터 아버지가 독일인이라는 사실을 알았다. 어머니는 끝내 이야기하지 않았지만(never speak of it) 할머니가 사실을 말해줬다. 어머니에겐 금지된 사안(a forbidden subject)이었던 것이다.

펭정은 2004년 프랑스 주둔 독일군에 관한 한 TV 프로그램을 본 뒤 독일군 문서보관서와 접촉하기(get in touch with the German army archives) 시작했고, 어느 정도 아버지에 관한 사실을 알게(learn the truth about her father) 됐다. 독일로 강제 귀국 조치된 그녀의 아버지는 감옥에 수감됐다가(be imprisoned) 탈옥을 시도했다. 그는 다시 재판을 받고 탈주 혐의로 기소돼 처형(be tried again, convicted of desertion and executed)됐다.

그가 탈옥을 기도한 것은 파리에 있던 자신의 딸 때문(because of his daughter in Paris)이었다. 재판 기록에도(in the minutes of the trial) 그는 아이를 보러 가려(want to go and see his child) 했다고 말한 것으로 적혀 있

었다. 결국 딸을 보고 싶은 마음이 그의 목숨을 앗아갔던(cost him his life) 것이다.

얼마 전 펭정은 아버지 가족과 연락이 닿아(be put in touch with her father's family) 지금은 그들 가족의 일원으로 받아들여졌다(be embraced as one of their own family). 그녀는 독일에 배다른 형제(a half-brother)가 있다는 사실도 알게 돼 지금은 가깝게 지내고 있다.

엘리안느 트렝킬의 사연은 훨씬 더 흐뭇하다(be even more heart-warming). 그녀는 사실 종전 2년 뒤 태어났다(be in fact born two years after the war ended). 그녀의 아버지 오토는 독일군 전쟁포로(a German prisoner of war)였다.

하지만 그녀는 자신을 전쟁고아로 여긴다(consider herself a war orphan). 학교에서 똑같은 희생을 당했기(suffer the same victimization at school) 때문이다. 어디를 가나 '더러운 독일X'(dirty boche) 소리를 들어야 했다.

트렝칼의 어머니는 농장에서 일하던 젊은 독일군 전쟁포로와 사랑에 빠졌다(fall in love with a young German POW). 그러나 현지 사람들이 알게 돼(locals find out) 그 커플을 고발하게(denounce the couple) 된다.

오토는 체포돼 다른 지역으로 압송되고(be arrested and taken away to another locality) 말았다. 당시 트렝칼의 어머니는 이미 임신 중이었지만, 오토는 그 사실도 모른 채 떠나갔다.

훗날 트렝칼은 자신의 아버지가 누구냐고 어머니에게 몇 번이고 물었지만, 끝내 대답해주지 않았다(refuse to tell her). 금기 대상(a taboo subject)

이었던 것이다.

그러던 2001년 어느 날 트렝칼은 어머니에게 아버지 이름만이라도 알려달라고 설득했고, 독일 여기저기에 편지를 내 아버지 소재를 수소문(send letters inquiring here and there)했다. 그리고 마침내 답장 한 통이 날아왔다(get a letter back). 아버지인 오토 본인이었다. 부녀는 이듬해인 2002년 처음 상봉했고, 지금은 정기적으로 그를 만나고 있다.

아버지 오토에겐 엄청난 놀라움(a huge surprise)이었다. 딸이 존재한다는 사실 자체를 모르고(have no idea his daughter exists) 있었기 때문이다. 하지만 그녀를 한번 보자마자(as soon as he takes one look at her) 그는 말했다. "부인할 수가 없구나(can't deny it). 너는 분명히 내 딸(be obviously my daughter)"이라며 부둥켜안았다.

트렝칼의 어머니는 1946년 오토가 옮겨간 농장에 편지를 썼지만, 가슴 아프게도(poignantly) 농장 주인(the farm-owner)은 이미 어떤 우편물도 전해주지 말라는 지시를 받은(be under instructions not to pass on any mail) 상태였다.

그리고 거의 60년이 흐르도록(nearly 60 years later) 오토는 왜 자신의 연인이 연락하지 못했는지(fail to contact him) 알지 못했다. 트렝칼에 따르면 오토는 당시 연애가 그저 단순한 외도가 아니었다(the affair was not a fling)고 말한다. 어떻게든 자신을 찾아왔더라면 결혼했을 것(would have married if she had come after him)이라고 한다.

트렝칼은 "아름다운 결말(a beautiful ending)이 났지만 그것은 어린 시절 겪었던(go through as child) 온갖 고통의 보상(just a recompense for all the misery)에 불과하다"며 눈물짓는다.

　최악의 경우(in the worst cases) 전쟁고아들은 바퀴벌레를 먹거나 자신의 오줌을 마시도록 강요 당하기도(be obliged to eat cockroaches or drink their own urine) 했다.

　묘한 일이지만(oddly enough) 가장 잔혹했던 사람은 바로 그들의 어머니였다. 한때 독일인 병사와 로맨틱한 연애를 즐겼다가(enjoy the romantic affair for a while with a German soldier) 이후로 줄곧 당시를 상기시키는 살아 있는 존재(due to a living reminder of it later on)와 함께 사는 고통을 겪다 보니 그 자식에게 냉혹해졌던 것이다.

Boche Babies' Trace German Roots

One of the last World War II taboos is being lifted in France.

So-called "Boche babies"—the illegitimate offspring of occupying enemy troops—are speaking openly for the first time about their family secret and hunting for long-lost German fathers.

Spurred by a 2004 investigative book, Enfants Maudits (Accursed Children), and a television documentary that came out at the same time, hundreds of men and women in their 60s have contacted the army archives department in Berlin to find out more about their lost parents.

"Everyone tells the same tale. They say: 'There's a hole in my life. Half of me is missing'," says Jeanine Nivoix-Sevestre, who heads the French National Association of War Children (ANEG).

The association was set up in 2005 following a visit by a small group of "enfants de la guerre" (war children) to the Wehrmacht Information Office for War Losses and Prisoners-of-War (WASt), where some 18 million index cards on World War II German soldiers are stored.

Today, ANEG has 335 members and has helped more than 130 of them locate paternal families in Germany. A handful have even found fathers who are still alive.

In all, it is estimated that as many as 200,000 French children were born to illicit liaisons during the German occupation between May 1940 and December 1944, though the figure is impossible to verify.

'Shocking blow'

Ms Nivoix-Sevestre's own story is typical.

In 1941, her mother was 16 and working in a shop-bar in the Normandy village of Cambes-en-Plaine, when she met a young German soldier called Werner.

Ms Nivoix-Sevestre was born in 1942. Two years later, her mother was killed in the Allied bombardment of Caen.

"My mother's family spurned me because of what had happened, and I was brought up by a foster mother," she says.

"I discovered the truth when I was 13. I asked a friend why my identity card said 'pere inconnu' (father unknown) and he told me my dad was German. It seemed everyone knew in the village except me."

"It was such a shocking blow. I literally was unable to speak for two and a half months. At the time, talk was still full of the horrors committed by the Germans. I was terrified that my own father might have been part responsible," she says.

Over the years Ms Nivoix-Sevestre picked up bits of information about her father.

A girlfriend of her mother remembered his first name and that he was Austrian. She said he was blond, not very tall, and something of an extrovert. He played the harmonica and could walk on his hands.

In 2003, she was among the first to contact the WASt, which then set out to trace soldiers who had been stationed at Cambes-en-Plaine in 1941.

Several were found and some had kept group photographs showing other soldiers. Sadly none fitted the bill. Ms Nivoix-Sevestre is convinced her father died later on the Eastern Front.

Half-brother

More fortunate is Marie-Christine Pingeon, who was born in Paris in 1943 after her mother fell in love with a German working at the navy ministry on the Place de la Concorde.

Willi Schober took the bold step of moving into her flat, which was frowned on by his superiors.

In 1944, Mr Schober had been posted to the port of Saint-Malo when he got news that his baby was ill.

He forged a permit of leave and went to Paris, but he was caught and sent for punishment in Germany. Mother and daughter never saw him again.

"I knew from a young age that my father was German, because my grandmother told me. But my mother never spoke of it. It was a forbidden subject," says Ms Pingeon.

"In 2004, I saw the television programme and got in touch with the WASt."

"There, I learned the truth. My father had been imprisoned and then tried to escape. He was tried again, convicted of desertion and executed."

"In a way it was because of me. In the minutes of the trial, he says that he wanted to come and see his child. You could say I cost him his life."

Ms Pingeon was put in touch with her father's family, who embraced her as one of their own.

She also discovered that she had a half-brother almost exactly her age—her father throughout had a wife in Germany—and the two are now very close.

'Huge surprise'

Eliane Trincal's story is even more heart-warming.

She was in fact born two years after the war ended – her father, Otto, was a German prisoner of war. But she considers herself a war child because she suffered the same victimisation at school.

"They called me a 'dirty boche' and all that. It was a very hard time," she says.

Eliane's mother had fallen in love with the young German POW, who was working on a farm in the Auvergne.

But locals found out and denounced the couple.

Otto was arrested and taken away to another locality, not knowing that his lover was pregnant.

"I often asked my mother who my father was, but she refused to tell me. It was a taboo subject," says Ms Trincal.

"Finally, in 2001, I persuaded her to give me his name. I sent out letters to about 30 people in the Leipzig region who could have been him. Then one day, I got a letter back. It was him!"

Ms Trincal met her father for the first time in 2002, and now sees him regularly.

"It was a huge surprise for him. He had no idea I existed. But he took one look at me and said - 'Well, I can't deny it: you're obviously my daughter!'"

Poignantly, Ms Trincal's mother had written a letter to Otto at his new place of work in 1946. But the farm-owner was under instructions not to pass on any mail.

Nearly 60 years later, Otto still wondered why his lover had failed to contact him.

According to Ms Trincal: "He said that for him the affair was not just a fling. He would have married her if she had come after him."

It is a sign of the enduring sensitivity of such family stories that Ms Trincal refuses to reveal her father's full name and will not permit photographs to be shown.

"It is a beautiful ending, but I regard it as just recompense for the misery I went through as child," she says.

'Law of silence'

For many of the war babies, childhood was indeed a trial.

Memories still rankle of being singled out, teased or maltreated.

In the worst cases, children were made to eat cockroaches or drink their own urine, says Ms Nivoix-Sevestre.

"Oddly enough, it was often the mothers who were the cruellest," she says. "They and their families."

"When you think about it, the mothers may have enjoyed their romantic affair with a German soldier, but what they certainly did not want was a living reminder of it later on," she adds.

On the other hand, Ms Pingeon says she never suffered as a child.

"Partly it was because my father was well-liked in the neighbourhood of Paris where I was born," she says. "I think he had been fed all this propaganda in Germany, and when he came to know my mother and to live among the French, it opened his eyes."

"As a child I knew I had a German father - though of course nothing about him. But I did not seek to hide it. In a way I was proud."

"In that sense I am not typical of the 'enfants de la guerre'. But in another way I am - I always had a very difficult relationship with my mother. She refused to tell me anything about my father. But you cannot build your life on a lie and not expect there to be emotional consequences," she adds.

The complex maternal relationship may explain why it is only now that so many war children are finally coming out with the truth.

"If we kept quiet for so many years, it was really to protect our mothers and also their husbands - our step-fathers. We respected the law of silence," Ms Pingeon says.

"But time has passed. Our parents have died or are very old. It is now that we can talk."

✅ 기억하면 좋을 구절!

be born to ~의 상태로 태어나다

She *was born to* a woman.
그녀는 천상 여자다.

be spurred by ~에 자극받다 / 고무되다

I *was spurred* into action *by* the film.
나는 그 영화에 자극받아 행동에 나섰다.

a handful of 소수의 / 한 움큼

Only *a handful of* humans have been killed by tigers.
소수의 사람들이 호랑이에 의해 살해되었다.

be brought up 길러지다 / 양육되다

He *was brought up* in a poor family.
그는 가난한 가정에서 자라났다.

fit the bill 만족시키다 / 딱 알맞다 / 딱 필요한 것을 주다

Nobody *fits the bill*.
조건을 만족하는 사람이 없다.

be frowned on 빈축을 사다 / 비난을 받다

Her behavior *was frowned on* by everyone.
그녀의 행동은 모두의 비난을 받았다.

내 인생의 명언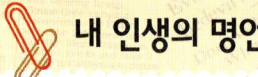

▶ 투표가 뭔가를 바꿀 수 있다면 정치인들은 그것도 불법화할 것이다.
엠마 골드먼 (미국 무정부주의자)

> If voting changed anything, they'd make it illegal.
> Emma Goldman

▶ 민주주의는 당신이 가장 덜 싫어하는 후보자에게 투표함으로써 굴러간다.
로버트 바이런 (미국 정치인)

> Democracy is being allowed to vote for the candidate you dislike least.
> Robert Byron

▶ 민주주의에선 반대도 신념의 행동이다.
제임스 풀브라이트 (미국 정치인)

> In a democracy, dissent is an act of faith.
> James William Fulbright

▶ 투표 참여 거부에 대한 형벌 중 하나는 결국 당신보다 못한 사람들의 지배를 받게 된다는 것이다.
플라톤 (그리스 철학자)

> One of the penalties for refusing to participate in politics is that you end up being governed by your inferiors.
> Plato

Favorite famous sayings!

▶ 자신의 권리를 위해 투쟁하고자 하는 사람들이
이 나라에 많이 있기에 민주주의라고 불릴 수 있는 것이다.
로저 볼드윈 (미국시민자유연맹 공동 설립자)

> So long as we have enough people in this country
> willing to fight for their rights, we'll be called a democracy.
> Roger Baldwin

▶ 정치에 쏟아져 들어오는 돈의 범람은 민주주의의 오염 공해다.
시어도르 와이트 (미국 정치저널리스트)

> The flood of money that gushes into politics today
> is a pollution of democracy.
> Theodore White

▶ 가장 적게 공약하는 사람에게 투표하라.
그러면 그는 가장 적게 실망시키는 사람이 될 것이다.
버나드 바루크 (미국 정치인 · 재정전문가)

> Vote for the man who promises least;
> he'll be the least disappointing.
> Bernard M. Baruch

▶ 어렸을 때 아무나 대통령이 될 수 있다는 이야기를 듣고 자랐다.
그걸 이제 믿기 시작했다.
클레어런스 대로우 (미국 시민자유연맹 변호사)

> When I was a boy I was told that anybody
> could become President; I'm beginning to believe it.
> Clarence Darrow

News English

"Europe's Richest Woman and a Man"

A French court will examine whether the elderly heiress to the L'Oreal fortune, Europe's richest woman, was in her right mind when she lavished gifts worth close to $1.4 billion on a younger male friend. Prosecutor Philippe Courroye, who has been probing for over a year the gifts made by Liliane Bettencourt to photographer and socialite François-Marie Banier, told Reuters on Wednesday the case would come to trial in September. Bettencourt, 62, a fixture in fashionable Paris circles for four decades, has received artwork, checks, cash, life insurance and other gifts from Bettencourt since 2002. Judicial sources estimate the total value of the gifts at about 1 billion euros.

"What I have given to François-Marie Banier, though it's a lot, it is not that much when you put it in perspective," Bettencourt told the French weekly Le Journal du Dimanche in December in her only interview on the case. Bettencourt, 86, daughter of the founder of cosmetics giant L'Oreal, has a fortune estimated at $13.4 billion by Forbes, placing her 21st on the magazine's list of billionaires. Bettencourt's only daughter Françoise Bettencourt Meyers filed a complaint in 2007, accusing Banier of taking advantage of her mother's weakened mental state to extract gifts. Bettencourt, who has refused to speak to her daughter, has angrily denied that version of events.

Bettencourt to accept an independent psychiatric evaluation, but she has refused. Her daughter alleges that Banier has been bullying her at times when she was mentally and physically frail.

Prosecutor Philippe Courroye, who has been probing for over a year the gifts made by Liliane Bettencourt to photographer and socialite François-Marie Banier, told Reuters on Wednesday the case would come to trial in September. Bettencourt, 62, a fixture in fashionable Paris circles for four decades, has received artwork, checks, cash, life insurance and other gifts from Bettencourt since 2002. Judicial sources estimate the total value of the gifts at about 1 billion euros.

"What I have given to François-Marie Banier, though it's a lot, it is not that much when you put it in perspective," Bettencourt...

...lavished gifts worth close to $1.4 billion on a younger male friend.

Prosecutor Philippe Courroye, who has been probing for over a year the gifts made by Liliane Bettencourt to photographer and socialite François-Marie Banier, told Reuters on Wednesday the case would come to trial in September. Bettencourt, 62, a fixture in fashionable Paris circles for four decades, has received artwork, checks, cash, life insurance and other gifts from Bettencourt since 2002. Judicial sources estimate the total value of the gifts at about 1 billion euros.

"...have given to François-Marie Banier, though it's a lot, it is not that much when you put it in perspective," ...Bettencourt.

...with her daughter, has angrily denied that version of events.

She says Banier is a dear friend whom she has known for two decades and who has introduced her to interesting artistic circles. She was in full possession of her wits every time she gave him presents, the heiress has said.

"Life would be no fun if you only saw people from the same background as your own," she said in her December interview.

"My daughter has to realize that I am a free woman."

Banier, who has refused to comment publicly on the matter, could face up to three years in prison and 375,000 euros in fines if he is convicted of taking advantage of Bettencourt.

Bettencourt says her daughter filed the complaint about as she wants her stake in L'Oreal, which holds the bulk of Bettencourt's fortune.

She says that if any of the money to Banier is recovered it will be donated to charities.

A French court will examine whether the elderly heiress to the L'Oreal fortune, Europe's richest woman, was in her right mind when she lavished gifts worth close to $1.4 billion on a younger male friend. Prosecutor Philippe Courroye, who...

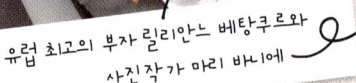

유럽 최고의 부자 릴리안느 베탕쿠르와 사진작가 마리 바니에

유럽에서 가장 돈 많은 여자와 한 남자

한 남자에게 10억 파운드에 달하는 돈과 선물을 줬다. 우리 돈으로 무려 2조 원에 달하는 엄청난 액수다.

여자는 87세, 남자는 63세. 연인 관계는 아니다. 예술에 눈뜨게 해주고 인생의 재미를 알게 해준 것이 고맙다며 여자가 남자에게 '무조건' 준 것이다.

여자의 이름은 릴리안느 베탕쿠르. 1907년 아버지에 의해 창업된 프랑스 화장품 기업 로레알의 상속녀(the heiress to the French cosmetics company L'Oreal founded by her father in 1907)이자 최대 주주(the biggest shareholder in L'Oreal)이다. 세계에서 세 번째, 유럽에서는 가장 돈이 많은 여자(Europe's richest woman)다.

총 재산이 약 100억 파운드(약 20조 원)인 것으로 추산(be estimated at £10 billion this year)된다.

그녀로부터 약 2조 원 상당의 돈과 선물을 받은 남자는 프랑스와 마리 바니에라는 사진작가다. 지난 40여 년간 파리 패션계의 터줏대감(a fixture in fashionable Paris circles for four decades)이었던 그는 2002년 이후 베탕쿠르로부터 현금, 수표, 생명보험, 예술품과 기타 선물들을 받아온(receive cash, checks, life insurance, artwork and other gifts from her since 2002) 것으로 알려졌다.

문제는 베탕쿠르의 딸인 프랑스와즈 베탕쿠르 메이예르(56세)가 어머니의 행위에 불만을 품고 법원에 금치산 선고를 신청하고 나선 것. 메이예르는 또 바니예가 자신의 어머니의 정신적 · 육체적 약점을 이용했다며 지난 2007년 고소했다(file a complaint in 2007 accusing Banier of taking advantage of her mother's mental and physical frailty).

이처럼 메이예르가 프랑스 당국에 수시를 의뢰(call in the French authorities to investigate)함에 따라 바니예는 베탕쿠르를 협박해서 10억 파운드 가까운 돈과 선물을 자신에게 건네도록 괴롭힌 혐의로(be accused of bullying Bettencourt into giving him money and gifts worth close to £1 billion) 조사를 받게 됐다.

딸 메이예르는 "어머니가 정말 자유 의지에 따라 내린 결정이겠느냐"면서 "믿기 어렵다는 것을 알게(find it hard to believe) 됐다"고 주장한다.

하지만 베탕쿠르 본인은 자신이 제정신이 아니어서(be not in her right mind) 나이 어린 남자친구에게 전 재산의 10분의 1을 줘버렸다는(lavish a tenth of her wealth on her young male friend)는 딸의 주장에 노여움을 표시하고 있다.

그녀는 한 프랑스 신문과의 인터뷰를 통해 "내가 바니예에게 준 것이 많기는 해도(though it's a lot) 진상을 알고 보면 그렇게 많은 것이 아니다(be not that much when you put it in perspective)"고 말했다.

딸과 말도 하지 않을 정도로 사이가 나쁜(be not on speaking terms with her daughter) 그녀는 "바니예는 20여 년간 알고 지내온 절친한 친구(a dear friend whom she has known for two decades)"라며 "나를 흥미로운 예술계로 이끌어준(introduce me to interesting artistic circles) 것도 바로 그였다"고 두둔한다.

베탕쿠르는 자신이 바니예에게 선물을 줄 때마다(whenever she gives him presents) 온전히 제정신인 상태였다(be in full possession of her wits)면서 "자신의 것과 같은 배경만으로 사람들을 바라본다면(only see people from the same background as your own) 인생은 재미없을 것(life would be no fun)이라는 사실을 딸도 알게 되기를 바란다"고 밝혔다.

바니예는 베탕쿠르의 딸 메이예르의 주장들에 대해 언급을 회피하고(refuse to comment on the allegations) 있다.

메이예르는 바니예에게 건네진 돈 중 회수되는 것이 있으면(if any of the money given to Banier is recovered) 모두 자선 단체에 기부할(donate all the money to charity) 것이라며, 자신이 돈 때문에 그러는 것이 아님을 강조하고 있다.

L'Oreal Heiress Faces Court Scrutiny of Huge Gifts

A French court will examine whether the elderly heiress to the L'Oreal fortune, Europe's richest woman, was in her right mind when she lavished gifts worth close to $1.4 billion on a younger male friend.

Prosecutor Philippe Courroye, who has been probing for over a year the gifts made by Liliane Bettencourt to photographer and socialite Francois-Marie Banier, told Reuters on Wednesday the case would come to trial in September.

Banier, 62, a fixture in fashionable Paris circles for four decades, has received artwork, checks, cash, life insurance and other gifts from Bettencourt since 2002. Judicial sources estimate the total value of the gifts at about 1 billion euros.

"What I have given to Francois-Marie Banier, though it's a lot, is not that much when you put it in perspective," Bettencourt told the newspaper Le Journal du Dimanche in December, in her only interview on the matter.

Bettencourt, 86, is the biggest shareholder in cosmetics giant L'Oreal, the company her father founded. Her fortune was estimated at $13.4 billion by Forbes this year, placing her in 21st position on the magazine's list of billionaires.

Courroye's investigation into the gifts stems from a complaint filed in late 2007 by her daughter, Francoise Bettencourt-Meyers, who accuses Banier of taking advantage of her mother's frailty to extort staggering sums from her.

Courroye has been trying to persuade Bettencourt to accept an independent psychiatric evaluation, but she has refused. Her daughter alleges that Banier has been bullying her at times when she was mentally and physically frail.

"Did she really make her decisions freely? I find that hard to believe," Bettencourt-Meyers told French magazine Le Point.

French media have leapt on the scandal over the past few months, publishing stories portraying Bettencourt as a lonely widow hooked on her friendship with the dashing Banier and helplessly giving in to his increasingly outrageous demands.

Bettencourt, who is not on speaking terms with her daughter, has angrily denied that version of events.

She says Banier is a dear friend whom she has known for two decades and who has introduced her to interesting artistic circles. She was in full possession of her wits every time she gave him presents, the heiress has said.

"Life would be no fun if you only saw people from the same background as your own," she said in her December interview.

"My daughter has to realize that I am a free woman."

Banier, who has refused to comment publicly on the matter, could face up to three years in prison and 375,000 euros in fines if he is convicted of taking advantage of Bettencourt.

The elderly billionaire says her daughter has nothing to complain about as she will inherit the stake in L'Oreal, which represents the bulk of Bettencourt's immense fortune.

The daughter says that if any of the money given to Banier is recovered, it will go to charitable causes.

☑ 기억하면 좋을 구절!

file a complaint against ~를 상대로 고소하다

I'm going to *file a complaint against* you.
나는 당신을 고소하겠다.

take advantage of ~를 기회로 삼다, 이용하다

I wouldn't feel right *taking advantage of* someone that way.
누군가를 그런 식으로 이용하는 것은 옳지 않다고 생각한다.

be out of one's mind (be not in one's right mind) 제정신이 아니다

He must *be out of his mind*.
그는 제정신이 아닌 것이 틀림없다.

be in possession of ~을 보유하다 / 소유하고 있다

The company *is in possession of* key technology.
그 회사는 핵심 기술을 보유하고 있다.

be not on speaking terms with ~와는 말도 하지 않는 사이다

She's *not been on speaking terms with* her younger brother for years.
그녀는 수년 동안 남동생과는 말도 하지 않는 사이다.

내 인생의 명언 — 평화의 값은 비싸다

▶ '눈에는 눈'은 결국 이 세상 모두를 장님으로 만들 뿐이다.
마하트마 간디 (인도 민족해방지도자)

> An eye for eye only ends up making
> the whole world blind.
> Mahatma Gandhi

▶ 오로지 전쟁 준비를 통해서만 평화를 지킬 수 있다는 것은
참으로 불행한 사실이다
존 F 케네디 (미국 35대 대통령)

> It is an unfortunate fact that we can secure peace
> only by preparing for war.
> John F. Kennedy

▶ 양이 늑대와 평화를 논의한다는 것은 미친 짓이다.
토마스 풀러 (영국 성직자 · 역사가)

> It is a madness for sheep to talk peace with a wolf.
> Thomas Fuller

▶ 비폭력은 내 신념의 제1조이자 내 신조의 마지막 조항이기도 하다.
마하트마 간디 (인도 민족해방지도자)

> Non-violence is the first article of my faith.
> It is also the last article of my creed.
> Mahatma Gandhi

Favorite famous sayings!

▶ 평화와 정의는 동전의 양면과 같다
아이젠하워 (미국 34대 대통령)

> Peace and justice are two sides of the same coin.
> Dwight David Eisenhower

▶ 평화는 웃음으로 시작된다
데레사 수녀 (노벨평화상 수상 가톨릭 수녀)

> Peace begins with a smile.
> Mother Theresa

▶ 평화는 그 자체가 보상이다.
마하트마 간디 (인도 민족해방지도자)

> Peace is its own reward.
> Mahatma Gandhi

▶ 평화로울 때 땀을 더 흘리면 전쟁에서 피를 덜 흘린다.
하이먼 리코버 (미국 제독 · 교육자)

> The more you sweat in peace, the less you bleed in war.
> Hyman Rickover

News English

"From an Ugly Duckling to a Beautiful Swan"

따돌림 당하던 뚱보에서 미녀로 거듭난 사라 에반스

영국판 '미녀는 괴로워'

국내영화 〈미녀는 괴로워〉의 여주인공 한나는 엄청 못생긴 뚱보였다. 그런데 어느 날 갑자기 날씬하고 섹시한 얼짱으로 변신, 성공과 사랑을 동시에 손에 거머쥔다.

영국에서 이런 일이 실제로 일어났다. 하지만 영국의 이 주인공은 영화에서처럼 전신 성형수술을 한 것이 아니다. 철저한 자기 금욕과 절제로 인생역전을 이뤄냈다. 영국 웨일스에 사는 21세의 사라 에반스.

과체중과 외모 때문에(because of her overweight and appearance) 학창시절 내내 놀림을 받아야(be bullied throughout her school days) 했다. 몸무게가 89㎏까지 불어나면서 혹독한 교실 내 조롱을 고스란히 감수해야(have to unavoidably endure cruel classroom taunts) 했다.

괴롭히는 친구들의 조롱(the bullys' taunts)은 어느 날 폭력으로 바뀌었고(turn to violence one day), 에반스는 얼굴을 플라스틱 자로 얻어맞아 피를 흘리는(be bloodied after being slashed across the face with a plastic ruler) 지경에 이른다.

하지만 에반스는 분노를 긍정적 동기로 사용할 결심을 하게(decide to use her anger for a positive reason) 된다. 그녀가 할 수 있는 유일한 것(the only thing to do)은 체중을 빼는(lose weight) 것뿐이었다.

좋아하는 모든 음식들을 당장 끊었다(give up all her favorite foods). 포테이토 칩, 사탕, 과자, 초콜릿, 햄버거, 피자와 기름진 음식(fatty food)은 일절 입에 대지 않았다. 그리고 3년 뒤 에반스의 체중은 48kg로 줄어들었다. 몸무게를 절반 가까이 줄이는데(shed nearly half the body weight) 성공했다.

엄청난 체중 감량(the massive weight loss)은 소기의 성과를 가져다(pay off handsomely)주었다. 에반스는 급기아 모델로 데뷔해 모델에이전시와 전속계약을 맺었고(land a modelling contract), 곧이어 미인대회 준결승까지 진출해 자신을 놀렸던 사람들에게 질투심을 불러일으켰다(make the bullies jealous by winning her way through to the semi-finals of a major beauty contest).

에반스는 언론과의 인터뷰를 통해 "나는 내 스스로 뚱뚱한 몸을 불만스러워 하면서도 먹는 것을 낙으로 삼았고(take comfort in eating), 그럴수록 몸은 더 커져가고(make me even bigger) 외모에도 영향을 주기(affect the complexion) 시작했다"고 말했다.

그녀는 "나는 내 인생을 바꿔보자(turn my life around)고 결심했고, 그 결과 미운 오리 새끼에서 아름다운 백조로 변신(go from an ugly duckling to a beautiful swan)할 수 있었다"며 흡족해했다. "옛날엔 친구들과 패션쇼에 가서 그림자 속에 숨곤(get used to go to fashion shows with my friends and hide in the shadows) 했다"면서 "하지만 이제는 패션쇼 무대 위에 올라 서 있는(up there on the catwalk) 것이 내 모습"이라고 자랑한다.

에반스는 "그동안 많은 의지력과 결단력이 필요(take a lot of willpower and determination)했다"면서 "다시 힘을 내야 할(need a boost) 때면 내가 겪었던 그 모든 괴롭힘을 생각하며(think of all the bullying I suffered) 이를 악물었다(clench my teeth)"고 밝혔다.

에반스가 참가했던 미스웨일스미인대회 대변인은 "우리도 에반스의 학생 때 옛 사진을 보고 지금의 에반스와 동일 인물이라는(be the same person) 것을 도저히 믿을 수 없었다"면서 "그녀가 자신을 아름다운 젊은 여성으로 탈바꿈시킨(transform oneself into a beautiful young woman) 피나는 노력과 끈기에 모든 사람들이 경외감을 표하고(pay reverence to her strenuous effort and perseverance) 있다"고 전했다. 그리고 덧붙였다. "에반스는 자신을 괴롭힌 사람들을 향해 최후에 웃는 승자가 됐다(have the last laugh on her tormentors)"고.

How 14st Bullying Victim Shed Half her Weight to Become 7st Beauty Queen

A teenager targeted by bullies for being overweight has shed almost half her body mass to become a beauty queen with a modelling contract.

Sarah Evans, 19, was ridiculed about her size and appearance after ballooning to almost 14st and hated going to school every day in her size 18 uniform.

Bullies even slashed her across the face with a plastic ruler.

But the attack only served to encourage Miss Evans to give up all her favourite foods including chips, sweets and crisps.

Three years later and she has dropped to seven-and-a-half stone, has landed a modelling contract and has reached the semi-finals of a major beauty contest.

Miss Evans said: 'I was unhappy with my size and I took comfort in eating which made me even bigger. It affected my complexion, my hair—everything.

'But I turned my life around and feel as if I've gone from an ugly duckling to a beautiful swan.'

The teenager, of Merthyr Tydfil, South Wales, has shrunk to a size six and has been signed up with the Vibe modelling agency.

She has also reached the semi-finals of this year's Miss Wales beauty contest.

'I used to go to fashion shows with my friends and hide in the shadows,' she said. 'But now it's me up there on the catwalk.

'It took a lot of willpower and determination, but every time I needed a boost I would think of all the bullying I suffered.

'Now when I look at my old school photograph, I can't believe it's me.'

A spokeswoman for the Miss Wales contest said: 'When we saw Sarah's old school photograph we could not believe it was the same girl.

'She has transformed herself into a beautiful young woman.'

☑ 기억하면 좋을 구절!

pay off   성공하다 / 성과를 올리다

Years of hard work finally *paid off*.
여러 해 동안의 노력이 마침내 성과를 올렸다.

clench one's teeth   이를 악물다

I endured the pain by *clenching my teeth*.
나는 이를 악물고 아픔을 참았다.

pay reverence to   ~에 경의를 표하다 / 존경하다

She *paid reverence to* the artist.
그녀는 그 화가에게 존경을 표했다.

take comfort in   ~을 낙으로 삼다

A lot of people *took comfort in* the news.
많은 사람들이 그 소식을 위안으로 삼았다.

get used to   ~에 익숙해지다

Hopefully he will *get used to* things soon.
그가 빨리 적응하기를 바란다.

내 인생의 명언 — 기회란 잡는 자에게 행운

▶ 기회는 언제나 힘든 일로 변장을 하고 있다.
그래서 대부분 사람들은 알아보지 못한다.
앤 랜더스 (미국 칼럼니스트)

> Opportunities are usually disguised as hard work,
> so most people don't recognize them.
> Ann Landers

▶ 한문으로 '위기'라는 단어는 두 글자로 구성돼 있다.
하나는 위험을 뜻하고, 다른 하나는 기회를 뜻한다.
존 F 케네디 (미국 35대 대통령)

> When written in Chinese the word crisis is
> composed of two characters. One represents
> danger and the other represents opportunity.
> John F. Kennedy

▶ 기회의 창이 나타나거든 차양을 내리지 마라.
톰 피터스 (미국 경제경영서 작가)

> If a window of opportunity appears,
> don't pull down the shade.
> Tom Peters

▶ 사소한 기회가 위대한 일의 시작이 되는 경우가 흔하다.
메모스테네스 (그리스 웅변가)

> Small opportunities are often the beginning
> of great enterprises.
> Memostenes

News English

"Michael Jackson, Desperate to Clone himself"

Michael Jackson was so terrified of dying he was desperate to clone himself in a bizarre bid to extend his superstar legacy. Jackson, who was obsessed with the idea of immortality, attended a Las Vegas conference on human cloning with his friend, the spoon bender Uri Geller. And the King of Pop was so blown away by the teachings of a sect called the Raelians he asked if they would clone him. Jacko's chauffeur Al Bowman, who drove the singer and Geller to the event in 2002, said: "Jackson was very excited. He bounced out of that conference like a small child. He was smiling and on a high. I heard him and Uri talking in the back of the limo.

"He was talking about the prospect of being cloned. He grabbed Uri by both arms and told him, 'I really want to do it, Uri, and I don't care how much it costs.'" The Raelian movement is a strange religious sect that believes the human soul dies when the body does but the key to eternal life is cloning – where individuals form their own followers.

The sect also has a scientific wing, Clonaid, which holds a genius list of clients to share its secret of cloning, among the great and good of Hollywood. Jacko always remember Jackson also witnessed the cloning of Dolly the Sheep in Scotland in 1996. Impressed by what he heard

about the Raelians he became utterly convinced this weird religious group could clone humans.

"It was really weird..."

마이클 잭슨과 브리지트 봐슬리에 박사

believed Jacko made contact with the Raelians after the conferences in Las Vegas and spoke with Dr Brigitte Boisselier about the idea of a Jacko clone.

Boisselier, a trained scientist with a master's degree in biochemistry and a doctorate in physical chemistry, is a Raelian bishop and the managing director of Clonaid, which was set up in the Bahamas in 1997. In December 2002 she told the world that the Raelians had created the first cloned child, a baby girl

but they're also the most stupid people around. They believe almost anything and then they hand over all their millions to these groups."

have their own children through our cloning technology."

Last night the Daily Mirror was unable to speak to anyone from Clonaid.

But Al, who now organises music events in Phoenix, Arizona, said: "When I heard Clonaid had cloned the first human being, I couldn't help thinking there was a mini Michael Jackson running around somewhere. With Michael, anything is possible."

Michael Jackson was so terrified of dying he was desperate to clone himself in a bizarre bid to extend his superstar legacy. Jackson, who was obsessed with the idea of immortality, attended a Las Vegas conference on human cloning with his friend, the spoon bender Uri Geller.

자기 복제를 간절히 원했던 마이클 잭슨

팝의 제왕 마이클 잭슨은 죽는 것에 공포를 느껴(be terrified of dying) 슈퍼스타로서의 유산을 이어가기 위한(in a bid to extend his superstar legacy) 방법으로 자신을 복제하기를 간절히 원했던(be desperate to clone himself) 것으로 밝혀졌다.

10년 넘게 잭슨의 운전기사(Jackson's chauffeur for over a decade)로 일했던 앨 바우먼에 따르면, 영생에 집착했던(be obsessed with the idea of immortality) 잭슨은 숟가락 구부리는 마술사 친구 유리 겔러와 함께(with his friend, the spoon bender Uri Geller) 2002년 인간 복제에 관한 회의에 직접 참석(attend a conference on human cloning in 2002)했다.

잭슨은 라엘리안이라는 종파의 가르침에 홀딱 빠져(be blown away by the teachings of a sect called the Raelians) 그들에게 자신을 복제해줄 수 있는지 문의하기도(ask if they would clone him) 했다.

2002년 라스 베이거스에서 열린 행사에 잭슨과 겔러를 태우고 갔던(drive the singer and Geller to the event at Las Vegas in 2002) 운전기사 바우먼은 "당시 잭슨은 굉장히 흥분한 상태(be very excited)였다"고 말한다.

그에 따르면 잭슨은 만면에 희색이 가득한 상기된 표정(with a face beaming with joy and on a high)으로 어린아이처럼 그 회의장에서 뛰어나왔다(bounce out of that conference like a small child)고 한다.

이어 겔러와 함께 리무진 뒷자리에(in the back of the limo) 탄 잭슨은 복제 가능성에 대해 이야기하며(talk about the prospect of being cloned) 두 팔로 겔러를 붙잡고(grab Geller by both arms) "나 정말 그거 하고 싶어. 비용이 얼마 들든 상관없어(do not care how much it costs)"라고 말했다고 바우먼은 전한다.

라엘리안 무브먼트(Raelian Movement)는 인간의 영혼은 육체가 죽으면 함께 죽는다(the human soul dies when the body dies)고 믿는 종파(a religious sect)로, 영생을 위한 열쇠(the key to eternal life)는 본인의 유전 구조에서 개체를 재생하는(recreate individuals from their own genetic make-up) 복제(the cloning) 뿐이라고 설파한다.

이 종파는 '클로네이드'로 불리는 과학 조직을 거느리고(have a scientific arm called 'Clonaid') 있으며 정기적으로 기금 모금 행사를 개최(hold regular fund-raising events)하기도 한다.

바우먼은 "잭슨이 1996년 영국에서 성공한 양 돌리 복제에 대해 늘 말하곤(talk about the cloning of Dolly the sheep in Britain in 1996) 했다"면서 "잭슨은 그 사실에 완전히 매료돼 있었다(be totally fascinated by it)"고 전한다.

그리고 라엘리안에 대한 이야기를 듣고(hear about the Raelians) 나서는 그 종교그룹이 인간을 복제할 수(can clone humans) 있다고 전적으로 믿게 됐다(become utterly convinced)는 것이다.

정말 터무니없는 얘기(a really oddball stuff)였지만 잭슨은 갈수록 더욱 깊이 빠져들었다. 잭슨은 자신의 유산을 이어갈 자신의 축소판 복제를 원했다(want a mini-version of himself cloned to carry on his legacy).

1990년대 들어 잭슨은 신체의 극저온 냉동이 가능한지 문의(inquire about being cryogenically frozen)하기도 했으며, 수명 연장을 위해 개발된 약품 GH3를 복용(take GH3, a drug designed to prolong life expectancy)했던 것으로 알려지고 있다.

잭슨은 특히 프랑스 언론인 출신 클로드 보릴롱이 창시한(be founded by French journalist Claude Vorilhon) 종파 라엘리안 무브먼트에 탐닉했다. 지금은 라엘로 알려진(Rael as he is now known) 보릴롱은 지난 1973년 자신이 비행접시에서 나타난(emerge from a flying saucer) 외계인과 만났다며(be contacted by an extra-terrestrial being), 그 외계인이 유창한 프랑스어로(in fluent French) "인간은 다른 행성에서 온 사람들에 의해 2만 5000년 전 실험실에서 만들어졌다(be created in laboratories 25000 years ago by people from another planet)"고 말했다고 주장한다.

이 초지능 인종(this race of super-intelligent beings)은 엘로힘(Elohim)으로 불리며, 엘로힘은 고대 히브루어로 '하늘에서 온 자들(those who came from the sky)'이라는 뜻이다. 보릴롱은 엘로힘을 옅은 녹색 피부에 길고 짙은 머리칼을 가진 약 1미터 키의 존재(a being about a meter tall with pale green skin and long dark hair)라고 말한다.

라엘리안 무브먼트는 현재 약 5만 5000명의 교도들을 갖고 있으며(now have up to 55000 members), 이들은 모두 엘로힘이 다시 지구를 찾을 때를 준비하고 있다(be all preparing for the expected return of the Elohim to Earth)고 한다.

잭슨은 라스 베이거스 대회 이후 라엘리언과 접촉하기 시작했으며(make contact with the Raelians after the conference in Las Vegas) 자신의 복제에 대해 브리지트 뵈슬리에 박사와 상담했던(speak with Dr. Brigette Boisselier about the idea of Jackson clone) 것으로 알려지고 있다.

뵈슬리에 박사는 생화학 석사학위와 물리화학 박사학위를 가진 정규 과학자(a trained scientist with a master's degree in biochemistry and a doctorate in physical chemistry)이며 라엘리안의 주교직과 1997년 바하마에 설립된 클로네이드의 소장(a Raelian bishop and the managing director of Clonaid set up in the Bahamas in 1997)을 맡고 있다.

뵈슬리에 박사는 지난 2002년 이브라는 이름의 여아인 최초의 복제 아기를 탄생시켰다(create the first clone child-a baby girl named Eve)고 발표하기도 했다. 그녀는 이어 공개되지 않은 북유럽의 한 레즈비언 커플에게 곧 두 번째 복제 아기가 태어나게 될 것(a second cloned baby will be born to a lesbian couple in an disclosed northern European location)이라고 공개했었다.

클로네이드는 웹사이트를 통해 인간복제 서비스는 20만 달러, 불임여성을 위한 난자 서비스는 5000달러부터 시작한다고 광고하고(advertise human cloning services for $200,000 and egg services for infertile women starting at $5,000)있다.

현재는 애리조나 주(州) 피닉스에서 음악행사 관련 일을 하고 있는 바우먼은 "지금도 어디에선가 작은 마이클 잭슨이 돌아다니고 있을 것이라는 생각을 떨칠 수 없다(cannot help thinking there is a mini Michael Jackson running around somewhere)"면서 "잭슨에게는 무슨 일이든 안 되는 것이 없었다(with Michael Jackson, anything is possible)"고 말했다.

Michael Jackson Wanted to Clone himself

Michael Jackson was so terrified of dying he was desperate to clone himself in a bizarre bid to extend his superstar legacy.

Jackson – who was obsessed with the idea of immortality – attended a Las Vegas conference on human cloning with his friend, the spoon bender Uri Geller.

And the King of Pop was so blown away by the teachings of a sect called the Raelians he asked if they would clone him.

Jacko's chauffeur Al Bowman, who drove the singer and Geller to the event in 2002, said: "Jackson was very excited.

"He bounced out of that conference like a small child. He was smiling and on a high. I heard him and Uri talking in the back of the limo.

"He was talking about the prospect of being cloned. He grabbed Uri by both arms and told him, 'I really want to do it Uri, and I don't care how much it costs'."

The Raelian movement is a strange religious sect that believes the human soul dies when the body dies so the key to eternal life is cloning ? recreating individuals from their own genetic make-up.

The sect also has a scientific arm called Clonaid which holds regular fund-raising events to share its latest research with the great and good of Hollywood.

"I always remember Jackson talking about the cloning of Dolly the sheep in Britain in 1996 ? he was totally fascinated by it," said Al, 50, Jacko's chauffeur for over a decade.

"Then when he heard about the Raelians he became utterly convinced this weird religious group could clone humans.

"It was really oddball stuff, but it interested Michael. One day in the limo he said, 'They did it with Dolly'. I said, 'Dali… you mean Salvador Dali'. We both laughed.

"Michael said he wanted a mini-version of himself cloned to carry on his legacy. He was hoping that Michael Jackson could live for ever."

In the 90s Jackson inquired about being cryogenically frozen before he died and it was also rumoured that he took GH3, a drug designed to prolong life expectancy.

But he was particularly fascinated by the Raelians, which were founded by French journalist Claude Vorilhon.

In December 1973, Vorilhon – or Rael as he is now known – claimed he was contacted by an extra-terrestrial being who emerged from a flying saucer and told him – in fluent French – that humans were created in laboratories 25,000 years ago by people from another planet.

This race of super-intelligent beings was called the Elohim, which in ancient Hebrew means "those who came from the sky" and in Jewish prayers refers to God.

Rael describes the Elohim as being "about a metre tall, with pale green skin and long dark hair".

Some estimates suggest that the Raelian movement now has up to 55,000 members, who are all preparing for the expected return of the Elohim to Earth.

Al, who was once given a cat by Jackson who then insisted on dressing it himself, said: "I used to drive so many celebrities around LA, and so many of them became obsessed with these weird religious sects – Michael was no different.

People in Hollywood are the most creative people you'll ever meet, but they're also the most stupid people around. They believe almost anything and then they hand over all their millions to these groups."

It's believed Jacko made contact with the Raelians after the conference in Las Vegas and spoke with Dr Brigette Boisselier about the idea of a

Jacko clone.

Dr Boisselier, a trained scientist with a master's degree in biochemistry and a doctorate in physical chemistry, is also a Raelian bishop and the managing director of Clonaid, which was set up in the Bahamas in 1997. In December 2002 she told the world that the Raelians had created the first cloned child—a baby girl named Eve.

She popped up on American, French, British and Belgian TV promising that a second cloned baby would soon be born to a lesbian couple in an undisclosed northern European location.

There has been no evidence of any such baby but the following year, in 2003, Al said he got a call from one of Jacko's publicists. "I wasn't chauffeuring for Michael anymore, but then this woman calls me out of the blue saying she was his publicist," said Al.

"She wanted contact details for the Raelian people. She said Michael was furious with them and she needed to get hold of them. She wouldn't say why.

"I thought that surely Michael or one of his people had a contact number, but the woman said he'd lost it. I gave them a number and then didn't hear anything back."

It remains unclear whether Jacko ever pursued his cloning ambition any further.

On its website, Clonaid advertises human cloning services for $200,000 and egg services for infertile women starting at $5,000.

It says: "Eve, the first cloned baby, was born on December 26, 2002, thanks to our team of highly skilled scientists. Since then, we've been able to help a number of patients have their own children through our cloning technology."

Last night the Daily Mirror was unable to speak to anyone from Clonaid.

But Al, who now organises music events in Phoenix, Arizona, said: "When I heard Clonaid had cloned the first human being, I couldn't help thinking there was a mini Michael Jackson running around somewhere. With Michael, anything is possible."

✓ 기억하면 좋을 구절!

be fascinated by ~에 매료되다

He *was fascinated by* her beauty.
그는 그녀의 미모에 매료됐다.

be obsessed with ~에 사로잡혀 있다 / 강박증이 있다

He *is obsessed with* the idea that he always has to be the best.
그는 늘 최고여야 한다는 생각에 사로잡혀 있다.

beam with joy 희색이 만면하다 / 좋아서 웃음이 가득하다

He *beamed with joy* when he received the letter of acceptance.
그는 합격증을 받고 좋아서 활짝 웃었다.

bounce out of ~서 뛰쳐나오다

He *bounced out of* the conference room.
그는 회의장에서 뛰쳐나와 버렸다.

emerge from 나오다 / 벗어나다, 헤어나다

She wants to *emerge from* the same routine.
그녀는 매일 반복되는 일상에서 벗어나길 원한다.

cannot help but ~하지 않을 수 없다 / ~할 수밖에 없다

I *cannot help but* like him.
그를 좋아하지 않을 수가 없다. (그가 참 좋다.)

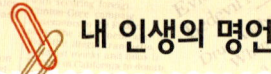

내 인생의 명언 — 시간은 황금이다

▶ 시계를 지배해야지 지배를 받아서는 안 된다.
골다 메이어 (이스라엘 여성정치인)

> You must govern the clock, not be governed by it.
> Golda Meir

▶ 잃어버린 시간은 다시는 찾을 수 없다.
벤저민 프랭클린 (미국 정치가 · 외교관 · 저술가 · 과학자)

> Lost time is never found again.
> Benjamin Franklin

▶ 낭비한 시간에 대한 후회는 더 큰 시간 낭비다.
메이슨 쿨리 (미국 격언작가)

> Regret for wasted time is more wasted time.
> Mason Cooley

▶ 시간이 간다고 당신은 말하는가. 아니다.
아아, 시간은 그대로 있는데, 우리가 가는 것이다.
오스틴 돕슨 (영국 시인 · 수필가)

> Time goes, you say? Ah, no! alas, time stays, we go.
> Austin Dobson

▶ 시간은 우리가 가장 원하는 것이면서 가장 최악으로 써버리는 것이다.
윌리엄 펜 (영국 신대륙 개척자)

> Time is what we want most, but what we use worst.
> William Penn

Favorite famous sayings!

▶ 돈을 낭비하면 돈만 없게 된다. 그러나 시간을 낭비하면
인생의 일부를 잃어버리게 된다.
마이클 르뵈프 (미국 기업소설가 · 교수)

> Waste your money and you're only out of money,
> but waste your time and you've lost a part of your life.
> Michael LeBoeuf

▶ 한 시간을 감히 낭비하는 사람은 인생의 가치를 발견하지 못한 사람이다.
찰스 다윈 (영국 박물학자 진화론 제창자)

> A man who dares to waste one hour of his life
> has not discovered the value of life.
> Charles Robert Darwin

▶ 현명한 사람은 허송세월을 가장 슬퍼한다.
단테 알리기에리 (이탈리아 시인)

> It is the wisest who grieve most at loss of time.
> Dante Alighieri

▶ 시간은 위대한 스승이기는 하지만 불행히도 자신의 모든 제자를 죽인다.
헥토르 베를리오즈 (프랑스 작곡가)

> Time is a great teacher, but unfortunately
> it kills all its pupils.
> Hector Berlioz

News English

"War over Chicken Feet between U.S. and China"

China and the United States are kicking up a trade war over chicken in which Beijing effectively has given the boot to millions of dollars worth of U.S. chicken, about half of which is chicken feet.

This action comes as Congress begins deliberating the 2010 federal budget for agriculture, which could extend a U.S. ban on imports of Chinese chicken products sparked by food...

according to trade statistics. Chinese importers last week told U.S. chicken companies that Beijing was not issuing import permits for U.S. chicken, effectively blocking the poultry for the rest of 2009.

It is believed some U.S. chicken could still enter China via Hong Kong, but industry sources said...

range of products. China has banned U.S. pork since the outbreak of a new strain of H1N1 flu virus, commonly called swine flu, even though the flu is not transmitted by hogs or pork.

Senior officials from the U.S. Trade...

import permits for U.S. chicken, effectively blocking the poultry for the rest of 2009. It is believed some U.S. chicken could still enter China via Hong Kong, but industry sources said it is not known if the quantities would be comparable.

CHINA MAY BE RETALIATING

No reason was given for China's action, but U.S. poultry officials claim it is related to a Congressional measure that prevents imports of chicken from China.

"They want to get rid of the DeLauro Amendment. So this might be a shot over the bow," Paul Aho, an economist with the consulting firm Poultry Perspective, said of the Chinese efforts.

The measure, championed by Representative Rosa DeLauro, prevents the U.S. Agriculture Department from allowing imports of poultry from China...

중국과 미국은 '닭발' 수출입 때문에 '치킨게임' 중

미국과 중국의 닭발 전쟁

미국과 중국이 '닭발'(chicken feet) 때문에 신경전을 벌이고(wage a nerve war) 있다.

양국이 닭 수출입을 둘러싼 무역분쟁을 고조시키고(kick up a trade war over imports and exports of chicken) 있는 가운데, '닭발'이 주요 변수가 되고(become a decisive factor) 있는 것이다. 중국은 최근 미국산 닭 수백만 달러어치를 퇴짜 놓았다. 그중 절반이 닭발이었다.

중국의 이 같은 조치는 미 의회가 2010년 연방예산 농업 부문 심의에 착수하면서(begin deliberating the 2010 federal budget for agriculture) 실시되었다. 미 의회가 식품안전 우려로 촉발된 중국산 닭 제품 수입금지를 연장할 수도(could extend a U.S. ban on imports of Chinese chicken products sparked by food safety concerns) 있기 때문이다.

미국의 수입금지는 중국 정부를 자극했고, 중국 측은 곧바로 미국산 닭 수

입을 중단(halt imports of U.S. chicken)했다. 중국 정부가 공식적으로는 "수입이 차단된 것은 아니다(be not blocked)"고 밝히고 있지만, 보복조치를 취했다(take the retaliatory measures)는 것은 누구나 다 아는 얘기다.

중국은 미국 닭발의 최대 시장(the largest market for U.S. chicken feet)이다. 미국 가금류·달걀수출위원회에 따르면(according to the USA Poultry and Egg Export Council) 중국은 지난해 2억 8000만 달러어치 42만 1000톤의 닭발을 수입해 갔다.

중국에선 닭발이 국, 탕 및 간단한 먹을거리로 널리 쓰이지만(be popular in soups, stews and as snack items) 미국에선 거의 팔리지 않는다(very few are sold in the United States).

중국 시장이 없으면(without the Chinese market) 미국산 닭발 대부분(most of the U.S. chicken paws)은 사료 또는 다른 비식품 용도로 처리돼야(be processed into feed or other non-food uses) 하고, 그러면 미국 닭 업체들에겐 돈이 덜 될 수밖에(bring less money to U.S. chicken companies) 없는 것이다.

중국의 수입금지 조치가 지속된다면 타이슨 푸드와 샌더슨 팜 같은 미국 닭 공급업체들의 수입은(earnings for chicken producers Tyson Foods Inc or Sanderson Farms Inc)은 큰 타격을 입게 될 것이라는 보고서도 나왔다.

중국은 미국산 닭날개와 닭다리 부분도 수입하고(buy some U.S. chicken wings and leg quarters) 있다. 무역통계에 따르면(according to trade statistics) 중국은 한 해에 약 6억 7600만 달러어치 75만 4000톤의 미국산 닭을 수입하는 것으로 집계되고 있다.

중국은 델라우로 수정안의 폐기를 원하고(want to get rid of the DeLauro Amendment) 있는 것으로 보인다. 이 안은 로사 델라우로 하원의원(민주당 · 코네티컷)이 주도하고 있는(be championed by Representative Rosa DeLauro) 것으로, 식품안전 우려를 이유로 미 농무부가 중국 가금류 수입 허가를 내주지 못하게 하는(prevent the U.S. Agriculture Department from allowing imports of poultry products from China because of food safety concerns) 내용을 골자로 하고 있다.

델라우로 의원은 미 농무부와 식품의약국을 감독하는(oversee the U.S. Agriculture Department and Food and Drug Administration) 영향력 있는 하원 세출소위원회의 민주당 대표(the Democratic head of an influential House Appropriations Subcommittee)를 맡고 있다.

중국은 미 의회의 조치와 관련해 미국을 상대로 세계무역기구에 소를 제기(launch a dispute with the World Trade Organization against the United States over the Congressional measure)한 바 있으며, 가금류 문제(the poultry issue)는 많은 상품들을 둘러싼 양국 간의 여러 무역분쟁 중 가장 최신 사례(be the latest of several trade skirmishes between the two countries covering a range of products)이다.

한편 중국은 이른바 '신종플루'라고 불리는 H1N1 인플루엔자 바이러스의 새 변종이 발생한 이후(since the outbreak of a new strain of H1N1 flu virus, commonly called swine flu) 인플루엔자가 돼지나 돼지고기에 의해 전염되는 것이 아님에도(be not transmitted by hogs or pork) 불구하고 미국산 돼지고기 수입을 금지하기도 했다.

War over Chicken Feet between U.S. and China

China and the United States are kicking up a trade war over chicken in which Beijing effectively has given the boot to millions of dollars worth of U.S. chicken, about half of which is chicken feet.

This action comes as Congress begins deliberating the 2010 federal budget for agriculture, which could extend a U.S. ban on imports of Chinese chicken products sparked by food safety concerns.

The ban has angered the Chinese and now, according to U.S. exporters, Beijing has halted imports of U.S. chicken, although officially China is saying imports are not blocked.

China is a huge market for U.S. chicken feet, commonly called paws, and bought 421,000 tons, or $280 million worth, in 2008, according to the USA Poultry and Egg Export Council, a trade group.

In China, paws are popular in soups, stews, and as snack items, but very few are sold in the United States.

Without the Chinese market, most of the paws will have to be processed into feed or other non-food uses, which brings less money to U.S. chicken companies.

In a note to clients last week, Stephens Inc analyst Farha Aslam said earnings for chicken producers Tyson Foods Inc or Sanderson Farms Inc would be impacted if the ban lasted past September.

China also buys some U.S. chicken wings and dark meat leg quarters. In total, China bought 754,000 tons of U.S. chicken in 2008, or $676 million worth, according to trade statistics.

Chinese importers last week told U.S. chicken companies that Beijing was not issuing import permits for U.S. chicken, effectively blocking the poultry for the rest of 2009.

It is believed some U.S. chicken could still enter China via Hong Kong, but industry sources said it is not known if the quantities would be comparable.

CHINA MAY BE RETALIATING

No reason was given for China's action, but U.S. poultry officials claim it is related to a Congressional measure that prevents imports of chicken from China.

"They want to get rid of the DeLauro Amendment. So this might be a shot over the bow," Paul Aho, an economist with the consulting firm Poultry Perspective, said of the Chinese efforts.

The measure, championed by Representative Rosa DeLauro, prevents the U.S. Agriculture Department from allowing imports of poultry from China. DeLauro is the Democratic head of an influential House of Representatives appropriations subcommittee that oversees the U.S. Agriculture Department and Food and Drug Administration.

Her committee has effectively blocked imports of Chinese poultry products because of food safety concerns.

An annual spending bill, which the House of Representatives is expected to debate on Wednesday, could extend that ban through fiscal 2010, which starts October 1.

The Senate has not yet deliberated its version of the USDA appropriations bill. In April, China launched a dispute with the World Trade Organization against the United States over the Congressional measure.

The poultry issue is the latest of several trade skirmishes between the two countries covering a range of products. China has banned U.S. pork since the outbreak of a new strain of H1N1 flu virus, commonly called swine flu, even though the flu is not transmitted by hogs or pork.

Senior officials from the U.S. Trade Representative's office will travel to China next week to meet with officials about bilateral trade issues.

☑ 기억하면 좋을 구절!

wage a war 전쟁을 벌이다

They *waged a war* of liberation in their country.
그들은 자국에서 해방전쟁을 벌였다.

become a decisive factor 결정적 변수가 되다

Air power is *the decisive factor* in modern warfare.
공군력은 현대전의 결정적 요소다.

call a hault to ~에게 정지를 명하다

We must *call a hault* to this childish behavior.
이런 유치한 행동은 그만두어야 한다.

retaliatory duties(tariff) 보복관세

We have to prevent the imposition of us *retaliatory duties*.
우리는 미국의 보복관세 부과를 저지해야 한다.

launch a boycott 불매운동을 벌이다

After the incident, they *launched a boycott* campaign against the products of the company.
그 사건 이후 그들은 그 회사 제품 불매운동을 벌였다.

at the latest (아무리) 늦어도

Applications should be in by next Monday *at the latest*.
원서는 늦어도 다음 월요일까지는 접수되어야 한다.

내 인생의 명언 — 분노는 결코 힘이 될 수 없다

▶ 언제나 너의 적에게 분노에 찬 편지를 써라. 그러나 절대 보내지는 마라.
　제임스 팰로우스 (미국 언론인)

　　Always write angry letters to your enemies.
　　Never mail them.
　　James Fallows

▶ 분노한 사람은 입을 열고 눈은 감는다.
　카토 (로마의 정치가)

　　An angry man opens his mouth and shuts up his eyes.
　　Marcus Porcius Cato

▶ 분노와 질투는 사랑보다 더 목표를 보이지 않게 한다.
　조지 엘리엇 (영국 소설가)

　　Anger and jealousy can no more bear
　　to lose sight of their objects than love.
　　George Eliot

▶ 노여움은 바보들의 가슴 속에만 산다.
　앨버트 아인슈타인 (독일 출신 미국 물리학자)

　　Anger dwells only in the bosom of fools.
　　Albert Einstein

Favorite famous sayings!

▶ 분노는 마음의 등불을 꺼버리는 바람이다.
로버트 잉거솔 (미국 정치지도자 · 웅변가)

> Anger is a wind which blows out the lamp of the mind.
> Robert Ingersoll

▶ 분노를 품고 있는 것은 다른 누구에게 던질 의도로 뜨거운 숯을 움켜쥐고 있는 것과 같아서, 화상을 입는 사람은 당신이 되고 만다.
석가모니 (불교 창시자 · 인도의 성자)

> Holding on to anger is like grasping a hot coal with the intent of throwing it at someone else; you are the one who gets burned.
> Buddha

▶ 잠자리에 눕기 전에 분노는 잊어버려라.
마하트마 간디 (인도 정치가 · 민족운동지도자)

> Forget your anger before you lie down to sleep.
> Mahatma Ghandi

▶ 분노로 시작된 것은 무엇이든 수치스러움으로 끝난다.
벤저민 프랭클린 (미국 정치가 · 외교관 · 저술가 · 과학자)

> Whatever is begun in anger ends in shame.
> Benjamin Franklin

독자가 영어로 꿈꿀 수 있는 날을 위해

내가 그나마 몇 마디 할 줄 아는 언어는 '꼬스빠뇰'(Cospañol)이다. 콩글리시(Konglish) 식으로 스페인어의 '꼬레아노'(Coreano · 한국어)와 '에스빠뇰'(Español · 스페인어)을 합한 말이다. 한국외대 스페인어과와 동시통역대학원 한 · 서 · 영(韓 · 西 · 英)과 3년 과정을 졸업하고, 6개월 석사장교로 군대를 마친 뒤 외대 · 한양대 · 동시통역대학원 등에서 시간강사를 3년 했으니 도합 10년간 스페인어를 한 셈이다.

1980년대에 특수전문요원(석사장교) 제도라는 것이 있었다. 석사 학위를 취득한 뒤 국사 · 영어 · 제2외국어 등 필기시험에 합격한 자에 한해 주던 병역 특례로, 훈련 3개월과 전방 근무 3개월 뒤 소위를 달고 곧바로 제대할 수 있는 병역 특례였다. 대학 4학년 졸업 때쯤 해군사관학교 스페인어 교관 제의를 받았고, 미군 카투사 시험에도 합격한 상태였다. 하지만 둘 다 포기하고, '육개장'(6개월 석사장교)에 도전하기로 했다.

갈등이 생겼다. 석사장교는 일반대학원 졸업생만 대상으로 했다. 동시통역대학원은 무역대학원, 경영대학원 등과 함께 특수대학원으로 분류돼 있었다. 하지만 그 비싼 등록금을 내면서 일주일에 6~9시간 강의만 듣는 일반대학원에 가고 싶지는 않았다. 기왕 대학원에 갈 바에야 고3 시간표처럼 강의가 빡빡한 동시통역대학원에 가서 외국어 하나는 확실하게 해두고 싶었다.

병무청을 상대로 '도박'을 해보기로 했다. 서·영과는 3년 과정이니 그 사이에 특수대학원까지 응시자격이 확대될 것으로 기대했다. 결국 그렇게 됐다. 문제는 석사장교 시험 응시에 필요한 대학원 졸업이 동시통역대학원에선 녹록하지 않다는 것이었다.

동시통역대학원은 논문 대신 졸업시험으로 학위 수여 여부를 결정했다. 2년 과정의 한국어-외국어(한-영, 한-불, 한-독, 한-서 등) 전공자는 다섯 과목, 3년 과정의 외국어-외국어(서-영, 불-영, 독-영 등)는 열 과목 시험을 봐서 단 한 과목이라도 80점 이하 과락을 하면 졸업장을 주지 않았다.

절박할 수밖에 없었다. 서-영 동시통역 전공이니 열 과목(한-서 서-한 동시·순차통역, 한-영 영-한 동시·순차 통역, 영-서 동시·순차 통역 등) 중 하나라도 삐끗하면 아예 석사장교 시험에 응시조차 해볼 수 없는 상황이었다.

당시 내 담당 교수는 불어-독어-스페인어-화란어-영어를 자유자재로 구사하는 벨기에 출신 국제통역사였다. 자그마한 키에 늘 콧수염을 기르고 다녔는데, 까탈스럽기 그지없는데다 무슨 사정이 있어도 공과 사를 구분하는 데 에누리 없는 사람이었다. 늘상 나에게 "Que mala memoria tienes!(넌 왜 그렇게 기억력이 나쁘냐!)"고 타박해오던 터여서 여간 불안하지 않았다.

다른 방도가 없었다. 우선은 졸업시험 열 과목을 통과하는 것이 급선무였다. 그때부터 스페인어 신문에 나오는 요긴한 관용구와 좋은 표현들을 깨알같이 적어가며 외우기 시작했다. 신문 기자들이 쓴 문장이니 현지인들이 구사하는 언어 중에서도 가장 세련되고 고급스러운 표현들이었다. 같은 말이라도 품격이 배어 있는 것이어서 시험 대비용으로 제격이었다.

외국에서 태어나 자라지 않은 우리 같은 사람은 외국어로 말할 때 일단 머릿속에서 번역을 한 뒤 입으로 내뱉어 읊는 과정을 거치게 된다. 제아무리 언어감각이 뛰어나도 이 한계를 뛰어넘는 것은 쉽지 않다. 외국어를 잘 하려면 관용구와 관용적 표현들을 가능한 한 많이 외워둘 필요가 있다. 그러면 입에서는 외워놓은 관용적 표현들이 자동적으로 나오게끔 하고, 그사이에 머릿속으로는 다음에 무슨 말을 할지 생각할 짬을 가질 수 있게 된다. 따라서 말이 끊어지거나 우물쭈물하지 않게 돼 마치 '머릿속 번역 과정' 없이 유창한 외국어를 구사하는 것처럼 보일 수 있다.

《조선일보》기자로 신문에 '윤희영의 News English'를 연재하게 된 것도 그때의 경험이 바탕이 됐다. 재미있게 읽을 수 있는 외신기사들을 통해 어느 시험에서나 요구하는 시사상식과 요긴한 영어표현을 독자들에게 동시 서비스하면 좋겠다는 생각에서 비롯된 것이다.

영문 기사에 직접 나온 표현이 아니면 절대 인용하지 않는다. 어설프게 아는 것을 임의로 쓰거나 영작을 해서 넣지 않는다. 그래서인지 지금까지 오류를 지적받은 적이 거의 없었다. 인용 부분은 모두 영문 기사 원문에서 그대로 따온 것이기 때문이다.

동시통역대학원 졸업시험을 겪어봤기 때문에 독자들이나 수험생들이 어떤 수준의 어떤 표현들을 가장 필요로 하는지 더 절실히 공감할 수 있다. 그래서 나 스스로 같이 시험을 준비하며 함께 공부한다는 자세로 기사들을 선별하고, 유용한 영어 표현들을 골라봤다. 부디 부모가 자녀들과 함께 읽으며 공감하고 공유할 수 있는, 수험생들에겐 잠시 머리를 식혀주면서 자연스레 공부도 되는 책이 되기를 바란다.

지저분해진 책(a dirty book)에는 먼지가 거의 없다고(be rarely dusty) 했다. 좋은 책은 마지막 장을 넘기고 나면(turn the last page) 친구를 잃어버리는 것 같은 느낌이 든다고(feel as if you have lost a friend) 한다. 언감생심, 다만 한 사람의 독자로부터라도 그런 말을 들을 수 있는 책이 되기를 감히 바란다.

2011년 10월
윤희영

NEWS ENGLISH

1판 1쇄 발행 2011년 10월 28일
1판 6쇄 발행 2019년 7월 5일

지은이 윤희영
펴낸이 김성구

단행본부 류현수 고혁 홍희정 현미나
디자인 이영민
제 작 신태섭
마케팅 최윤호 나길훈 김영욱
관 리 노신영

펴낸곳 ㈜샘터사
등 록 2001년 10월 15일 제1-2923호
주 소 서울시 종로구 창경궁로35길 26 2층 (03076)
전 화 02-763-8965(단행본부) 02-763-8966(마케팅부)
팩 스 02-3672-1873 이메일 book@isamtoh.com 홈페이지 www.isamtoh.com

ⓒ 윤희영, 2011, Printed in Korea.

이 책은 저작권법에 따라 보호를 받는 저작물이므로 무단 전재와 복제를 금지하며,
이 책의 내용의 전부 또는 일부를 이용하려면 반드시 저작권자와 ㈜샘터사의 서면 동의를 받아야 합니다.

ISBN 978-89-464-1813-4 13740

이 도서의 국립중앙도서관 출판시도서목록(CIP)은 e-CIP 홈페이지
(http://www.nl.go.kr/cip.php)에서 이용하실 수 있습니다. (CIP제어번호: CIP2011004462)

값은 뒤표지에 있습니다.
잘못 만들어진 책은 구입처에서 교환해 드립니다.

• 이 책에 수록된 이미지와 원문 뉴스는 대부분 저작권자의 동의를 얻었으나,
  일부는 저작권자를 찾지 못했습니다. 저작권자가 확인되는 대로 정식 동의 절차를 밟도록 하겠습니다.